Echolalias

Echolalias
On the Forgetting of Language

Daniel Heller-Roazen

ZONE BOOKS · NEW YORK

2005

© 2005 Daniel Heller-Roazen
ZONE BOOKS
1226 Prospect Avenue
Brooklyn, New York 11218

Frontispiece: Woodcut, folio 15v, from Ovid, *Le grand olympe*
(Paris, 1538). Typ 515.39.663, Department of Printing and
Graphic Arts, Houghton Library, Harvard College Library.

Printed in the United States of America.

Distributed by The MIT Press,
Cambridge, Massachusetts, and London, England

Library of Congress Cataloging-in-Publication Data

Heller-Roazen, Daniel.
        Echolalias: on the forgetting of language /Daniel Heller-
Roazen.
        p.   cm.
    Includes bibliographical references and index.
    ISBN 1-890951-49-8
    1. Language attrition. 2. Language and languages.
    I. Title.

P40.5.L28H45   2004
401—dc22   2004052135

I hear some of our Sea-*Yahoos* find fault with my Sea-language, as not proper in many Parts, nor now in Use. I cannot help it. In my first Voyages, while I was young, I was instructed by the oldest Mariners, and learned to speak as they did. But I have since found that the Sea-*Yahoos* are apt, like the Land ones, to become new fangled in their Words; which latter change every Year; insomuch, as I remember upon each return to mine own Country, their old Dialect was so altered, that I could hardly understand the new. And I observe, when any *Yahoo* comes from *London* out of Curiosity to visit me at my own House, we neither of us are able to deliver our Conceptions in a Manner intelligible to the other.

Jonathan Swift, *Gulliver's Travels*

Contents

CHAPTER ONE

The Apex of Babble

As everyone knows, children at first do not speak. They make noises, which seem at once to anticipate the sounds of human languages and to be fundamentally unlike them. As infants approach the point at which they will begin to form their first recognizable words, they have at their disposal capacities for articulation that not even the most gifted of polyglot adults could hope to rival. It is no doubt for this reason that Roman Jakobson found himself drawn to the prattle of infants, in addition to such things as Russian futurism, comparative Slavic metrics, and structural phonology, the science of the sound shapes of language. In *Child Language, Aphasia, and Phonological Universals*, which he wrote in German between 1939 and 1941 while living in exile in Norway and Sweden, Jakobson observed that "a babbling child can accumulate articulations which are never found within a single language or even a group of languages: consonants with the most varied points of articulation, palatalized and rounded consonants, sibilants, affricates, clicks, complex vowels, diphthongs, and so forth."[1] Drawing on the research of linguistically trained child psychologists, Jakobson concluded that at what he termed the "apex of babble" (*die Blüte des Lallens*), no limits can be set on the phonic powers of the prattling child. As far as articulation is concerned, infants, he maintained, are

9

capable of everything. Without the slightest effort, they can produce any—and all—sounds contained in human languages.

One might think that with such capacities for speech, the acquisition of a particular language would be a quick and easy task for the child. But it is not. Between the prattle of the infant and the first words of the child there is not only no clear passage but evidence of a decisive interruption, something like a turning point at which the hitherto-limitless phonetic abilities of the infant seem to falter. "As all observers acknowledge with great astonishment," Jakobson related, "the child loses nearly all of his ability to produce sounds in passing from the pre-linguistic stage to the first acquisition of words, that is, to the first genuine stage of language."[2] A partial atrophy of the phonic abilities, to be sure, is not altogether surprising at this point; as the child begins to speak a single language, he obviously has no use for all the consonants and vowels he could once make, and it is only natural that, ceasing to employ the sounds not contained in the language he is learning, he soon forgets how to produce them. But when the infant begins to learn a language, he not only loses the capacity to produce sounds that exceed its particular phonetic system. Much more "striking" (*auffallend*), noted Jakobson, is that many of the sounds common to his babble and the adult language also now disappear from the stock of the infant's speech; only at this point can the acquisition of a single language be said truly to begin. Over several years, the child will gradually master the phonemes that define the sound shape of what will be his mother tongue, according to an order that Jakobson was the first to present in its structural and stratified form: starting, for example, with the emission of dentals (such as *t* and *d*), the infant will learn to pronounce palatals and velars (such as *k* and *g*); from stops and labials (such as *b*, *p*, and *m*), he will acquire the ability to form constrictives (such as *v*, *s*, and *ʃ*); and so forth, until, at the end of the process of his language learning, the child comes to be a "native speaker," to use the expression with which we are all familiar but whose imprecision is manifest.

What happens in the meantime to the many sounds the infant once easily uttered, and what becomes of the ability he possessed, before he learned the sounds of a single language, to produce those contained in all of them? It is as if the acquisition of language were possible only through an act of oblivion, a kind of linguistic infantile amnesia (or phonic amnesia, since what the infant seems to forget is not language but an apparently infinite capacity for undifferentiated articulation). Could it be that the child is so captivated by the reality of one language that he abandons the boundless but ultimately sterile realm that contains the possibility of all others? Or should one instead look to the newly acquired language for explanations: is it the mother tongue that, taking hold of its new speaker, refuses to tolerate in him even the shadow of another? Everything is complicated by the fact that at the moment the infant falls silent, he cannot even say "I," and one hesitates to attribute to him the consciousness of a speaking being. It is difficult to imagine, in any case, that the sounds the child was once capable of producing with such ease have departed from his voice forever, leaving behind nothing but a trail of smoke (and even smoke is something). At the very least, two things are produced in the voice left empty by the retreat of the sounds the speaking child can no longer make, for a language and a speaking being now emerge from the disappearance of babble. It may well be inevitable. Perhaps the infant must forget the infinite series of sounds he once produced at the "apex of babble" to obtain mastery of the finite system of consonants and vowels that characterizes a single language. Perhaps the loss of a limitless phonetic arsenal is the price a child must pay for the papers that grant him citizenship in the community of a single tongue.

Do the languages of the adult retain anything of the infinitely varied babble from which they emerged? If they did, then it would be only an echo, since where there are languages, the infant's prattle has long ago vanished, at least in the form it once had in the mouth of the child who could not yet speak. It would be only an echo, of another speech and of something other than speech: an echolalia, which guarded the memory of the indistinct and immemorial babble that, in being lost, allowed all languages to be.

Chapter Two

Exclamations

In one sense, the sounds children forget how to make never leave them, for there is a field of speech in which they recur with striking regularity: those utterances traditionally termed, with more or less precision, "onomatopoeias." It has often been observed that when children in the process of learning a language seek to imitate the inhuman noises around them, they consistently use not the sounds that they are capable of making in their new mother-tongue but those they seem otherwise unable to make, which they once produced without the slightest effort. Jakobson dwelled on the phenomenon at some length in *Child Language, Aphasia, and Phonological Universals*, arguing for its systematic and universal role in the acquisition of language. "Thus," he wrote, "in children who do not yet have any velar phonemes, one observes *gi* as an imitation of falling blinds, *kra-kra* of the raven's cawing, *gaga* as an indication of pleasure, *ch-ch* as a sound of joy, *kha* = 'pfui,' etc. Although fricatives are still replaced by stops in the 'objective denoting language' of the child, the former can still appear as sound imitations with onomatopoetic function. The noise of a trolley car is reproduced by *zin-zi*; the cat, by one child, and the fly, by another, is imitated by *ss*; and there are frequent attempts to imitate the sound of an airplane or to chase away chickens or dogs with *f*. The liquid *r* can

13

still be lacking in words which the child borrows from an adult, but the sound of a bird or of rattling can nonetheless be reproduced by it, and children who do not yet make use of any *i* imitate the barking of dogs with *didi* or the cry of the sparrow with *titi*, *bibibi*, and *pipi*."[1]

Imitations of animal and mechanical noises seem to belong to a curious and complex dimension of the child's speech whose exact status in the evolution of language is far from clear. Do the sounds that the child uses in onomatopoeias represent the last remnants of an otherwise-forgotten babble or the first signs of a language still to come? The exclamations of the child, in any case, indicate that language evolves in a time that is neither unitary nor linear; they suggest that however resolutely one speech may develop, it continues to bear within it elements—traces or announcements— of another.

Children are in this sense not at all unlike the adults they will become. In the very same years that Jakobson wrote his path-breaking work on the acquisition and loss of language, his good friend Nikolai Sergeevich Trubetskoi, with whom he had founded the Prague Linguistic Circle years before, demonstrated that ono-matopoeias belong to a specific type of utterance common to the speech of both children and adults. At the end of the fourth chapter of his unfinished and yet monumental *Principles of Phonology*, having defined every individual language as a finite "phonological system of distinctive phonetic oppositions," determining its characteristic vowels, consonants, and prosody, Trubetskoi added a final section, which he presented as something of an appendix: a brief but far-reaching discussion of what he defined as the "distinctive anomalous phonological elements" of languages. "Beyond the normal phonological system," he wrote, "many languages also present special phonological cases, which appear with altogether particular functions."[2] To this category belong all the "foreign sounds" made by speakers of one language when trying to imitate another: phonemes present in words borrowed from other languages that in the passage from one tongue to another inevitably change shape and often acquire a new and singular form, which is ultimately reducible neither to the tongue from which they came nor to the one in which they are invoked. Trubetskoi, who was living in Vienna when he wrote his book, cited the occasions when speakers of German use a French or Slavic word containing a sounded form of ʃ (that is, ž), or nasal vowels, all sounds normally absent from the phonological system of the German language. Wanting to indicate the foreign origin of the term "telephone," in distinction to the German word *Fernsprecher*, the Viennese, for example, would pronounce the final syllable of the word with a half-open, posterior nasal vowel: they would say "telefõ," calling to mind a Gallic sound that is indeed foreign to German (the nasal õ) but that, as it happens, is also absent from the actual pronunciation of the French term for "telephone," *téléphone*. To this category of "distinctive anomalous phonological elements," wrote Trubetskoi, also belong all the sounds found in "interjections and onomatopoeias, as well as calls and orders aimed at domestic animals," made by both children and adults.[3]

These exclamatory utterances, Trubetskoi argued, "have no representative function [*Darstellungsfunktion*], in the strict sense of the term." In the terms of the contemporary philosophy of language, one might say that they are "speech acts," which, without being utterly meaningless, do not assert or deny anything. Unlike classical propositions, they do not "state one thing concerning another thing"; their sole function consists of the very force of their utterance. In itself, this was, of course, not a new claim. That an exclamation is not a statement was a thesis familiar to the theory of language at least since the time of Aristotle, who, for this reason, excluded all exclamations, such as prayers and cries, from the field of logic at the start of the decisive treatise on the proposition known to the philosophical tradition as *De interpreta-tione*.[4] Trubetskoi's true insight pertained to the field of linguistics that he in large part defined, phonology, for he showed that to the logico-formal singularity of exclamations there corresponds an altogether exceptional phonetic structure. Trubetskoi demon-strated that the sounds a human being uses in interjections, imita-tions of inhuman noises, and commandments to animals are rarely found in regular expressions within the speaker's tongue. They typically lie well beyond the limits that define the sound shape of a particular language. As usual, the linguist had no trouble pro-viding examples: for the European languages alone, he cited "the interjection transcribed as *hm*; the clacking and clicking sounds made to spur on horses; the labial *r* made to stop horses; the inter-jection 'brrr!' used to express a shudder."[5] It would not be difficult to extend the list, restricting oneself to the exorbitant and exces-sive sounds regularly found in exclamations made by the speakers of a single tongue. In English, for example, consider the common exclamation of disgust "ukh," which involves a constrictive con-sonant *kh* (reminiscent of the sounds transcribed by the Castil-ian letter *jota* or the Arabic letter خ), and which appears in some languages in distinctive opposition to a velar *k* or a more fully guttural *h*, but which has no proper place in the sound system of English; or take the "apico-alveolar" or "rolled" *r* that Anglophone children once used in imitating the sound of a ringing telephone; or the "dorso-velar" or "trilled" *r* often produced to mimic the purring of a cat, which strikingly recalls the liquid consonants in modern French and German; or, finally, the sound that intervenes at the center of the contemporary English expression of dismay "Uh-oh," which closely resembles the glottal stop that plays an important role in languages such as Arabic and Danish but is not generally thought to have a distinctive function in the phonology of standard English. In each case, interjections open one sound system to phonemes that normally lie outside it; and they carry, in this way, a language to a point at which, as Trubetskoi wrote, "the usual phonological system no longer holds."[6] Passing beyond the borders that normally define it, a single tongue now moves into an indistinct region of sound that belongs to no one language—and that often seems, in truth, not to belong to any human idiom at all.

It is not easy to define the precise position that such exclamatory sounds occupy in a single language, and Trubetskoi's decision to restrict his discussion of "distinctive anomalous phonological elements" to the final section of his chapter on phonological systems seems to belie a certain reluctance to confront the question directly. What relation, after all, do exclamations, both infantile and adult, bear to the languages in which they are uttered? On the one hand, interjections seem to represent a dimension common to every language as such, for it is difficult, if not impossible, to imagine a form of speech in which such sounds could not be made. And yet on the other hand, exclamations necessarily mark an excess in the phonology of an individual tongue, since they are made of specific sounds that by definition are not otherwise contained in the language. "Distinctive anomalous phonological elements," in short, are at once included in a language and excluded from it; they seem, more exactly, included in a language to the very extent that they are excluded from it. Phonetic equivalents of the paradoxical entities that set logic banished from its discipline at its foundation, the noises of exclamations constitute the "elements" within every language that do, and do not, belong to the set of its sounds. They are the unwelcome yet inalienable members of every phonological system that no language can do without and that none shall recognize as its own.

That such phonetic elements are less "anomalous" than they

might seem is suggested by no less a thinker and maker of language than Dante, who claimed in his unfinished treatise on language, *De vulgari eloquentia*, that ever since the Fall, human speech has always begun with an exclamation of despair: "Heu!"[7] (Hence—it is worth noting—with an utterance whose written form, at least, contains one letter representing a sound that must have been absent from the medieval Latin Dante knew: the pure aspirate consonant *h*). The poet's suggestion is worth considering seriously. What would it mean for the primary form of human speech to be not a statement, a question, or a naming but an exclamation? Dante's remark is perhaps misinterpreted if taken too literally, for it defines less the empirical conditions of speech than the structural conditions that allow for the definition of language as such. These conditions, Dante suggests, are those of the interjection: as soon as there can be an exclamation, the poet-philosopher implies, there can be a language, but not until then; a language in which one could not cry out would not truly be a human language at all. Perhaps this is because the intensity of language is nowhere as great as in the interjection, the onomatopoeia, and the human imitation of what is not human. Nowhere is a language more "itself" than at the moment it seems to leave the terrain of its sound and sense, assuming the sound shape of what does not—or cannot—have a language of its own: animal sounds, natural or mechanical noises. It is here that one language, gesturing beyond itself in a speech that is none, opens itself to the nonlanguage that precedes it and that follows it. It is here, in the utterance of the strange sounds that the speakers of a tongue thought themselves incapable of making, that a language shows itself as an "exclamation" in the literal sense of the term: a "calling out" (*ex-clamare*, *Aus-ruf*), beyond or before itself, in the sounds of the inhuman speech it can neither completely recall nor fully forget.

CHAPTER THREE

Aleph

The Hebrew language contains a letter that no one can pronounce. It is not that it represents a particularly demanding sound, such as the notoriously difficult emphatic dental of classical Arabic (ض), which many native speakers never fully master, or the complex sibilant liquid of Czech (ř), which gives foreigners so much trouble and which even Roman Jakobson, in a rare moment of personal disclosure, confessed he could not always produce in his dreams.[1] The Hebrew letter *aleph* (א) cannot be pronounced, not because its sound is too complex but because it is too simple; none may utter this letter because, unlike all others, it represents no sound at all. Of course, it is thought that this was not always so. *Aleph* is said to have originally indicated the movement of the larynx in the production of a glottal stop. The counterpart less of the Arabic *alif* (ا) than of the *hamza* (ء), the Hebrew letter would have represented a mere gesture of articulation; its sound would have been like that of "a sudden spasm of the chest that needs some effort to produce," as Sībawayh, the great grammarian of classical Arabic, once described the *hamza*.[2] In his *Compendium grammatices linguae hebraeae*, Spinoza described the phonetic character of the letter *aleph* with great precision, writing that it "cannot be explained by any other in the European languages."[3]

19

Strictly speaking, *aleph* represents no fully articulated noise, being merely, in Spinoza's terms, the sign of "the beginning of sound in the throat that is heard by its opening."[4] But such an account of the letter conceals to a certain degree its true nature, which is even more modest than the grammarians would allow. The Hebrew *aleph* has not possessed the "articulatory" value indicated by the *hamza* in classical Arabic for a very long time, and the belief in its past existence can be nothing more, and nothing less, than the work of philological and linguistic reconstruction. It is as if the sound of *aleph* had been forgotten by the people who once produced it: of the many modern pronunciations of Hebrew, not one assigns any sound to the letter, and in all of them *aleph* is treated as the silent support for the vowels it bears, deprived of even the non-sound, the interruption in articulation, it is thought to have once expressed.[5]

Despite its phonetic poverty, however, *aleph* is a letter of prestige in the Jewish tradition, and it is certainly no accident that the Hebrew grammarians consider it the first in the alphabet. One of the earliest great works of the Kabbalah, *The Book Bahir* (ספר הבהיר), defines it as older than all signs and more primordial than their combination in Scripture: "Aleph preceded everything, even the Torah" (היתה קודם לכל ואפי' לתורה).[6] It is almost as if the silence of *aleph* were not only the sign but also the reason for its distinction. The introductory section of the *Zohar* explains the letter's privileges as the just rewards for its exceptional modesty:

> When the Holy One, Blessed be He, was about to create the world, the letters [of the Hebrew alphabet] were with Him. And He contemplated them and played with them for the two thousand years that preceded the creation. When He decided to create the world, each of the letters came before Him, from the last to the first.[7]

It is only natural, of course, for each to wish to be the instrument of creation, and every letter, from *tav* (ת) to *gimel* (ג), furnishes good yet ultimately insufficient grounds for her candidacy (letters in Hebrew are feminine). *Tav* points out that she constitutes "the seal of truth" (אמת), *shin* (ש) that she marks the beginning of the divine name "Almighty" (שדי), *tsadi* (צ) that she is the inception of the "righteous" (צדיקים), as each member of the alphabet, beginning with the last, steps forward to extol her virtue. Finally we reach *bet* (ב), who reminds God that "it is thanks to me that you are blessed [ברך] both above and below," thereby earning her distinguished position in the opening two words of the Torah: "In the beginning [God] created..." (בראשית ברא). "'Of course!' the Almighty, Blessed be He, responded. 'It is with you that I will create the world; you will be the one to inaugurate the creation of the world.'"[8]

During the entire proceedings, we read, *aleph* hid herself:

Aleph abstained from coming forward. The Holy One, Blessed be He, said to her: "Aleph, Aleph, why did you not come forward before Me like all the other letters?" Aleph responded: "Master of the World, I saw all the other letters come before you to no end, and what was I then to do? Moreover, You have already given this precious gift to the letter Bet, and it is not proper for the great King to take back the gift that He has just given to one servant to give it to another." The Holy One, Blessed be He, said to her: "Aleph, Aleph, even though I will create the world with Bet, you will be the first among all the letters of the alphabet. I will have unity in you alone, and you will also be the beginning of all calculations and all works in the world. All unification will rest in the letter Aleph alone."[9]

Excluded from the first word of creation, *aleph* nevertheless becomes the fundamental principle of all construction. Placed at

21

the inception of the alphabet, the letter is accorded the numerical value "one," and its silence in the beginning proves the reason for its subsequent elevation among all others.

The first portion of *Bereshit rabbah*, one of the most famous of the ancient commentaries on the Hebrew Bible, dwells at some length on the absence of *aleph* from the beginning, recording a number of interpretations of the seeming lacuna at the opening of the Torah. Here Rabbi Yoma starts the discussion, asking, on behalf of Rabbi Levi, "Why was the world created with the letter *bet?*"[10] Another *midrash aggadah* is even more pointed. "The text [of Genesis] could also have read 'God in the beginning created,' in which case the first letter would have been *aleph*" (*aleph* being the letter of the divine name used in the opening verses of Genesis, אלהים).[11] Various reasons for the worthiness of *bet* are adduced, but before long the sages explicitly pose the question of the absent *aleph*: "Why not *aleph?*"

> Because it is the sign of cursing [ארירה, which begins with an *aleph*]. Another interpretation: so as not to give reasons to the heretics who would then say, "How can a world exist if it is created under the sign of cursing?" ... Truly, the Holy One, Blessed be He, said, "I will thus create [the world] under the sign of blessing [ברכה], so that it may exist thus."[12]

Before causing consternation among the Palestinian rabbis, however, the incipit is said to have troubled no one more than the letter herself:

> A saying of Rabbi Eliezer on behalf of Rabbi Aha: For twenty-six generations [the twenty-six generations between Adam and the revelation at Sinai], Aleph grieved before the Throne of glory of the Holy One, Blessed be He. "Master of the world," she said, "You did not

create the world with me, although I am the first of the letters!" The Holy One, Blessed be He, answered, "The world and that which fills it were only created for the sake of the Torah, as it is written: 'The Lord has made the earth with wisdom [that is, the Torah]' [Proverbs 3.19]. And indeed tomorrow, giving the Torah at Sinai, when I begin to speak, I will utter no other letter than you: 'I [אנכי, which begins with the letter *aleph*] am the Lord your God' [Exodus 20.20]."[13]

Recalling the form of the opening of the Decalogue, the tale (which is repeated again in a much later midrash[14]) moves the discussion from one beginning to another, substituting the absence of the letter from one capital passage for its decisive presence at the scene of the giving of the Torah in its entirety. If one recalls that the revelation at Sinai is in every sense the fundamental event in the history of the Jewish tradition, it is not difficult to measure the honor thus accorded *aleph*. The prestige of the letter in the history of Israel, quite simply, could not be greater.

When the precise nature of the revelation became an explicit topic of investigation, the commentators were naturally forced to confront the original form of the divine words inaugurated by *aleph*. The Talmudic treatise *Makkot*, which contains a fundamental discussion of the matter, established that the only words directly heard by all the children of Israel at the foot of the mountain were those of the two phrases that, in Exodus, immediately follow the initial *aleph* of "I" (אנכי): the commandments "I am (the Lord thy God)," and "Thou shalt have no other (gods before Me)."[15] Considering the "speech at Sinai" at some length in the second book of *The Guide of the Perplexed*, Maimonides drew on this Talmudic source while departing from it significantly. He argued that the rabbinic claim that the Israelites heard "I am [the Lord thy God]" and "Thou shalt have no other [gods before Me]" directly from the mouth of the Almighty was purely speculative: it indicated that "the principles of divine existence and unity can be conceived by [mere] human understanding."[16] Maimonides could then add the following, more modest answer to the question of what the Israelites themselves actually heard: "It is clear to me that in the scene of Mount Sinai, not everything that reached Moses reached the Israelites in its totality."[17] Noting that God addresses himself in this passage exclusively to a second-person singular, and that the text of Scripture relates only that the Israelites perceived a "voice" (קול), the philosopher concluded that the people "heard a mighty voice, but not distinct words" (אלצוט אלאטים לא תפשיר אלכלאם, literally "the mighty voice, but not the distinction of speech").[18] "In the whole scene," Maimonides thus reasoned, not without a certain severity, "the Israelites heard only one sound, and they heard it only once."[19] The philosopher in this way both rewrote a rabbinic gloss on the biblical passage and anticipated its most radical mystical interpretations. The "one sound" of *The Guide of the Perplexed* recalls the Talmudic reading of the first word uttered at Sinai, "I" (אנכי), as the stenogram of an entire Aramaic phrase, "I decline my soul in writing."[20] But at the same time, only the smallest gap separates it from the doctrine of the eighteenth-century Hassidic rabbi Mendel of Rymanów, which Gershom Scholem once summarized as follows: "All that Israel heard was the Aleph with which in the Hebrew text the first Commandment begins, the Aleph of the word *anokhi*, 'I.'"[21]

Through a series of contractions of increasing intensity, the divine revelation is thus reduced to its smallest element: from the text of the entire Torah as it was given at Sinai, we pass to the only text that was heard by all, the first two commandments, which are then said to be contained in the single word "I" (אנכי) and, in the most extreme case, compressed into its initial *aleph*, which *The Book Bahir* defines as "the essence of the Ten Commandments" (עקרהון דעשרת הדברות),[22] and the *Zohar* as the "head and end of

24

all degrees," "the inscription in which all degrees are inscribed."[23] The single, "mighty voice" of which Maimonides wrote thus shows itself, in the end, to be curiously silent: all revelation is reduced to a single letter whose sound none can recall. The point is perhaps less startling when it is grasped in its theological dimension. Could God have shown himself to human beings in anything other than a letter that they had always already forgotten? The sole material of divine speech, the silent letter marks the forgetting from which all language emerges. *Aleph* guards the place of oblivion at the inception of every alphabet.

Chapter Four

Endangered Phonemes

Sooner or later, every language loses its sounds. There is nothing to be done about it. The phenomenon can be observed not only diachronically, during the centuries a tongue develops, decays, and disappears. The synchronic analysis of a single moment in the course of a language suffices to illuminate the sounds its speakers are always already forgetting. In his *Principles of Phonology*, Trubetskoi demonstrated in systematic detail that every language can be characterized by a finite set of distinctive oppositions, which come to light once its vowels and consonants are classified according to their particular traits. A linguist wishing to study the sound shape of French, for instance, can begin by distinguishing oral vowels (such as *i*, *y*, and *u*) from nasal vowels (such as *ɛ*, *œ*, and *ã*) and by classifying consonants according to whether they are occlusive (such as *p*, *t*, and *k*), constrictive (such as *f*, *s*, and *ʃ*), lateral (*l*), or semi-consonants (*j*, *ɥ*, *w*). From the identification of such general differences, the scholar of language can pass to more precise and minimal distinctions. Within French oral vowels, for instance, closed vowels may be opposed to open vowels, half-closed ones can be opposed to half-open ones, and within each series of oral vowels of a certain opening one may divide the anterior from the anterior-labialized and the posterior; among consonants, one may similarly distinguish between the elements of each series until, at the end of the phonological portrait, it is possible to ascertain which sounds may be significant in a language and which sounds, by definition, may not. But the study of the language cannot end there; the specialist in sound and sense must go still further. The presentation of the sound shape of French will not be complete until the linguist has added to the set of significant sounds that the language includes and to the set of sounds that it excludes a third class: those phonemes that lie at its borders, those meaningful sounds the language is still in the process of acquiring—and those vowels and consonants that it is already losing.

Linguists who have studied the sound shape of French have thus observed that the Gallic tongue contains at present thirty-three full-fledged phonemes while being affected by an additional three sounds, classified by phonologists alternately as "problematic," "threatened," or "endangered phonemes" (*phonèmes en voie de disparition*).[1] No longer full members of the set of sounds in a language, these "problematic phonemes" are not yet utterly foreign to it. They cannot be clearly classified within the sounds of a tongue, but at the same time the "threatened" sounds cannot be said to lie outside it. "Endangered phonemes" inhabit the indistinct region at the limits of every sound system; they reside in the phonic no-man's-land that both separates and joins every language to what it is not. In contemporary French, they are all vowels, and their disappearance, which has been well under way for some time now, cannot but bring about the obsolescence of distinctive oppositions that traditionally characterized the language. They are the rare α of the word *tâche* (tɑʃ), "task," as distinguished from the "middle" *a* of the word *tache* (taʃ), "stain"; the nasal vowel œ in the word *brun* (bʀœ), "brown," as opposed to the nasal vowel in *brin* (bʀɛ), "sprig"; and the ə traditionally reckoned to be the vowel of the first-person pronoun *je* (ə) and the word *mesure*

28

(mǝzyʀ), "size," considered somehow, although not distinctively, opposed to the anterior vowels ø of nœud (nø), "knot," as well as the œ of heure (œʀ), "hour," to say nothing of the half-closed e of nez (ne), "nose," and the half-open ɛ of naît (nɛ), "born."

The third of the "endangered phonemes" is surely the most elusive of the set. It has always been numbered among the sounds of the language, yet its definition presents contemporary linguists with the greatest of difficulties. In the authoritative Grammaire méthodique du français of Martin Riegel, Jean-Christophe Pellat, and René Rioul, one encounters it not as a phoneme in its own right but as a "problem" that proves singularly resistant to all pho-nological classification and that, in the absence of clear, distinctive properties, proves susceptible to bearing all sorts of names. "It is here," the authors of the primer in linguistics write as they offer an account of the vocalic series containing the phonemes y, ø, and œ, "that we must confront the problem of the e. The sound sometimes transcribed as ǝ is generally described, in terms of articulation, as a central sound that is half-open, half-anterior, and half-posterior; yet the reality, as we see, is in fact slightly different. It has sometimes been termed 'the obsolete e' [e caduc], and it is indeed true that at times it does 'fall' and disappear; at times it has also been called 'the silent e,' yet it is when it is not silent that it can be characterized as a phoneme, for otherwise it does not correspond to any observable reality—in other words, otherwise it is nothing at all; and at still other times it has been said to be 'the non-tonic e.'"[2] Later, in a section dedicated to the enigmatic vowel, the authors go so far as to raise serious doubts as to its very existence: "The phonological reality of ǝ, or, if one wills, its distinctive function, can be strongly called into question. On the one hand, it cannot be phonetically opposed to its close neighbors ø and œ.... And above all, it can be observed that even in the words which include it, its frequent disappearance seems to

have no effect on communication: whether one says 'lafənɛtʀ' or
'lafnɛtʀ' it is still *la fenêtre* [the window]; and *une bonne grammaire*
[a good grammar] can be just as easily 'ynbɔngʀam(m)ɛʀ' or 'ynə
bɔngʀam(m)ɛʀ.' A mere 'phonetic lubricant' (Martinet), it seems
to have no function other than to help avoid, as much as it can,
certain consonant clusters."[3]

One might well wonder why linguists do not abandon the
"problematic phoneme" altogether. Why devote such attention
to a single sound that seems not even to be one, that cannot be
strictly opposed to any other in phonological terms, that seems
not to play any functional role in semantic terms, that is a "phonetic lubricant" at best? The answer is simple. There is a domain
in which the "obsolete," "silent," or "non-tonic" *e* plays a decisive
role: poetry. One cannot perceive the rhythm of a French verse
if one does not take into account the possibility of its presence in
the syllable count. Take, for example, Mallarmé's verse "Ce lac dur
oublié que hante sous le givre."[4] Although it cannot be established
with certainty when examined in isolation, this linguistic seg-
ment, which is composed of twelve syllables and divided by a syntactic caesura after six, constitutes an alexandrine. But it can be
perceived as such only as long as one sounds, either silently or out
loud, the "obsolete" final *e* of *hante*: if one utters the words as they
might well be pronounced in contemporary French, "sølakdyru-
bliekeãtsulezivʀ," one produces a hendecasyllable and entirely
misses the meter of the verse.

The "endangered phoneme" may have vanished from the coun-
tryside of the French language, but it nevertheless survives, albeit
behind bars, in its poetry. No reader of French verse can let the
threatened sound escape from his field of vision. None who would
wish to perceive the music of the language can forget the "problematic *e*" altogether, for without it it is not possible to discern
the repeated series of syllables that constitutes the rhythm of the

poem. One has no choice: if one wishes to have anything at all to do with the music in the language, one must leave an acoustic door open in case the threatened syllable should wish to present itself. Here nothing, however, is certain. The elusive sound may make itself heard within the verse, but it also may not; its presence or absence depends on a series of complex linguistic, historical, and prosodic factors. Specialists in French metrics, of course, have long sought to specify these factors, but their task is clearly not an easy one: how, after all, is one to be sure of the characteristic movements of an animal that is no longer to be found?

One recent work on French versification defines the sound as "the unstable *e*" and, more precisely, "the optional *e*," in the sense that it is a phoneme characterized by the possibility that within a given word it may or may not appear. "This possibility, which is a characteristic of the 'word' insofar as it can appear in either of two forms," Benoît de Cornulier has written, "can be called ... the *e* option."[5] Such a definition succeeds admirably in accounting for the presence of the "threatened phoneme" in the verse: wherever the *e* is sounded, it will always have been possible for it not to have been. But what of the times when the phoneme is absent? As the inventor of the "*e* option" cogently notes, if the elusive sound does not manifest itself in the verse, it is difficult to see how one could presume to identify it there. When the *e* does not appear in the syllable count, the scholar writes with scientific precision, "one cannot seriously call it a *vowel* or assign it the name of a vowel, because it does not exist. Concerning this position, one can only mention that a vowel—the vowel named *e* in accordance with orthographic conventions—could (under certain conditions) have been actualized; but this non-usage, or this omission of *e*, ... is not truly an *e*, a vowel, a non-actualized one. An absence of sound is not a voiceless or mute sound, even when it is localized by a letter."[6]

What is a sound that "could ... have been actualized," but was not? Admittedly, the phonologist "cannot seriously call it a *vowel* or assign it the name of a vowel, because it does not exist." But even he cannot do without it altogether. He must still—if only—"mention" the fact that it could have been actualized but was not, recalling that a certain "option" in the language might have been actualized, even if, in fact, it was not. Imperceptible and inexistent, the named but unnameable *e* thus remains within the poem, haunting it; not even the most rigorous analysis of the structure of the verse can fully banish the "problematic phoneme" from its terrain. Having fallen silent in its language, having retreated from sight even in its final abode in poetry, the "unstable" letter is now in truth more than "endangered"; it is dead. As the linguist points out with mortuary precision, it would be going too far even to call it a "voiceless or mute sound." But it nevertheless persists: the "absence of sound" remains in its disappearance, and it is the task of poets to shape it as they draw from the vanishing letters of their language the matter of their art.

CHAPTER FIVE

H & Co.

A letter, like everything else, must ultimately meet its fate, and over time every written sign of speech falls out of use. No matter how eminent its place in the idiom to which it belongs, a letter ultimately grows quaint, then rare, falling finally into utter obsolescence. A grapheme, however, has more than one way to go. Its demise can be more or less natural, as it were, the result of a gradual and irrevocable occurrence that owes nothing to resolutions on the part of a writing community. One thinks of the archaic Hellenic letters that had already begun to vanish from Greek scripts before the classical literary tradition as we know it came to be transcribed: from the most illustrious and often commented on of the set, the semi-consonantal *digamma* (Ϝ), which was once the sixth letter of the alphabet and whose traces can still be found in Homer, to the *koppa* (Ϙ), the *sampi* (Ϡ), and the *san* (Ϻ), to name only three figures to which the memory of marks has not been kind.[1] But one need not look as far away in space and time as ancient Greece for evidence of the disappearance of members of alphabetic systems. English suffered its own losses: after the invasion of the Normans, the Anglo-Saxon *eth* (ð), thorn (þ), *aesc* (Ϝ), *ash* (æ), and *wynn* (Ƿ) slowly went their way, and the last of the representatives of the old script, the *yogh* (ȝ), followed them soon afterward, once a contrasting continental *g* established itself in the *abecedarium* of the language.[2]

Elements of writing, however, can also grow obsolete on account of deliberation and decision. For better or worse, their fates can rest on the judgment of those who would, or would not, write them. A glance at the history of writing reveals the brute fact: letters can be forcibly evicted from the scripts to which they once belonged. In a drastic orthographic reform of 1708, Peter the Great, for example, decreed that a series of rare figures of Greek origin (such as the θ, the ξ, and the ψ) were to leave the Cyrillic alphabet immediately, and shortly after the October Revolution the linguistic representatives of the new Soviet state declared that a host of letters were in truth superfluous and henceforth never again to be printed. Nineteen seventeen thus became the year of the official obsolescence of an unusual *z*-mark (the зело, ς), two rare types of *i*-graphs (the восьмиричное, i, and the десятиричное, ï), and a sign for a vowel (a closed *e*) of considerable age and respectability (the ять, ѣ), which had entered the script from that most venerable of tongues, Old Church Slavonic, and found itself, in revolutionary times, suddenly banished to the linguistic terrain of Bulgaria (where, it should be added, it did not last long, removed in turn from the Balkan script in 1945).[3]

Letters can also vanish more than once, and, like spirits, they can return to make themselves perceptible long after some would pronounce them quite defunct. A classic case is the grapheme *h*, from the spelling of whose current English name, "aitch," the initial letter itself, tellingly, is now often absent. The sign of the sound characterized by linguists as a pure aspiration or a glottal fricative, *h* belongs to the alphabets of almost all the languages that use the Roman script. But the value it designates often remains imperceptible in speech; and in the passage between languages, it is almost always the first to go. The implications of this can be severe, as Heinrich Heine, a poet of multiple *h*'s and two distinct types of aspiration (the pure *h* and the more constrictive *X*), knew well. In the memoirs he composed between 1850 and 1855, he commented on the alteration his name had undergone following his emigration from Germany:

> Here in France my German name, "Heinrich," was translated into "Henri" just after my arrival in Paris. I had to resign myself to it and finally name myself thus in this country, for the word "Heinrich" did not appeal to the French ear and the French make everything in the world nice and easy for themselves. They were also incapable of pronouncing the name "Henri Heine" correctly, and for most people my name is Mr. Enri Enn; many abbreviate this to "Enrienne," and some called me Mr. Un Rien.[4]

From "Heinrich Heine" to "a nothing" in four steps: the "translation," geographic and linguistic, was in this case more than treacherous. Had the poet chosen to move not westward but eastward, however, the consequence could have been at least as grave. He might in his own lifetime have assumed an equally unrecognizable appellation, in which the initial letter of his first and second names vanished into not "a nothing" but "a something" at least as startling: "Geynrich Geyne" (Гeинрих Геинe), as he is known to this day in Russia.

The truth is that the breathy letter posed delicate problems from the beginning. Pre-Euclidean Greek inscriptions contained an *h*, no doubt the distant ancestor of the Roman letter. The mark of a consonantal aspirate, it is thought to derive from an earlier letter (Ｂ), which represented an adaptation of the Semitic letter *ḥēt* (which, in turn, engendered both the Hebrew ח and the Arabic ح). The Greek *h*, however, did not last long, at least as the sign of an aspirate. By the early fifth century B.C., the grapheme

35

h had acquired a vocalic value, which eventually brought it to its classical form as the Greek letter *eta* (ê); at the same time, the aspirate phoneme, by contrast, came to be indicated in writing by a "half-*H*," namely, Ⱶ.[5] From there, *h* followed a double path to obsolescence, both as a sound and as a sign. During the centuries in which classical Greek was spoken, the once-consonantal phoneme gradually gave way to a soft but audible "initial aspiration." In Hellenistic times, the weakened aspiration began to leave the language altogether, and documentary sources indicate that by the fourth century A.D., if not sooner, the sound had long since disappeared. During the same period, the Ⱶ graph, a fragment of its former self, shrank in size, losing its right to a full position in the writing of letters. The philologists and grammarians of Ptolemaic Alexandria reduced it to a small mark above the letter it modified. Still later, scholars and copyists abbreviated the sign further, making it a diacritic, placed before the modified vowel, that was barely more sizable than a period and closely resembled our modern apostrophe. Hence the final form of the grapheme in the Hellenic script: ', designated by specialists in the Greek tongue ever since not as a letter but as a "spirit" (to be exact, a "rough breather," *spiritus asper*, or πνεῦμα δασεῖαν, as distinguished from the "smooth breather," *spiritus lenis*, or πνεῦμα ψιλή, which indicated the absence of aspiration before vowels).

On the surface, the Latin script, by contrast, recognized *h* as a full-fledged member of its alphabet. But the grapheme of the Roman language seems to have represented a sound of as little substance as the Greek aspirate: "basically a weak articulation," as one historical linguist has written, "involving no independent activity of the speech-organs in the mouth, and ... liable to disappear."[6] It is no doubt for this reason that the Romans themselves seem to have been unsure of the exact status of the letter in their language. In a passage of the *Institutio oratoria*, Quintilian, for

36

example, voiced doubts about whether *h* constituted a "letter" at all.[7] Despite appearances, his was a generously open-minded position: later grammarians, such as Priscian and Marius Victorinus, defined the mark in no ambiguous terms as "not a letter, but merely the sign of breathing" (*h litteram non esse ostendimus, sed notam aspirationis*, we read, for instance, in Priscian's influential *Ars grammatica*).[8] Like its Hellenic counterpart, the Roman sound seems to have been infirm by nature, apt to vanish from whatever position in the word it occupied. Its historical demise was thus both gradual and irrevocable. First it vanished in the classical period between vowels (*ne-hemo* became *nemo*); then it disappeared, in the middle of the word, after certain consonants (*dis-habeo* became *diribeo*); finally, by the end of the Republic, it departed from its last holdout, the beginning of the word (in common inscriptions, *Horatia, hauet* thus became *Oratia, auet*).[9]

Before long, only the most educated Latin speakers could be sure where the elusive sound had once been. The stakes of subtracting—or adding—a breath or two became quite marked. In a poem, Catullus ridiculed one Arrius, who, to appear erudite, added aitches at the start of his words, where they did not in fact belong.[10] And in a famous passage of the first book of his *Confessions*, Augustine, denouncing the teachers of his day, took as his target the grammatical obsession with aspiration among Carthaginian *magistri*:

O Lord my God, be patient, as you always are, with the men of this world as you watch them and see how strictly they obey the rules of grammar which have been handed down to them, and yet ignore the eternal rules of everlasting salvation which they have received from you. A man who has learnt the traditional rules of pronunciation, or teaches them to others, gives greater scandal if he breaks them by uttering the first syllable of "human being" [(*h*)*ominem*] without aspiration [that is, as *ominem*] than if he breaks your rules and hates another human being, his fellow man.[11]

The teachers' punctilious attention to orthography was clearly meant to distinguish them from the uncouth multitude, which knew nothing of the etymologically correct placement of breaths.

Among themselves, however, even the learned of the age expressed uncertainty about why some words possessed or lacked aspirations. Aulus Gellius, for example, lived a good two centuries closer to the original aspirate than Augustine, but he was already well aware of the problematic status of the Latin "letter," and in a passage of his *Attic Nights* he devoted a chapter to the question of its presence in selected words. It was, he argued, an entirely gratuitous addition, made by the Romans of ancient times who had wanted to increase the "force and vigor" (*firmitas et vigor*) of certain expressions and at the same time to recall the characteristic accents of the classical Athenians:

> The letter *H*—or perhaps it should be called a spirit rather than a letter—was added by our forefathers to give strength and vigor to the pronunciation of many words, in order that they might have a fresher and livelier sound; and this they seem to have done from their devotion to the Attic language, and under its influence. It is well known that the people of Attica, contrary to the usages of the other Greek races, said *hikhthus* (ἰχθύς, fish), *hippos* (ἵππος), and many other words besides, aspirating the first letter. In the same way our ancestors said *lachrumae* (tears), *sepulchrum* (burial-place), *ahenum* (of bronze), *vehemens* (violent), *incohare* (begin), *helluari* (gorman-dize), *hallucinari* (dream), *honera* (burdens), *honustum* (burdened). For in all these words there seems to be no reason for that letter, or breathing, except to increase the force and vigor of the sound by adding certain sinews, so to speak. (*In his enim verbis omnibus litterae*

seu spiritus istius nulla ratio visa est, nisi ut firmitas et vigor vocis quasi quibusdam nervis intenderetur.)[12]

A graphic sign with no semantic "reason" of its own, *h* had clearly become in Aulus's time a thing of some mystery. The erstwhile-aspirate phoneme was, at least by the second century A.D., a breath in need of explanation.

Since it had been marked by an orthographic figure and iden-tified as such by the grammatical authorities of classical and late Antiquity, the ancient "breather" did not vanish in the centuries that followed the demise of the Roman Empire. It persisted in the written language of the schools and universities of the Mid-dle Ages; and even those such as Petrus Helias, who, following Priscian, later denied it the status of a "letter," did not go so far as to question its place in the alphabet.[13] The real challenge to the letter came later. With the emergence of the grammatical sciences of the European vernaculars in early modernity, the "spirit" sud-denly found itself the object of the most critical scrutiny. Start-ing in the mid-fifteenth century, grammarians, typographers, and teachers in Italy, Spain, France, and England called the grapheme to the courthouse of national orthography, often threatening to do away with it altogether. At one extreme were the Italians. The first to extol the rights of the vernacular in the face of Latin, they were inevitably also the most hostile to this classical mark. In *Il polito*, a treatise on orthography published in 1525, Claudio Tolomei thus considered the possible functions of the grapheme at some length before reaching his verdict, which was unsparing. "I say," he declared, "that no force obliges us to want this *h* among our letters."[14] And in the same years, Giovan Giorgio Trissino noted in his *I dubbî grammaticali* (Grammatical Doubts) that *h* "is no letter," subsequently adding: "It is a totally useless mark of breath" (in his reformed spelling, *nota di fiatω tωtalmente ωzioSa*).[15]

The grammarians of French and Spanish seem to have been more moderate in their judgments of the old aspirate. Like the Italian humanists, they were of course aware of its singularity as a sign. In his 1529 *Champfleury:Art et science de la vraie proportion des lettres*, Geoffroy Tory, for example, qualified *h* as "neither a Vowel, nor a Consonant, nor a Mute, nor a Liquid, and by consequence no Letter at all."[16] And in his groundbreaking *Liber de differentia vulgarium linguarum et Gallici sermonis varietate* (Book of the Differences of Languages and the Variety of the French Language) of 1533, Charles de Bovelles wrote of the sound indicated by the mark that "one barely notices it on the lips of the French, unless the eyes come to the aid of the confused and almost indistinct perception of the ears."[17] But the philologists nowhere suggested that *h* be removed from the script of the language. Antonio de Nebrija, the first grammarian of Spanish, justified the modern use of the figure in systematic terms in his *Reglas de orthografía en la lengua castellana* (Rules of Orthography in the Castilian Language) of 1517. Going so far as to treat *h* as a letter in its own right, he argued that it "held" no fewer than "three offices" in the modern language, in addition to recalling the aspirations that had once been sounded in Latin. It marked the Spanish successor of the Latin *f* (as in *hago*, which represents the modern form of *facio*); it helped in several cases to separate the vowel and the consonant, marking a vocalic *u* (as in *huerto* [uerto]); and, finally, when placed after *c*, it indicated "that sound that is proper to Spain, for which we have no other letters, *mucho, muchacho*" (in modern linguistic terms, the constrictive consonant ч).[18]

The threatened mark found at least as many friends in early-modern England. Modern English, to be sure, had erected itself over the tomb of Anglo-Saxon aspiration. By the sixteenth century, the modern *l* had completely eclipsed the older *hl-* (as "loaf" had taken the place, for example, of the Old English *hlāf*), the solitary n- was well established where *hn-* had once dwelled ("nut," for instance, being the modern form of *hnutu*), and the single r- had acquired all rights over those positions that had belonged to the *hr-* in the older tongue ("roof," in this way, having supplanted *hrōf*).[19] The English grammarians, one could imagine, were perhaps unwilling to lose that last remnant of breath designated by *h*. The first orthographers of the language were in any case united in their defense of the contested grapheme. Sir Thomas Smith, the author of the first published treatise on English spelling (*De recta et emendata linguae Anglicae scriptione* of 1568), declared himself aware that "some people, over fond of the Greek, have, as it were, expelled *h* from the senate of letters" (*quidam nimium grœcissantes, è litterarum tanquam senatu moverunt*), and that still others had "replaced" it. Nevertheless, like Nebrija, he treated the sound alongside all the letters, maintaining that "whether you choose to call it a letter or a spirit," the English "use it freely."[20] And in 1669, over a century later, William Holder argued in a similar vein that even if certain authorities rejected *h* as a letter in the full sense of the term, there were in truth good grounds for its official and integral inclusion within the territory of the English language. "In that it causes a sensible, and not incommodious discrimination of sound," he wrote, "it ought to be annexed to the alphabet."[21]

Well after the canons of grammar and spelling had been established in the modern European vernaculars, the question of the precise status of the elusively pure aspirate achieved a central place in the intellectual program of the Enlightenment. In 1773, Christian Tobias Damm, a distinguished theologian and disciple of Christian Wolff's, published a "Betrachtung über die Religion" (Reflection on Religion), in which he provided a reasoned and methodical critique of the traditional German practice of employing the grapheme in the middle and at the end of certain words, where, he argued, it could not possibly reflect any convention of speech. "Universal, sound, and practical human reason," Damm wrote, "authorizes our German minds *newly to say* how the letter *h*, which is never pronounced, came to be inserted *between syllables* by *careless, unthinking bread-writers* and so-called pulpiteers [unachsamen, unbedenkenden Brodtschreibern *und so genannten Kanzellisten*], and to say that the aforementioned *h* must be done away with [*abgeschafft*], insofar as it is a useless, unfounded, and barbaric practice that is insulting to our nation in the eyes of all foreigners."[22] That more than "the aforementioned *h*" itself was at issue in such a "reflection" became particularly clear in the final lines of Damm's polemic. Here the Protestant theologian declared, in threatening terms, that "he who, in spelling, is unfaithful with respect to that little letter, *h*, is also, in the *great* revelations and mysteries of the universal, sound, and practical human religion, willingly *unfaithful* and *unjust*."[23]

Today Damm's "Betrachtung" is best known for the response it provoked from one of the dissenting voices of the age, Johann Georg Hamann, who quickly came to the defense of the grapheme in his "Neue Apologie des Buchstaben *H*" (New Apology for the Letter *H*), also published in 1773. Accepting the challenge of what he called an "orthographic duel" (*orthographischer Zweikampf*), Hamann reflected on the two reasons adduced by his adversary for the proposed spelling reform: that *h* is not pronounced; and that, when unsounded but written, it cannot but bring disgrace upon the German nation among the peoples of Europe.[24] Hamann concluded that both reasons were spurious. Damm's proposal, it followed, was a barely disguised "crusade against an innocent breath," an act of unmotivated aggression against a being whom "speech-brooders [*Sprachgrübler*] have more than once wished to recognize as a letter."[25] Why, the apologist wondered, had Damm singled out *h*, among all the letters, for reproach? Hamann noted that if the letter's fault lay in its unsoundedness, the double *l*, the double *s* (or *ß*), and the double *t*, all unquestioned, would also have to go.[26] He sketched the dire consequences that would surely issue from such changes in the landscape of the German tongue: "What fragmentation! What Babylonian confusion! What hodgepodges of letters!"[27] And he dismissed Damm's attempt to convince his readers that "foreigners" considered the Germans "barbarians" on account of their silent aitches. Did not the English, the French, and the Latins before them all behave with the same "irresponsibility" (*Unverantwortlichkeit*) with regard to the etymological *h* they, too, had inherited from Antiquity?

At the end of his tract, the self-styled apologist revealed that his commitment to the letter was an interested one, in a double sense: it was, he explained, both professional and more intimate. Hamann now assumed a *persona ficta*, claiming for himself the mask of a poor schoolteacher who wished nothing more, in his modest life, than to impart some sense of spelling to his three classes, who awaited him with growing impatience even as he wrote. The author claimed, moreover, to be bound to the disputed grapheme by his own Christian name: Heinrich. In fact, however, the pseudonym concealed the more pressing pertinence of the question for the author, who was far more profoundly implicated in the entire affair than he wished to reveal. For the thinker's surname made him, quite literally, an "*H* man": precisely a *Ha-mann*, as the German language has it, in both spelling and sound. It was perhaps for this reason that the apologist-author felt qualified, in the closing paragraph of his essay, to give the last word to the contested character itself. "The small letter *h*," "Heinrich" now wrote, "may speak for himself, if there is any breath at all left in his nose." So the apology proper ended, and thus began its appendix and conclusion: "Neue Apologie des Buchstaben H von ihm selbst" (New Apology of the Letter *H* by Himself), in which the aspirate briefly rehearsed the schoolmaster's argument, defending himself at last, not without some impatience, in his own name. "Do not be amazed," *H* explained, "that I address you with a human voice, like the dumb and encumbered beast, to punish you for your misdemeanors. Your life is what I am—a breath!"[28]

In the course of the long and repeatedly threatened life of *h*, Hamann's apology was hardly the last. A little over a century later, Karl Kraus, to name only one of the grapheme's other great defenders, composed a poetic memorial for the fallen letter, "Elegie auf den Tod eines Lautes" (Elegy on the Death of a Sound), whose opening stanza sounded the following passionate injunction: "May the God of language protect this *h*!" (*Dass Gott der Sprache dieses h behüte!*).[29] But the eighteenth-century essay was perhaps the first vindication of the sign on its own terms, as it were, neither as a consonant nor as a vowel but as the singular being it had been held to be since the inception of grammatical learning in classical Antiquity: a written "breath." In this defense of the obsolescent mark, there spoke, if only once, and if only in a whisper, the most illustrious member of the company of dead letters: the one letter of the spirit. One might also call it the spirit of every letter. For there is no written sign, however widely recognized its rights and however well respected its functions, whose sound does not pass through the mute medium of the "rough breather"; there is none that does not come into being and fade away into nothingness in the aspiration and exhalation designated by the letter now called aitch. *H*, to paraphrase a poet who removed it from his name, is the trace that our breathing leaves in language.[30] That is perhaps why, in one way or another, it will not leave us: the rhythms of its appearances and disappearances are those of the inevitable, if irregular, expirations of our own speech.

Chapter Six

Exiles

A group of speakers can lose the capacity to produce not only some but even all the sounds and letters of its language as an entire idiom falls, for one reason or another, into oblivion. One then says that the language is dead or, more precisely, that a new language has begun to be spoken. Such terms belong to historical linguistics, a discipline that approaches its obsolescent objects with the benefit of hindsight. In the moment a people begins to forget what was once its language, of course, things are rarely so clear. The possibilities are many. A tongue can vanish without its ever being noticed; it can also be recalled by those who once spoke it at the moment it becomes for them only a memory. But no language, even one considered holy, can escape the time of its transience. It was thus that the language of the five books of Moses, for example, progressively gave way, within the single yet diverse collection of texts that form the Hebrew Bible, to the later forms of speech that supplanted it, ultimately ending with the "Syriack" in which the Chaldeans in the Book of Daniel are said to communicate, which modern philologists identify with a different yet related language, Aramaic. And it was thus that this second Semitic language, which in truth belonged not only to the advisers of Nebuchadnezzar but also to those who claimed to be descended

45

from Israel, ceded its place to a third, Arabic, at a still later point in the life of the people of the ancient Near East.

For the Jews, the loss of biblical Hebrew raised questions whose theological import could hardly be avoided. It is true that Scripture could be explained and translated at least in part, and the expressions of the Bible could be sifted through the idioms that followed them in time. As evidence, it suffices to call to mind a page of the Talmud, in which one finds as many as three languages invoked to gloss a single legal principle. One might also recall that monument of Arabic Jewry, the *Taj*: the polyglot edition of the Pentateuch in its original Hebrew, the Aramaic rendition called *Targum* and the singular translation, completed by Sa'adīa Gaon in the tenth century, in which Jewish Scripture finds expression in a form of Arabic that at more than one point noticeably recalls the characteristic diction and phrases of the Qur'ān while being written, as it happens, in the letters of the Hebrew alphabet. Both the *Talmud* and the *Taj* aimed to move back, by hermeneutical, exegetical, and philological techniques, through the time that separated one form of speech from another; both sought to traverse the layers of oblivion that tie, while separating, one moment in the course of a language to another that, by then, had been forgotten.

Certain dimensions of the lost language, however, proved particularly difficult to retrieve. One was that of sound. Early on, the phonetics of the holy tongue became a subject of discussion among the philologists of Hebrew, who worked in large part in the wake of the nascent grammatical schools of classical Arabic. It was only natural that the debates became most heated when it came to defining the conventions of that field of language in which sound shapes become the matrices of composition, namely, poetry. For those who believed that the original tongue of the Jews could give rise to compositions in verse equal to those of other languages, the question was pressing. How was Hebrew poetry to be written?

The Bible itself furnished only the most cursory indications, for it contained no utterances from which the critic or writer could extract clear principles of versification. In the tenth century, a Moroccan poet and philologist named Dunash ha-Levi ben Labrat proposed a novel idea. Hebrew poetry, he suggested, could be written in the meters used by the poets of the Arabian Peninsula since before the coming of Islam. Of course, certain adjustments had to be made for the Bedouin metrical system to be transplanted into the older Semitic tongue. The system of Hebrew vowels, in particular, differed substantially from that of classical Arabic, and certain Arabic meters proved incapable of being reproduced in the biblical language. But in a series of original poetic compositions, Dunash showed that once certain constraints were made clear, the Arabic system of versification could be applied to Hebrew. Of the original sixteen rhythms of classical Arabic verse, at least twelve could be recovered in metrical "translation" (and the fifteenth-century Spanish philologist Sa'adīa ben Maimūm Ibn Danan, who left us the most complete classical presentation of Hebrew Arabic prosody we have, was of the opinion that even the remaining four meters could be adapted to suit the biblical language).[1]

Not surprisingly, the systematic use of foreign rhythms in Hebrew caused more than consternation among the self-appointed custodians of the ancient language. In the twelfth-century defense of the Jewish religion by the Spanish poet and philosopher Yehuda ha-Levi, *A Book of Proof and Argument of the Despised Faith* (כתאב אלרד ואלדליל פי אלדין אלדליל), also known as *The Book of the Khazars*, it is even suggested that the use of Arabic meters in Hebrew contributed to the obsolescence of the holy tongue.[2] (One hesitates, however, to attribute the claim, which is itself formulated in Arabic, to the author of the dialogue, ha-Levi himself having been one of the unmatched masters of Arabic prosody in the Hebrew language.) In fact, there had been opposition to the

47

use of the Arabic system of versification from the moment Dunash introduced it. A particularly violent response came from the disciples of the great Spanish grammarian and lexicographer Menaḥem ben Saruq, who had written the first dictionary of biblical Hebrew at the end of the tenth century and whose work Dunash had denounced in a series of merciless philological "responses" (תשבות). When the students of the accused master came to his defense, they did so by drafting a series of "responses" to the "responses" of the rival grammarian, in which they submitted Dunash's system of versification, as well as the poems he had written in it, to criticisms every bit as unsparing as the ones that had provoked them. *The Book of the Responses of the Disciples of Menaḥem Against Dunash ben Labrat* opens with a summary inventory of all the solecisms in the verse Dunash had composed in the Arabo-Hebrew meters he had invented. "How can you say the meter of the Arabic language is appropriate for the Jewish language," the disciples demanded of their antagonist, "when all this evidence demonstrates the falsity of your words and calls into question your poems?"[3]

At one point in their opening reflections, the disciples of Menaḥem paused to consider the ultimate reason for all the lexical, grammatical, and phonetic debates in which they and their adversaries participated. It was simple. The identity of the Hebrew language was in need of definition, they explained, because it had slipped away from them long before, because, as the fourteenth-century Provençal thinker Joseph Caspi would repeat, "our language is lost" (נאבד לשוננו).[4] It is not difficult to see the significance of such a fact in the eyes of the medieval grammarians. How could the fate of the holy tongue be separated from that of the people to whom it was once entrusted? The Jews forgot their language, the disciples suggested, for the same reason they were banished from the land that had been given to them: they made

48

themselves unworthy of it. Their exile was not only geographic; it was also linguistic, and it separated them irretrievably from the sounds in which God had once revealed himself to them. "Had we not been sent into exile from our land [ואילו לא גלינו מארצינו]," the disciples wrote, using the technical Hebrew term for the divinely sanctioned banishment,

> we would possess our language just as we did in ancient times, when we lived safely in peaceful places. We would master all the details of our language and its different parts, and we would know its meter without having to transgress its borders. The language of every peo-ple contains its meter and its grammar. But from the day we went into exile, it was lost for us in accordance with the magnitude of our crime; it was hidden from us in accordance with the gravity of our guilt. The wealth it once possessed has been reduced and obscured; it has disappeared. Had God not worked miracles, taking account of the destitution of his people, what little remains today would have already been lost and consumed.[5]

What does it mean for a language to go into exile? It is more common, of course, to speak of an individual or a people being banished from its land. To be sure, sometimes language can be involved, as in the case of the exiled writer, of whom Joseph Brodsky gave a memorable portrait: "To be an exiled writer is like being a dog or a man hurtled into outer space in a capsule (more like a dog, of course, than a man, because they will never retrieve you). And your capsule is your language. To finish the metaphor off, it must be added that before long the capsule's passenger discovers that it gravitates not earthward but outward."[6] The situation described by the medieval grammarians, however, is more complex, for here it is not an individual writer but an entire language that is exiled. The capsule, to retain Brodsky's figure, contains no one, not even a dog: one cannot distinguish the receptacle from its contents, for the whole Hebrew tongue is now said to have left its mythical homeland behind, and passenger and vessel are one. Hence the fundamental difference between the exiled writer and the exiled language. The first can dream of being "retrieved" by those who still reside in the country from which he came, even if the dream takes the form of a disavowal, as when Brodsky notes, in a telling parenthetical remark, that "they will never retrieve you." But for the second, banishment is irreparable. "What little remains today" of the language shall remain in exile, for there can be no return to a land whose "wealth" has definitively disappeared.

One can certainly view the disciples of Menaḥem as partisans of a vain will to defend the purity of a language that they know they have already lost. And the assiduous grammarians were indeed soon vanquished by the efflorescence of the literature they had so strenuously sought to impede. Within a century of the disciples' "responses," there arose in Spain an entire body of poetry in Hebrew composed in Arabic meters that announced, in its unrivaled beauty and complexity, all the transgressions of the borders of the holy tongue that were to follow it in the history of Hebrew letters, from the verse of the medieval and Renaissance Italian and Provençal Jews, composed in Romance forms such as the *canso* and the sonnet, to the poetry of the Jews of eastern Europe, who were later to write in accentual meters borrowed from the Germanic and Slavic languages they spoke. But it is possible that the disciples had nevertheless grasped something few before and after them had seen: that a language, too, can be banished from its place of origin, that it can remain sacred, even though—or perhaps because—the wealth it once possessed has all but vanished. It is perhaps no accident that the golden age in the history of Hebrew poetry, that of Islamic Spain, arose in the moment the writers of the language let its native land fall definitively out of sight. Exile, in the end, may be the true home-land of speech; and it may be that one accedes to the secret of a tongue only when one forgets it.

CHAPTER SEVEN

Dead Ends

At times it seems that a whole language, having run its course, reaches a limit at which it ceases to be itself. The name we are accustomed to give to such an end is the one we use in reference to an organic being: death. The expression acquired currency long enough ago that it is often difficult to recall the exact meaning of the figure at its origin. In what sense can a language, after all, be said to "die"? The usage is of relatively recent date; and it seems to have been unknown to many of the cultures that have contributed to the reflection on language in the West. It did not occur to those inventors of the "art of grammar" (τέχνη γραμματική), the philosophers and philologists of Ptolemaic Alexandria, to consider the Homeric and Attic idioms to be either "alive" or "dead." And when Donatus and Priscian proposed the first systematic accounts of Latin in the wake of their Hellenistic predecessors, neither seems to have thought to use the biological terms with which we are so familiar today. The field of study that classical Islamic culture calls "grammar" (نحو), for its part, took as its object a linguistic being to which "life" and "death" would be equally inappropriate terms, namely, the inimitably "clear Arabic" (العربية المبينه) of the Qur'ān, after which much of the "eloquent speech" (اللغة الفصحة or الفصيحة) of Arabic literary discourse is modeled. And the

53

Jewish scholars who recorded the transience of the biblical tongue
would never have described ancient Hebrew in terms of a mortal
creature, since it was for them "the holy tongue" (לשון הקדש) and
therefore of a nature fundamentally different from that of cor-
ruptible things. The language of Scripture could certainly be forgotten by men; yet it could hardly be said, for that reason, to grow
old and perish on account of them. In the allegorical prologue to
Taḥkemoni, the literary masterpiece of the twelfth-century Spanish
writer al-Ḥarizi, the biblical tongue, for example, makes a remarkable appearance in human form, begging the poet to make of the
language of the Jews a tongue as eloquent as that of the Arabs.
Lamenting the neglect it has suffered at the hands of the people to
whom it was given, Hebrew nevertheless retains the form it could
never lose: for all the wrongs committed against it, the sacred
language remains an eternally beautiful "daughter of wisdom," "a
maiden as pure as the sun."[1]

How and when did it happen that, of all the things of which it
could be thought capable, a language was said to die? It has been
noted that in a passage of the *Ars poetica*, Horace described the
elements of language in terms of organic development and decay,
likening "words" (*vocabula*) to the leaves that come into bloom
and fall from the branches of trees.[2] And in his *Etymologiae sive
originum*, Isidore of Seville divided the history of Latin into four
distinct periods, which have been said to form something like the
"life stages" of a single being: *prisca*, *Latina*, *Romana*, and *mixta*.[3]
But one must wait until the Italian Renaissance to encounter a
depiction of the emergence and decay of language that resembles
the one with which we are familiar today and that fully assimi-
lates the time of language to the life span of a mortal being. Here
examples of the figure of linguistic life and death proliferate. One
of the first occurrences of the image can be found in Lorenzo de'
Medici's discussion of Latin and Italian, in which the vernacular is

54

said to be still in the stages of its "youth," having survived "child-hood" and promising to live well into the more perfect "ages of youth and adulthood."[4] In Sperone Speroni's *Dialogo delle lingue* (Dialogue of Languages) of 1542, Pietro Bembo portrayed the "modern tongue" as "a small and subtle branch, which has barely flowered and has not yet borne the fruit of which it is capable." As such, he opposed it to the two languages of classical Antiq-uity, which, he related, have already "grown old and died" and are, in truth, "no longer languages, but merely ink and paper."[5] The "Courtier" of Speroni's *Dialogo* went even further: Latin, he claimed, is but a "relic" that, "cold and dry by now," ought "to fall silent."[6] In this defense of the vernacular, one finds what may be the first explicit qualification of a language as dead. "You may well adore it," the Courtier says, speaking of Latin, "and hold it in your mouths, dead as it is; but speak your dead Latin words among yourselves, and let us idiots have our living vernacular ones, so that we may speak in peace in the language that God gave us."[7]

After Speroni, the figure became more and more common and, over a few decades, gradually came to play a fundamental role in reflections on the similarities and differences between classi-cal and modern languages in general. The argument of Joachim du Bellay's *Défense et illustration de la langue française* of 1549, whose importance in the history of the French national tongue can hardly be overestimated, relies at every step on the organic metaphor. As in the *Dialogo*, the vernacular appeared in du Bellay's treatise as a plant that had just begun to bloom, in distinction to the old tree of Latinity, said to have already borne "all the fruit it could bear." By the time Benedetto Varchi wrote his *L'Hercolano*, which was published in 1570, he could present the differences between types of languages in universal terms, alongside those of "articulate" (or written) tongues and "inarticulate" (or unwrit-ten) ones. In the chapter of the work dedicated to the problem

55

of the "division and declaration of languages," we thus find the following formulation, which at once recalls and complicates the distinction made by Speroni less than half a century earlier: "Of languages, some are alive, and some are not alive. There are two ways in which a language can be not alive: that of the ones we will call completely dead [*morte affatto*], and that of the ones that are half-living [*mezze vive*]."[8] The vital taxonomy began to admit of degrees. Whereas the European vernaculars, for example, could be said to be altogether alive, and such ancient tongues as "Etruscan" could be called "completely dead," other languages, such as Greek, Latin, and Old Occitan, though not regularly spoken, were nevertheless still in use, lying in a curious state at the borders between the life and the death of tongues.

Before long, the new linguistic categories were fully loosened from the tongues with which they had originally been identified, and it grew possible for every language to be either alive or dead. By the end of the sixteenth century, the first of all "living languages," Italian, had found itself, through a perfectly symmetrical inversion, the first of the European vernaculars to be dubbed "dead." Turning the rhetoric of the defenders of the *vulgar lingua* against the very tongue for which it had been advanced, Bernardo Davanzati remarked in a letter of 1599 that the vernacular championed at the start of the century (in which, it is worth noting, he wrote his letter) no longer differed in nature from the tongues of classical Antiquity. "It seems to me," he commented, "that we are not writing in our own living language, but in that common Italian in which one cannot write literature, which one learns, like dead languages, from three Florentine writers who could not have said everything." (*Come a me pare, che noi facciamo scrivendo non in lingua nostra propria e viva, ma in quella comune italiana che non si favella, ma s'impara come le lingue morte in tre scrittori fiorentini, che non hanno potuto dire ogni cosa.*)[9]

It is unlikely the humanists could have foreseen the success the organic figure they coined would enjoy. Since the time of its formulation in the Renaissance, it has only grown in influence, to the point that it now seems something of a truism to claim that every tongue, by definition, must be either alive or dead. In our time, the idea of the death of language certainly shows all the signs of being, if one may say so, alive as never before. There is today an entire field of linguistic studies dedicated to a phenomenon that bears the technical name "language death," in which scholars have distinguished a range of degrees of linguistic obsolescence far more baroque than any imagined by the scholars of the sixteenth and seventeenth centuries. While Varchi limited himself to defining one state of linguistic "half-life," contemporary sociolinguists have taken pains to distinguish a series of levels of linguistic obsolescence, drawing up a whole cast of ghostly tongues. According to many scholars, a tripartite classification is too simple and cannot do justice to the varieties of linguistic decay. It was to this end that in 1992, one linguist, Michael Krauss, introduced the influential notion of the "moribund" tongue, which he applied to those endangered languages caught at the point between being still spoken by the adults of a community and being no longer learned by its children.[10] And it was for the same reason that another scholar, with even greater subtlety, distinguished between two types of "unsafe" languages: those that are "endangered" *simpliciter* and those that are more properly termed "nearly extinct."[11] But still more elaborate taxonomies of fatality are also found in the literature on the subject. It has been argued that there are in fact no fewer than four distinct types of ailing languages, to be classed, according to the increasing gravity of their various troubles, from the "potentially endangered" to the "endangered," the "seriously endangered," and, finally, the truly "moribund," described by one scholar as having "only a handful of good speakers left, mostly very old."[12]

57

The large and often polemical literature on "linguistic endangerment" today leaves one with the distinct impression that for many, the contemporary age could well be characterized as the time of the rapidly intensifying extinction of languages. The last decade of the twentieth century witnessed the establishment of a number of organizations, national and international, governmental and humanitarian, that aimed to remedy what was considered a phenomenon of ever-increasing gravity, which threatened the entire globe with the specter of what some called the "monoglot millennium." In November 1993, UNESCO, for example, officially announced the creation of the Endangered Languages Project; and two years later the U.S. government instituted its own Endangered Language Fund, whose founding declaration, sounding a drastic note, called for an immediate response on the part of linguists worldwide. "Languages have died off through history," the statement read, "but never have we faced the massive extinction that is threatening the world right now. As language professionals, we are faced with a stark reality: Much of what we study will not be available for future generations. The cultural heritage of many peoples is crumbling while we look on. Are we willing to shoulder the blame for having stood by and done nothing?"[13] A newsletter published by the Foundation for Endangered Languages, established by the United Kingdom also in 1995, insisted on the extent and importance of the phenomenon, which it described as marking nothing less than a "catastrophic inflexion point" in the history of humanity. "There is agreement among linguists who have considered the situation," it reported, "that over half of the world's languages are moribund, i.e. not effectively being passed on to the next generation. We and our children, then, are living at the point in human history where, within perhaps two generations, most languages in the world will die out."[14]

It is rare to find a clear discussion in this field's literature of the precise sense that biological, botanical, and zoological figures may have in this setting, and not without reason has one contemporary scholar remarked that "as yet, there is no theory of language death."[15] That a language can be said to "die," in the same sense as an individual or even an entire species, seems the single presupposition on which much of the edifice of the burgeoning scholarly field rests, which may be stressed with more or less intensity and frequency but not questioned as such. A recent handbook on the relatively new field, which bears the programmatic title *Language Death*, for instance, opens with a declaratory statement that is as clear in form as it is obscure in content. "Language death," the author writes, "is real."[16] The gloss of the enigmatic phrase given on the first page of the work is of little assistance, for it reasserts, without explaining, the pertinence of the assimilation of linguistic and biological beings. "The phrase 'language death,'" we read, "sounds as stark and final as any other in which that word makes its unwelcome appearance and resonances. To say that a language is dead is like saying that a person is dead. It could be no other way—for languages have no existence without people."[17] It is not difficult to see the limitation of such reasoning. If it were sound, one would be logically obliged to maintain a number of claims to which one doubts the experts in language death would immediately subscribe, such as that pirouettes, time zones, taboos, and arpeggios must also be said to be born and to die, just like human beings, since they, too, "have no existence without people."

For those who believe in the death of tongues, in any case, the theoretical and practical consequences of the phenomenon seem clear. It falls to the expert in language death and language health to explain the causes of the maladies he studies, which may range from such decisive factors as natural catastrophes (volcanic eruptions, earthquakes, and so forth) and geopolitical events (banishments, massacres, and so on), to technological factors such as

communication media in a foreign language, which one sociolin-
guist, thoroughly committed to the biological figure, has termed
"cultural nerve-gas," and to less easily defined psychological and
sociological determinants, such as what one linguist has called
the "lack of confidence" that some speakers have in their tongue,
which can bring them to commit the act bearing the technical name "language suicide."[18] On the basis of such etiologies,
the expert can then propose some remedies, which can seem
of less than certain value to the untrained observer: examples
cited in the literature on the subject include increasing the prestige, power, and wealth of those who speak the ailing tongue;
encouraging the writing down of the endangered language; and
introducing its speakers to electronic technologies such as the
Internet, which, in the words of one hopeful author, "provides
an identity which is no longer linked to geographical location,"
thus enabling the speakers of an otherwise-moribund tongue to
"maintain a linguistic identity with their relatives, friends, and
colleagues, wherever they may be in the world."[19] For some, such
techniques function only as long as they are sponsored by larger
political establishments, such as the state. Certain sociolinguists
claim, therefore, that the maintenance of the well-being of a language must be an integral part of the political management of the
physiological health of a people. Here the assimilation of linguistic
and biological phenomena is often far-reaching in its implications. "My view," writes David Crystal, formulating a program that
seems at once biological, linguistic, and political, "is unequivocal:
in exactly the same way as doctors ... intervene with the primary
aim of preserving the physiological health of the patients, so linguists should ... intervene with the primary aim of preserving the
linguistic health of those who speak endangered languages."[20]

The phenomena understood to bring about the death of a language are of the most varied sort, and they often present experts

in the field with greater difficulties than they might like to admit. A small set of examples may suffice to illustrate the complexity of the problem. At the second meeting of the United Kingdom's Foundation for Endangered Languages, in 1998, Ole Stig Andersen presented a paper on what he called "The Burial of Ubykh," in which he offered what closely resembled an official report on the recent disappearance of a tongue. "The West Caucasian language Ubykh," he declared, in the technical terms of the field, "died at daybreak, October 8, 1992, when the Last Speaker, Tevfik Esenç, passed away. I happened to arrive in his village that very same day, without appointment, to interview this famous Last Speaker, only to learn that he had died just a couple of hours earlier. He was buried later the same day."[21]

Nearly half a century before the emergence of "language death" studies, the Italian philologist Benvenuto Terracini had recalled a similar event in the history of an Italian dialect once spoken by the inhabitants of the Franco-Provençal valley of Viù. The dialect, Terracini noted, hardly resembled those in the mountainous areas that surrounded the valley, since it was not related to them in historical terms, deriving instead from the language of a different region of northern Italy, eastern Piedmont, from which the dukes of Savoy had sent a small group of miners and ironworkers to the valley in the thirteenth century.[22] Terracini wrote:

> The first time I visited the colony, an elderly man was pointed out to me ... who was considered the best, almost the only one who still spoke in the old manner of the place. There was more: not only did he use his dialect; he knew it, and he loved it with the passion of a collector. Sitting on the porch of his little house, he liked to rehearse with me the memories of his simple life, mixed together with folk-loristic passages, anecdotes concerning the origins and history of the colony: that chapel was built by so-and-so's family; that point over

there, up on the mountain, was where his ancestors had once fought against the folk from another valley in that direction.... He often complained (and in those moments I discerned a gleam of pride) that the younger generation had forgotten their mother tongue, and so I came to think that I was in fact before the last representative of the colony.[23]

Similar tales of the extinction of language can be found well before the twentieth century. They are often startlingly precise in their detail. The great grammarian Joseph Vendryes once noted, for instance, that according to nineteenth-century sources, Vegliotic, a rare Romance dialect, became definitively obsolete on June 10, 1898, in the moment its last speaker, Antonio Udina, accidentally fell into the sea and drowned at the age of seventy-seven. And if one believes an expert of the eighteenth century, the Cornish tongue vanished from the earth when Mrs. Dolly Pentreath died December 26, 1777, leaving behind the significantly impoverished set of the surviving Celtic languages. Long before the modern scholars, however, Nennius already offered an account of the sudden disappearance of a language that was at least as precise as the modern ones, and a good deal more chilling. The Latin historian recounts that when they first arrived in Brittany, the Armoricans killed all the indigenous men of the area, leaving only women and children alive. But then they cut off the tongues of the remaining inhabitants, so that the children born from unions with the Armoricans would speak only the pure Breton language of their fathers.[24]

It is difficult to ignore the fabulous element in such tales, which is especially apparent in the last case, where a single act of extreme violence intervenes in the historical chronicle to efface from the earth an entire tongue. These tales are perhaps nothing other than fictions of the ends of language, which are invoked as the only possible answers to what would otherwise threaten to be an unsolvable question: how can one be certain that a language has truly been lost? Tales of the extinction of tongues certainly aim to provide the necessary documentation for absolutely incontrovertible death certificates, but even they are susceptible to more than one reading.

Commenting on Andersen's account of the "burial of Ubykh," one linguist thus observed that "in actual fact, Ubykh ... had effectively died long before ... Tevfik Esenç passed away. If you are the last speaker of a language, your language—viewed as a tool of communication—is already dead."[25] The structure of the linguistic decease would then be more complex than it might seem: the event would have happened before the time of its official happening, and on the day of the famous occurrence nothing, in truth, would have occurred. Vendryes raised a similar query about the dating of the disappearance of Cornish in the person of Dolly Pentreath. "God, in his grace," he commented, "accorded her an uncommon longevity. She lived beyond her 102nd birthday. Cornish should have died sooner, if one reckons in terms of the average human life expectancy. But did it truly die at this moment? Old Dolly was the only one to speak it; but for a language to be spoken, there must be at least two people. Cornish would then have died the day that last person who could answer her passed away."[26] Terracini, by contrast, admits to having erred in the opposite direction: the dialect of Viù, he relates, in fact remained in life well after the death of the elderly man with whom he had conversed about the fate of the sadly ailing isogloss. After recalling his impression of having stood "before the last representative" of the dialect, the philologist adds that he was in fact mistaken. The disappearance of the rare form of speech turned out not to be so easy to grasp, although the linguist, to be sure, remains convinced that the illness of the tongue is in any event quite fatal. "I was wrong,"

Terracini writes. "Ten years later I was able to return again to the village. My old man was dead, and with him all his stories were buried forever. But the ghostly tongue nevertheless continued to live. I could even see that the works of the elderly man had produced in his grandchildren and pupils (who called him 'Maestro') a kind of rebirth: the last gasping of a life condemned by history to disappear. When? I do not know, but I think that even such drawn-out agonies are destined to cease altogether at a certain point."[27]

What is the "certain point" at which a ghostly tongue finally comes to an end? The linguist who invoked it admitted he had failed to find it once; but still he would not doubt its existence. Here it is difficult to avoid the impression that even the most determined attempts to grasp the decisive point seem fated to miss the mark, as the specialists who would identify the elusive instant find themselves, in the end, pointing to a time already after its disappearance, as in the decease of Dolly Pentreath and Tevfik Esenç, or to one well before it, as in the death of Terracini's elderly friend from the valley of Viù. It is as if the critical moment continued to slip away from the scholar who would grasp hold of it, as if there were an element in the vanishing language that resisted every attempt to record and recall its definitive disappearance. Fabricating the death certificate of a language is no easy task, and it may be that even the most official document of linguistic decease reflects less the tongue to which it is assigned than the convictions of the bureaucrats who produce it. The attempt to demonstrate that a language has reached its end cannot but be motivated, for better or worse, by a powerful, albeit unstated, wish that has little to do with speech and a great deal to do with the desires of those who would be its keepers, who seem often desperately in search of the assurance that a language has truly been laid to rest, buried in a grave from which it will never rise again. Every death certificate remains written in the tongue of its makers, and in this case all documents of decease bear witness to the same obstinate will to set aside the one possibility the experts in the health and the sickness of tongues would rather not ponder: that in language there may be no dead ends, and that the time of the persistent passing of speech may not be that of living beings.

CHAPTER EIGHT

Thresholds

In the realm of languages, cataclysms, of course, are the exceptions. It is rare for a tongue to meet the fate of the inhabitants of Atlantis, who disappeared forever, one presumes, when the mythical continent sank to the bottom of the sea. More often than not, the end of a language is not sudden but gradual, and it can be all the more decisive for being almost imperceptible at the time of its occurrence. At what point did Hebrew, for example, turn into Aramaic, and when exactly did the Latin spoken in the streets of ancient Rome become the modern European language we now call "Italian"? Even those scholars willing to attribute exact dates to the death of languages hesitate to make pronouncements on their birth, although, in principle, if one can mark with certainty the moment at which a tongue ends, it should be possible to identify the point at which one begins. The problem is that noticeable events in the time of languages are rare; and where they can be perceived, they seem less of the order of death than of metamorphosis. Even the most stalwart proponents of the idea of language death must grant this fact. On the whole, "for a language to die," Terracini observed, "is for it to change into another";[1] and the period of the change, as Vendryes commented, is generally a "very long time."[2] When one examines it closely, the end of a tongue seems less a single point than a transition carried out over centuries. What some would liken to a moment of death, in many cases, seems not an event at all but a threshold, through which every form of speech, in its inevitable "transition from one linguistic system to another," must ultimately pass.[3]

The precise nature of this threshold, however, has presented historians of language with the gravest of difficulties, to which both theoretical and practical solutions often seem lacking. One scholar has likened the challenge faced by the specialist in "language shift and language death" to the one faced by the Homeric hero in the fourth book of the *Odyssey* when he sought to identify the sea god Proteus: how can one recognize a being who could easily elude the mortal observer by transforming himself into a lion, a snake, or even a large and stocky tree?[4] The problem is not simply that the metamorphoses of a language, like those of the mythological divinity, are continuous; it is not only that the transformations of speech seem not to admit of discrete points at which the transition from one form to another can be clearly indicated. There is more. Where in the field of language is the body that changes shape, and what are its parts? It has been observed that when the discipline of historical linguistics emerged in the nineteenth century, it did so in the wake of the neo-Lamarckian doctrine of the evolution of species: linguistic beings were thought to change over time just as living forms developed through the modification of their characteristic anatomical constituents. However seductive it may have proved to the founders of the discipline, the homology is in truth of little use, for the simple reason that a form of speech has neither limbs nor organs. As Bernard Cerquiglini has observed with acuity, "In a language there are no gills, fins, or wings, and no elements belonging to an organic system. There are only heterogeneous domains (syntax, lexis, semantics, and so on), which are complex in themselves and have their own historicity."[5]

To follow the course of any metamorphosis, one must know the traits that define the original and subsequent forms of the changing body. But in the observation of language, one may adopt a number of approaches that lead to differing and even contradictory conclusions. Consider, for instance, the passage from Latin to French, of which Cerquiglini has offered an enlightening analysis.[6] If one takes the pertinent trait of the ancient tongue to be its system of declination, one will date the emergence of the modern successor between the first and the fifth century; yet if one finds the kernel of the tongue in the architecture of its verbs, one will be obliged to set the decisive moment sometime between the sixth and the tenth century, for it is only then that one finds signs of a characteristically Romance set of conjugations, in which, for example, tenses are formed on the basis of the conjunction of the verb "to have" (*habere*) and the infinitive or the past participle. If, however, one takes not morphology but phonetics to be the linguistic domain by which one measures the evolution of speech, one will have to choose between a different set of possible dates, which will depend, in turn, on the nature of the phenomena that one takes to be decisive. If one believes that the essential trait of the new tongue, compared with the old, consists of its effacement of tonic vowels, one will maintain that the new language appears between the first and the third century A.D.; if one takes the important difference to lie in the passage from a melodic accent to an accent of intensity, one will set the date some time after the fifth century; and if one locates the decisive element of the transition between languages in the disappearance of final vowels, one will conclude that Latin becomes French only in the eighth century.

Questions of periodicity, to be sure, may be considered settled for practical purposes, even if they are strictly speaking unsolvable in epistemological terms. One may, for example, take as a heuristic criterion the canon proposed by Antoine Meillet, according to which a language is considered "dead" once there is evidence that in the eyes of a group of speakers it has changed into another.[7] The principle, for better or worse, makes the life and death of a language a matter decided entirely by the consciousness of its speakers. It will not permit the linguist to designate a language as extinct until it has been registered as such by the community that once communicated in it, even if, as far as the outside observer is concerned, the tongue is long gone. Until the inhabitants of the province of Gaul show signs of believing they are no longer speaking Latin, for example, the historian will not be able to claim they are speaking French, despite whatever documents he may find in a tongue he himself would consider quite foreign to the classical idiom. In historical research, such a criterion can give rise to results that are approximate at best. How can one be certain there was no consciousness of a language shift before one was recorded in those documents that we happen to retain today? And by what generally valid criteria can one establish the existence of a consciousness sufficient to register the emergence—or demise—of a language? All decisions of dating will rest not on strictly empirical data, which must be falsifiable by nature, but on interpretations, which allow the contemporary historian and philologist to make order out of a linguistically disparate set of surviving records.

Cerquiglini has argued that the French language emerged in 842 with that decisive declaration in the vernacular known to the historiography of the national language, through its transcription in Nithard's *De dissensionibus filiorum Ludovici pii* (History of the Sons of Louis the Pious), as the *Strasbourg Oaths*. To the classic question "Since when does French exist?," the historical linguist has thus given the following answer, which justifies attributing the "birth of French" to the precious Carolingian document: "from the day its difference and specificity, which are due to its own development, are recognized; from the day that they are used consciously, in the service of communication, in a relation of power, and that this usage takes the form of knowledge, that is, writing."[8] One may likewise conclude that by the time François Villon composed his "Ballade en vieil langage françoys" (Ballad in Old French Speech) at the end of the fifteenth century, a further transformation had taken place and a new idiom had already made its appearance: the form of speech that modern historians of the language call "Middle French" but that, for obvious reasons, could hardly have seemed "intermediary" in any straightforward sense to Villon at the time he wrote in it. In this ballad, the poet, setting out to compose a work in a language he himself called "old," produced something of a parody of the language of the twelfth- and thirteenth-century poets, indiscriminately adding to nouns the nominative suffix *s*, which had a distinctive function in the morphology of the *langue d'oïl* but was clearly obsolete in his own day.

The terms "life" and "death" seem of little use in such a setting, for they cannot but suggest a distorted image of the time of language, which is not segmented but continuous and in which emergence and decay cannot be isolated as distinct moments. On this matter, the medieval reflection on the identity and difference of tongues remains unsurpassed in our time, and one looks with great profit to the terms with which Dante characterized the vernacular in his treatise *De vulgari eloquentia*. The poet-philosopher took as his object the speech common to all men, which is learned, he wrote, "by children from those who surround them." Unlike many modern specialists in language, however, he defined the common tongue without reference to any set of rules governing the sounds and forms of meaningful speech. The characteristic trait of human language, Dante argued, is nothing other than its essential mutability in time: its intrinsic "variability" (*variebilitas*)

71

through the centuries, which necessarily brings about the plurality of human languages. "The language of a single people," he thus explained in the first book of his treatise, "varies in the course of time, and it can never remain the same; and this is why the languages of people who live far from one another must become different from one another in the most diverse ways."[9]

In a sense, everyone knows that, as Dante wrote, a language "can never remain the same." But the consequences of such a simple fact are more difficult to admit than it might seem, and they appear at times to have eluded those who have written on the nature and development of speech. Vendryes, for example, began his inquiry on "language death" by stating that "death is a natural act, which belongs to life"; and in his conclusion, he went so far as to define, at least implicitly, the "life" of a language by its capacity for change, writing that "one can tell that a language is dead when one does not have the right to make mistakes in it."[10] And Terracini, as we saw, also recognized that what is called the "death" of a language constitutes not an interruption in the course of its development but its inevitable transformation into another. But the force of the biological figure is strong, and in the end both linguists betrayed their own recognition of the essential mutability of language; they let themselves be swayed by the pathos of the fiction of the life and death of tongues. Vendryes closed his contribution to the subject with an impassioned plea for the maintenance of the identity of the French language: "It is in the interest of each of us to maintain intact this beautiful patrimony of the French language.... It is a collective task, the success of which depends on each of us."[11] Such a conclusion represents a striking retreat before the consequence that inevitably follows from the recognition of the intrinsic mutability of language: namely, that a language cannot be "maintain[ed] intact," for it lasts only as long as it changes. Confronted with the essential variability of all language, Terracini showed signs of a willingness to give up the figure of the "life" of a language, granting that it was ultimately inadequate to the nature of the object in question. But he immediately recovered a biological power of a higher level, writing that "in the final analysis, the mutability of language expresses the infinity of a vital force that stands above the concept of death and even above the concept of birth."[12]

What is a "vital force that stands above the concept of death and even above the concept of birth"? It is as if the scholar wished to retain the very figure he knew, for reasons of method, he had to abandon. The precise nature of the greater power is far from clear, and other names might be equally appropriate at this point. Could the philologist, one wonders, also have spoken of a "spectral force that stands above the concept of death and even above the concept of birth"? In matters of language, both "life" and "death" may be inadequate at whatever level one invokes them. They can, in any case, be avoided. It is possible to conceive of a passage that is not that of the generation and corruption of living beings; it suffices, for example, to think of the sand that desert winds continuously set in motion and that inevitably slips through the hands of the one who grasps hold of it. One finds a figure of this nature in the portrait that Montaigne drew of the perpetually fleeting language he had known in his life and in which he wrote his *Essays*. "I write my book for few men and for a few years," he commented sometime around 1540. "If it had been a question of making it last, I would have committed it to a firmer tongue. Given the continual variation that ours has followed to this very hour, who can hope that its present form will still be in use fifty years from now? Every day, it slips out of our hands, and in the time I have lived, it has changed by half. We say that it is perfect at this hour. So says every century of its own. I do not care to consider it such, as long as it runs away and deforms itself as it does."[13]

73

The beginning and the ending of a tongue are perhaps best grasped in the terms afforded by Montaigne. They can be seen as nothing other than two moments in the course of the "continual variation" by which every language "runs away" from its speakers and "deforms itself," two fleeting points at which, for a number of possible reasons, speaking beings suddenly catch sight of a fact they are all too prone to forget: that, often without having been noticed, "a" language has already ceased to be itself. Such points are not only, as many have argued, instances in which a community of speakers recognizes that it has effectively adopted a new language, which it now designates as such for the first time. By that very token, they are also the moments in which a community of speakers sees that it has already lost the language it once spoke. In the perpetual alteration that is language, formation and deformation, emergence and decay, "birth" and "death" can hardly be told apart, and memory and forgetting are inextricably linked. Have the authors of the *Strasbourg Oaths* realized that they are speaking French or that they have already forgotten Latin? The recognition of the advent of one tongue entails that of the passing of another; and the coming to consciousness of a new language must simultaneously imply a "coming to unconsciousness," so to speak, of the old, in which a community, giving a name to its newfound tongue, recalls the idiom to which it has already, perhaps unwittingly, bid farewell. Beginnings and endings are but two sides of a single threshold, and in the time of language they are figures of the transience that destines every tongue to vanish in its imperceptible and yet irrevocable passing into another.

Hence the vanity of all attempts to slow or stop the fleeting course of languages. Whether they are nationalist or international, philological or ecological, such projects are united in the belief that speech is an object in which linguists can, and must, intervene to recall and conserve the identity from which it seems to be departing. In their aim to hold on to the forms of speech a tongue has already cast off, such efforts are futile at best. One way or another, a tongue will continue in our time to change "by half," running away and deforming itself as it does, for a language, as Dante wrote, "can never remain the same," and, whether we like it or not, it will continue "every day," in the words of the essayist, to slip out of our hands. Essentially variable by virtue of the time that is its element, speech is incapable of being fully possessed and so, too, completely lost; always already forgotten, it can never be recalled. Despite their best efforts, the biographers will not catch the metamorphoses of this protean being.

CHAPTER NINE

Strata

In the passage from one language to another, something always remains, even if no one is left to recall it. For a tongue retains more than its speakers and, like a mineral slate marked by the layers of a history older than that of living beings, it inevitably bears the imprints of the ages through which it has passed. If "language is the archives of history," as Ralph Waldo Emerson wrote, it does, in this sense, without keepers and catalogs.[1] Its holdings can only ever be consulted in part, and it furnishes the researcher with elements less of a biography than of a geological study of a sedimentation accomplished over a period with no clear beginning or end. Like the multiple memories of indistinct and immemorial origins invoked by the nearly nameless narrator of *Remembrance of Things Past*, the remains of the past are superimposed on one another in speech with an often-impenetrable density and complexity. In language, as in the mind of the novel's protagonist, the present invariably contains the stratified residues of a past that, when examined, retreats beyond the memory of the individual who uncovers it. "All these recollections, superimposed upon one another, formed only a mass," he recalls, "but it was still possible to distinguish between them, between the oldest ones and the more recent ones, born from a scent, and still again from those that were but the recollection of another person, from whom I acquired them—perhaps they formed fissures, real geological fault lines, that variegation of coloring, which in certain rocks, in certain blocks of marbles, points to differences of origin, age, and 'formation.'"[2]

It seems to have been such a geological conception of speech that led an early-nineteenth-century Scandinavian scholar, Jakob Hornemann Bredsdorff, to propose a doctrine of language change that, for better or worse, has exerted great influence on historical and general linguistics from the time of its formulation in 1821 to the present day.[3] Bredsdorff's theory was simple: alterations of speech over time are reflections of historical changes in the ethnic consistency of speaking peoples. Conquest proved the classic example. In the period following the domination of one nation by another, he noted, two populations come to be inevitably fused. It may seem, to be sure, that the dominated group disappears under the force of the dominators. But the population produced in the historical encounter between the two peoples is in truth the child of both nations; it represents the progeny not only of the victors but also of the vanquished. So, too, Bredsdorff reasoned, in the contacts between peoples the language of one people might seem to give way to that of another. Yet it could still survive in the one that seemed to supplant it. Buried by a novel idiom, an old tongue could persist in the speech of its people; and hidden from view and all but forgotten by those who once spoke it, one language, the scholar maintained, could then exert a subterranean force on its successor, causing it in time to change.

"Substrate" is the name Bredsdorff gave to the persistent remainder of one tongue within another, the forgotten element secretly retained in the apparently seamless passage from one language to the next. The idea found almost immediate favor among specialists in the development of languages, and in the nineteenth

century it was invoked by many of the founding figures of historical linguists, especially those most competent in Romance philology. Claude Charles Fauriel, Friedrich Diez, Hugo Schuchardt,
and Graziadio Ascoli, for instance, all sought to explain aspects
of the development of the neo-Latin languages with reference
to the substrates they contained, which harked back to the indistinct time in the life of the inhabitants of the European regions
before the coming of the Romans.[4] In the twentieth century, what
has become known as "substrate theory" has been extended to a
number of linguistic fields largely unexplored by the nineteenth-
century scholars. It has been invoked, for example, to explain the
emergence and development of such diverse phenomena as the
modern Arabic dialects, Japanese, and Caribbean creoles. Since
Bredsdorff, the doctrine's terminology has grown more complex,
and today the student of language change has at his disposal at least
three technical terms for the mineral deposits left by one language
in another. Specialists in the field of language contact and language
change now distinguish "substrates" in the strict sense from those
linguistic entities called "superstrates" and "adstrates." Following
Walther von Wartburg, the scholar will speak of a "superstrate"
when discussing the changes brought upon the tongue of one
people through its adoption by another, as when one nation takes
on the language of the inhabitants of a territory it conquers and
thereby alters it.[5] And the expert will use the term "adstrate," an
expression coined by Marius Valkhoff, for those cases in which
one language changes on account of the proximity of its speakers
to another idiom to which it is related.[6]

The "strata" that compose a single language are many, and they
can be of varied form and importance. It can be a matter of a set
of lexical elements, for which no exhaustive principles of selection can be found. Take, for example, the many common words of
Scandinavian origin left in English from the time when the Nordic

peoples fought and lived with the Anglo-Saxons of the British Isles, such as the terms "skin," "shirt," "cake," "egg," and "fellow." Sometimes they constitute additions to the vocabulary of the language, as with the Scandinavian term "skirt," which persists beside the Old English word "shirt," and at others they represent substitutions of older Anglo-Saxon forms, as with the verb "to take," whose entry into English brought about the obsolescence of the Old English *niman*, cousin of the modern German *nehmen*. Lexical strata, however, can also be more systematic. One language can retain forms borrowed from another for terms belonging to a well-defined semantic field: consider the religious and juridical terms of Hebrew and Aramaic origins in Yiddish, or the Latin expressions that for so long composed the biological, zoological, and medical taxonomies of the modern European languages. In all such cases, one tongue persists in another. The vocabulary of a single language bears witness to the multiple historical strata that compose it.

The strata that tie one language to another, however, are not necessarily lexical. They can also be phonological, and if one believes those scholars who have argued in their favor, they can determine some of the most fundamental traits of the sound shape of a single tongue. Examples of the phenomenon are not lacking, even within the restricted linguistic terrain of the Romance family. It has been argued, for example, that the shift from the Latin *f* to the Spanish *h*, which plays such an important role in the historical phonology of the language, reflects the phonetic properties of the original tongue of the inhabitants of the Iberian Peninsula;[7] that the aspirated intervocalic *k*, *p*, and *t* that mark the Tuscan accent in contemporary Italian are due to an archaic Etruscan deposit in the speech of the region;[8] and that a host of phonetic features which unite the dialects spoken along the coasts of Spain, France, and Italy, and which distinguish them from other Indo-European languages, point to an original "ethno-linguistic Mediterranean substrate."[9]

One of the most widely debated and contested of cases is the French palatal vowel transcribed, according to the orthographic conventions of the language, by the single letter *u*, as in the current words *pur*, "pure," and *dur*, "hard." Today, linguists classify the sound as one of the three anterior, rounded vowels (*y*, *ø*, *œ*). In the words of the phonologists of the language, it "constitutes one of the original aspects of French and presents foreigners who do not have it in their language with great difficulties."[10] As early as the nineteenth century, scholars observed that in those French words that seem to derive from Latin, the phoneme consistently appears in the position occupied by the long vowel *ū* in the classical language: to retain the examples already cited, where the Romans said *purus* (pūrus), the French say *pur* (pyʀ), and where the ancients said *durus* (dūrus), their modern successors in the land that was once Gaul now say *dur* (dyʀ).[11] How, the philologists naturally asked themselves, is one then to understand and explain the passage of *ū* into *y*? The phonetic transformation seemed particularly in need of explanation because of its apparent singularity: one need merely glance at the physiognomy of the Romance languages to ascertain that the shift did not take place in all the modern languages that emerged in the European territories in which Latin was once spoken. The vocalic shift is attested exclusively in the forms of speech that developed in France and the regions near its borders. In the geographic domains of Portuguese, Catalan, and Castilian, as well as in Romanian and both peninsular and insular Italian, the classical vowel passed unchanged into the modern Romance languages, where, as a rule, it continues to appear today in the exact positions assigned to it by the vocabulary of the classical tongue.

In a philological study of an Old French literary work published in 1876, Eduard Koschwitz related an explanation for the phenomenon that was to become something of the classic case in the field. The account of the change, Koschwitz acknowledged, was not of his own invention. But it came from a most eminent authority—namely, Gustav Gröber, who later acquired a canonical position in the disciplines of medieval and modern literary scholarship by founding the *Grundriss der romanischen Philologie*, with whose multiple volumes and fascicles every student in the field must still reckon.[12] Koschwitz began by recalling Professor Gröber's observation that it is not exact to claim, as was often done, that the phonetic mutation took place exclusively in French. $\bar{U}$ also turned into *y* in the tongues and dialects "of the other Romance countries whose original populations belonged to the Celtic race, such as northern Italy and the Ladino linguistic regions."[13] The explanation for the shift then followed immediately. "One is justified," Koschwitz concluded, "in maintaining that the Celt, whose language completely lacked the *u* sound, was accustomed to pronouncing what was once a *u* as an *i*, and transformed in this way the Latin *u*, if not into *i*, then into *y*."[14] The cause of the vocalic shift, he argued, was a linguistic deposit left to the people of Gaul by the "race" defeated long before by the Romans, an irreducible Celtic substrate that persisted in the otherwise Romance tongue.

The explanation met with great favor among many scholars in the field, and it was not long before Gröber's account of the Celtic component in the phonetics of modern French came to number among the authoritative doctrines of the historiography of the language. Such eminent figures as Gaston Paris, Graziadio Ascoli, and Hugo Schuchardt, in particular, all subscribed, albeit in different ways and for different reasons, to the so-called Celtic hypothesis (*Keltenhypothese*).[15] But dissenting voices were soon heard; and in addition to works by those nineteenth- and twentieth-century philologists and linguists who have maintained that the emergence of the palatal vowel in French, Occitan, and Rhaeto-Roman (or Ladino) is due to a Celtic stratum, there is by now an equally significant literature on the contested phoneme by scholars who have denied that the birth of the sound could be explained in any such terms. The critics have adduced several reasons for the improbability of the hypothesis. The first of them is comparative, and it calls into question the supposed link between the *y* sound and Celtic linguistic communities. In his classic *Einführung in das Studium der romanischen Sprachwissenschaft* (Introduction to the Study of Romance Linguistics), Wilhelm Meyer-Lübke pointed out that both Vegliotic and Albanian contain the *y* vowel but can hardly be said to have a Celtic substrate, and that, by contrast, the Italian region of Emilia was once inhabited by Celts, yet its modern dialect bears no trace of the sound.[16] In an article titled "L'U long latin dans le domaine rhodanien" (The Long Latin *U* of the Rhône Region), Edouard Paul Lucien Philipon similarly observed that the presence of the Celtic people often did not imply that of the contested sound. In Aquitaine and central Italy, there were never any Celts, yet the speech of the region now contains the *y* sound; in the area around the Rhône, which was once Celtic, one still finds the old Roman *u*; and in contemporary Irish Gaelic, surely a Celtic tongue, the long *u* remains a member of the vocalic set.[17] Research on the Gaulish tongue itself, moreover, has furnished significant evidence against at least part of the original "Celtic hypothesis": for today it is generally accepted that, far from "completely lack[ing] the *u* sound," the language of the Gauls included it, in both short and long vocalic forms.[18]

Historical considerations, too, have led scholars to doubt that the formation of the characteristic vowel could be attributed to the ancient language of the people of Gaul. It seems only natural to assume that if the transformation of the Latin *u* into the French *y* was indeed the work of "the Celt," who was "accustomed to pronouncing what was once a *u* as an *i*," then the phonetic shift should be datable to a time when there were still Celts in France and when the Gallic tongue had not yet entirely been replaced by Latin. But there is little evidence that this is the case. At first, to be sure, scholars believed that the vocalic change could be attributed to an age when the Celtic tongue was still in use, even if no longer at its height. Gaston Paris, who considered the modern sound "one of the oldest monuments of our language,"[19] thus argued in 1878 that the vocalic change could be ascribed to the third century A.D.[20] But as the research on the historical phonology of the language became more precise, the date of the change began to slip further and further forward. In 1887, Rudolf Lenz argued that it could not have occurred before the sixth or seventh century;[21] three years later, Meyer-Lübke's *Grammatik der romanischen Sprachen* (Grammar of the Romance Languages) presented it as a phenomenon of the eleventh century, at the earliest;[22] and by the middle of the twentieth century, scholars had concluded that the phonetic change took place in the thirteenth century, that is, close to a millennium after the Gallic tongue ceased to be a language of regular use in France.[23]

How long can a language last? If one believes the theorists of the substrate, it would seem that well after vanishing, the ancient tongue nevertheless somehow remained in force. A good thousand years after its disappearance, something of the mother tongue of the Celts still survived and continued, beyond the grave, as it were, to exert its influence on its Latinate successor. It is remarkable that specialists in the French language did not abandon the "Celtic hypothesis" when they discovered that the change from the Latin *ū* to the French *y* occurred ten centuries after the obsolescence of the Celtic language. On the contrary, many historical linguists continued to maintain the theory of Gallic influences on the phonetics of modern French long after it had been established that such "influences" could not have been those of a living language. A number of explanations were then suggested. Some took recourse to physiological figures, which cast language as the object of biological heredity, as when Antoine Meillet claimed that speech habits could be transmitted from generation to generation in a way analogous to physical characteristics, and when Clemente Merlo defined variations in articulation over time as the signs of the various "phonetic predispositions of different peoples."[24] Such claims gave rise to often startlingly biologistic theories of sound change. In a famous article, Jacobus van Ginneken, for example, explained the phonetic change from $\bar{u}$ to y as the effect of the "recessive" components of the genetico-linguistic constitution of the inhabitants of France, and Philipp August Becker went so far as to write of the "Celtic inheritance of the speech organ," which, through the "awakening of dormant tendencies," had been led by its innate "palatal disposition" to produce the y phoneme.[25] It is not difficult to see that the science of language, in such cases, had little scientific about it. The claims of scholars seem at times barely separable from the ideologies of national and racial identity that marked the political landscape of the twentieth century.

Many scholars, however, have maintained that past languages can continue to influence present ones for reasons that have nothing to do with national identity and the supposed biological heredity of speaking beings. A number of explanations of the curiously belated influence of one language on another have been suggested. In a study of the Indo-European legacy of the Celtic languages, Julius Pokorny, for example, argued that the "mysterious reappearance of linguistic tendencies after several generations" could be understood in social terms as the equivalent in speech to the rise of "social classes that had until then been oppressed."[26] More faithful to the principles of philology, Ramón Menéndez Pidal appealed to the slow and gradual nature of all linguistic change as an explanation for the seeming persistence and even recurrence of long-obsolete forms of speech. In language, he noted, alterations are carried out over centuries, and every process implies a "latency period," in which the obsolescent and the incipient, conservation and innovation, inevitably coexist.[27] The substrate would be a being of this ambiguous state: situated in the indistinct region between one language and its successor, it would stretch beyond the tongue and the people to whom it once belonged, extending well into those that followed it.

Such an explanation is attractive but ultimately misguided. For it suggests that the "latency period" in language is one among others and that the overlapping of distinct forms in speech can therefore be restricted to a single moment in the development of language. Yet speech, in contrast to the history that is written of it, knows neither periods nor chapters; its movement remains everywhere as continuous as it is complex, and it is difficult to see how linguists could ever entirely exclude, at least in principle, the possibility of a foreign substrate in their object. The archaeological remainder, *a limine*, could lie concealed beneath any linguistic element at any point in the duration of a single tongue. What word, what sound, what phrase could not contain the persistent trace of another? The contested Gallic vowel may be not the exception but the rule; and it may be that more of a language than its speakers would like to think is the forgetting of another, which continues to resound, albeit in oblivion, in the sounds of its successor. The meticulous research of linguistic geologists certainly aims to identify the distinct strata, both indigenous and foreign, that compose and decompose a single language. But the search for lost time is no less arduous in speech than it is in memory, and the ages through which a tongue has traveled resist retrieval and representation. Confronted with the fault lines and fissures of language, the speaker and the scholar are in this sense less able than the narrator who, summoning the mineral mass of his recollections, believes he can "still...distinguish between them, between the oldest ones and the more recent ones." They cannot boast his powers of discrimination. For the "latency period" of speech knows neither beginning nor end, and in the continuum in which all languages move, one cannot ultimately distinguish with certainty between propriety and impropriety, emergence and decay; repetition and difference here grow indistinct. The slates of language are too many, and too diverse, for the rhythms of their incessant shifting to be perceived all at once.

CHAPTER TEN

Shifts

Sometimes one language retains so much of another that one may
wonder whether it is truly "a" language at all. The most obvious
cases are those politically, culturally, and socially marginal forms
of speech alternately termed "creoles" and "pidgins," which can
seem startlingly unlike national languages and yet often nearly
indistinguishable from them. In a lecture given to a German-
speaking public in Prague in 1912, Kafka, for example, characterized the language of the eastern European Jews, Yiddish (which
he called *Jargon*, in accordance with the scholarly conventions of
the day), as an idiom spoken "from the outskirts of the German
language" (*aus der Ferne der deutschen Sprache*), inseparable from
the major European tongue and yet also irreducible to it. And he
maintained, for this reason, that as a rule, the Judeo-German idiom
could be perfectly well translated into any European tongue, with
the one natural exception of German.[1] But even those languages
that now seem most august have been called into question, in
their time, as autonomous forms of speech. No less an authority
than Aelius Stilo, the first grammarian of Latin and the teacher
of both Cicero and Varro, was of the opinion that the language of
the Romans was in truth but a dialect of Greek. Although none
of his own works has survived, a number of sources indicate that

his judgment was widely shared in Antiquity, before being revived in a new form and forcefully defended by several humanists, such as Pietro Bembo and Guarino Veronese, in the second half of the fifteenth century.[2]

The foreign components in languages are not always easy to measure, and any theory of substrates must grant that the diverse slates that compose a single tongue are of differing extent. To be sure, the survival of one language within another can be a limited phenomenon: take the Yaku tongue, which, although now generally considered defunct, is said to persist in a number of plant names widely used today in Ethiopia.[3] Vanished languages, however, can also leave their traces on spoken ones in more complex ways, which are often difficult to define. A classic case is the Arabic dialects, which show a remarkable degree of lexical, phonetic, and grammatical diversity, despite being thought to derive from the same classical language that today remains, to a large degree, the sole written tongue of the Arab world. Faced with the difficulty of tracing the different idioms now spoken in Egypt, Iraq, North Africa, and the Syro-Palestinian region back to a common source in the archaic language of the Bedouins who conquered so much of the Middle East and Africa starting in the seventh century, many Orientalists long ago took recourse to the theory of substrates. The contemporary dialects, they argued, developed out of the various encounters of the classical tongue with the indigenous languages spoken at the moment of the Arab invasions.

Noting that "the forming of a language is a continuous process, albeit a slow one, and [that] any given stage thereof necessarily reflects, besides the overall patterns of the present, several remains of the past," Irene Garbell, for instance, argued in a study published in 1958 that the specific sound system common to many of the spoken idioms of Syria, Lebanon, and Palestine could be explained through the hypothesis of a residue left in Arabic

by the Semitic language spoken in the area before the Arab conquest. "It ... seems indicated to assume," she wrote, "that phonetic
changes in the Arabic dialects of the region are possibly or probably due to Aramaic influence."[4] In this case, much more than a
vowel was at stake. According to the scholar, the entire phonology
of Levantine Arabic was determined, in its development and systematic structure, by the persistence of the older Semitic language
within it. The argument has certainly been contested, but it is
hardly an *unicum* in the field.[5] Similar and even more far-reaching claims have been made for the vernacular of contemporary
Egypt, which has often been said to owe much to the Coptic
language spoken by the Christian inhabitants of the country at
the time of the Arab invasion. Using the classic terms of substrate
theory, George Sobhy formulated the doctrine as follows: "When
a Copt turned into a Muslim, he was bound to learn Arabic. That,
he could not do in a day or two. It was only natural then, that he
was obliged to speak and have relations with his co-religionists
in a mixture of Coptic and Arabic. Thousands did that—and thus
a new Arabic dialect was evolved for the inhabitants of Egypt—a
mixture of Coptic and Arabic."[6] Almost twelve hundred years
after falling out of regular use among the inhabitants of Egypt,
Coptic, according to such a view, would have thus still survived.
It would have been not so much incorporated into Arabic as fused
with it, in a "mixture" that brought about the characteristic idiom
of modern Egypt.

As always, there is little scholarly unanimity on the subject,
and the critics of the Coptic thesis are numerous. It is hardly
surprising: how, after all, could one expect to measure the persistence and power of a vanished language with any scientific
exactitude? The specialists differ considerably in their estimates
of the nature and extent of the linguistic remnant. For some,
not only many of the sounds but even much of the grammar of

contemporary Egyptian bears witness to the hidden presence of the foreign element in the apparently Arabic tongue: some of the characteristic consonants and vowels of the vernacular, as well as a number of its typical syntactic structures, would be traceable to a common Coptic stratum. For others, by contrast, the examples of influence are more limited. But even those most skeptical of the Coptic inheritance admit that the remains of the old tongue may well be more than phonological and extend into the grammar of the modern language.[7]

Any consideration of the nature and extent of the strata that compose a language ultimately confronts a question that is not strictly linguistic but philosophical and involves the very concept of a language as such: how much can one tongue retain of another? How much Aramaic can the eastern Mediterranean dialect, for example, contain if it is still to be largely distinct from it, and to what extent can Coptic determine the sounds and grammar of the Egyptian vernacular if this contemporary form of speech is to remain a variety of Arabic?

Such questions become most heated when the linguistic objects in question are those official idioms of political associations known as national languages. Charged with representing a single people, a form of speech can often prove singularly resistant to analysis and identification. One may take as an example Hebrew, which, after having remained in use without being tied to any single political entity for almost two thousand years, was suddenly summoned to become the official language of a nation little over half a century ago, at the time of the establishment of the state of Israel in 1948. Those who oversaw the transformation of the ancient language into a national vernacular dubbed the process "language revival," but it is not difficult to perceive the imprecision of such a phrase. In the field of speech, the words "rebirth" and "resurrection" are at least as unclear as "birth" and "death"; and in this case, there are a number of good historical and linguistic reasons, as several scholars have indicated, to treat them with great caution. It has been pointed out, first of all, that if one takes the "death" of a language to be the moment it ceases to have any function in a community, then Hebrew cannot be said ever to have died, for after it ceased to be used as a spoken idiom, the ancient tongue remained a commonly used means of written expression among Jews, for whom it was a "diglossic half-language."[8] Others have remarked that if one understands the term "revival" in its usual sense, as the restoration of vitality to a creature long dead, then Hebrew was never truly revived, for the modern idiom does not coincide with the ancient variety of the tongue.[9] As many linguists have shown in detail, those who aimed to "revive" the ancient language were thus ultimately obliged to do something quite different: to constitute a new tongue on the basis of an old one as they established, in particular, new rules of pronunciation for a language that had largely lost them and a suitably modern vocabulary for an idiom whose *realia* had until then been characteristically biblical.

The new national language that thus emerged seemed clearly Hebrew, but at the same it inevitably contained unmistakable traces of the various mother tongues of its twentieth-century European inventors. Such traces continue today to extend well beyond the lexicon of the novel twentieth-century idiom. After just a few moments of attentive listening, one notices that the sound system of the modern language possesses some elements that are unlikely to have belonged to the ancient tongue and lacks others that most likely were a part of it. Take, for example, the uvular or "trilled" r of the contemporary language, which is far closer to the letter r in modern High German than to the apical liquids or "rolled r's" of Semitic languages (such as the letter rā' [ر] in Arabic, to which the Hebrew letter resh [ר] typologically corresponds); or consider the distinctive oppositions in biblical

Hebrew between such letters as *aleph* (א) and 'ayin (ע), *tet* (ט) and *tav* (ת), *kaf* (כ) and *qof* (ק), to which there remain equivalents in modern Arabic but not modern Hebrew, even if its script retains them for etymological reasons. In its morphology and grammar, moreover, the Israeli language shuns a number of characteristic Semitic structures, opting instead for ones closer to the Indo-European languages: examples include the widespread tendency to avoid the construct state, as well as suffixed nominal forms, and to replace them by analytic expressions of belonging formed on the basis of the preposition של, which recall symmetrical constructions in the modern European languages. And where the modern language does retain the morphology of the old, it often alters its semantic value to make its forms homologues to those of modern European languages. A case in point is the verbal system of Israeli Hebrew, which resembles that of biblical Hebrew in its morphology but not in its semantics, which is closer to that of Indo-European languages.[10]

Such traits are all undeniable, and it is only natural they have been remarked on by scholars of the language, who have interpreted them in different ways. For some experts, they seem of relatively minor importance, signs of an Indo-European "adstrate" in the modern Semitic language bearing witness to the mother tongue of the majority of the Hebrew-language revivalists, namely Yiddish.[11] For other scholars, however, such characteristics are significant enough to call into question the Semitic identity of the modern national language as a whole. In his *Einführung in die semitischen Sprachen* (Introduction to the Semitic Languages) of 1928, Gotthelf Bergsträsser already observed that the new tongue spoken by the Zionists of Palestine seemed less a Semitic idiom than "a European language in transparent Hebrew clothing";[12] and twenty years after the foundation of the Jewish state, an Israeli linguist went so far as to characterize the modern language of his country as "nothing other than a translation of eastern European languages."[13]

The most radical thesis on the subject to be advanced so far may be that of Paul Wexler, a professor of linguistics at Tel Aviv University, who in 1990 published a slim but highly provocative monograph bearing the unmistakably polemical title *The Schizoid Nature of Modern Hebrew: A Slavic Language in Search of a Semitic Past*. The idiom of the biblical people, Wexler argued, has little to do with that of the state of Israel, both in its typology and in its genesis, and the use of the single glottonym "Hebrew" for both languages cannot but obscure the fundamental difference that separates them. The first is an ancient Semitic tongue that ceased to be spoken approximately eighteen centuries ago; according to the linguist, the second is an Indo-European language fashioned at the end of the nineteenth century as a modern form of Hebrew. The emergence of the Israeli national language, Wexler maintained, was not the "resurrection" of the ancient tongue of the Bible; it was not even its continuation. The modern vernacular, in his view, arose instead in the moment the language planners of Israel, aiming to restore the ancient Semitic tongue, exchanged their native Yiddish vocabulary for a biblical one and altered their pronunciation so as to make it seem more Mediterranean than eastern European, in a "compound process" Wexler termed "relexification *cum* rephonologization." The language that then resulted superficially resembled the tongue of the ancient Jews, but it could not truly be classified as Hebrew. As Wexler remarked, "A Semitic lexicon hardly suffices to turn an Indo-European language like Yiddish into the 'direct heir' of Old Semitic Hebrew." Without knowing it, the Zionists had produced something much stranger: in the words of the researcher, "a form of Yiddish with a bizarre vocabulary."[14]

"Partial language shift" is the name given by the linguist to the complex process at the origin of the modern national language.

The eastern European tongue, seeming to give way to another, would have lived on, albeit hidden from sight, in the artificial "Hebrew" of the new state. Pronounced obsolescent by all, Yiddish would in truth have found a new life, so to speak, in being forgotten by both its speakers and its observers. The movement of such a "partial language shift" is certainly subtle, and it might have provoked the scholar who defined it to reconsider one of the fundamental, if unstated, axioms of substrate theory, which holds that it is possible to distinguish in speech between element and set, between the single stratum and the complex geological mass to which it is added. Here the presumed Yiddish "component" of the Israeli language would have extended well beyond the limits of the part, determining the sound and the grammar of the national language as a whole. But the scholar, holding fast to the terms of the discipline, continued to believe that even in such a complex displacement of slates, major and minor plates could still be distinguished; and reversing the traditional judgment, he thus argued that modern Hebrew is not a Semitic tongue with a European overlay but rather a European language with a Semitic addition ("a bizarre vocabulary," in his terms). One cannot help wondering, however, whether the linguist did not thus betray his own insight, ultimately repeating the very gesture he had shown to be untenable. After having called into question the identity of the national language through a reconsideration of its heterogeneous components, he reasserted it in a new guise, defining the modern tongue as nothing other than the continuation of the one commonly thought to have been supplanted by it.

The shifting of language, however, could be more far-reaching still, and its movement might well be more difficult to track than the scholar would like to admit. It is possible that the displacement of the contiguous and multiple slates of speech does not admit of a single order of succession and substitution, in which fundamental plates can be clearly distinguished from each other and from the lesser ones superimposed on them over time. The scholarly partisans of the mineral deposits in speech, to be sure, concentrate on those particular slates they believe they can identify with relative certainty and attribute, therefore, to the tongues from which they derive and to which they are added. But in this they may ultimately err, not by going too far, as many would think, but by not going far enough, and by restricting their inquiries for reasons of scientific scrupulousness to those particular slates that can be represented as the drifting parts of otherwise firm and established languages. Could one not define *all* of speech through the incessant shifting of its plates, too many and too diverse to be represented as the members of a single set? Language has no being beyond its drifting parts, and its sole consistency may lie in the layers of forgetting and remembrance that tie and untie it, in ever-changing ways, to those before it, like the national tongue still traversed by the statelessness from which it arose, the defunct vernaculars that persist in the "Arabic" dialects of today, or, finally, the Latin and Celtic idioms that, surviving the peoples who once communicated in them, gave rise to the modern Romance language now called "French." One might consider "a" language in this sense to be a measureless mass, bearing, in each of its slates, the perceptible and the imperceptible absence of those worn away from it: the shifting sum, so to speak, of those continually subtracted from it in time.

Chapter Eleven

Little Stars

It is always possible to perceive in one form of speech the echo of another. Depending on the idiom and the sensitivity of the ear turned toward it, however, the nature and significance of the resonance may vary considerably. At times it can be a matter of a single sound, even a letter, that recalls those of other forms of speech, like the Russian palatal constrictive consonant *tche* (ч), which seems close to the sound transcribed in modern High German by the letters "tsch" (as in "bye-bye," *tschüss*), or the interdental consonant at the start of the English word "thing," which seems almost indistinguishable from the letter *thā'* (ث) of classical Arabic. At other times, it can be a matter of prosody. The music of one tongue can summon that of another: consider the cadences of Argentinean Spanish, which are often thought to resemble those of Italian. At other times still, entire words in one language may sound strikingly like those of another. Innumerable documents bear witness to such similarities; and in many cases, the consciousness of the affinities between tongues seems as old as the reflection on language itself. In offering a systematic elucidation of the terms of Jewish law, the rabbinic exegetes of the Talmud, for instance, already interpreted a number of obscure biblical expressions with reference to terms of similar phonetic form in Aramaic and Arabic. Centuries later, the Jewish philologists of the Middle Ages followed in their footsteps when, offering the first systematic analysis of Hebrew, they studied the vocabulary and grammar of the Bible in relation to those of the Qur'ān.[1] And in the classical West, the awareness of the similarities between apparently disparate tongues appears also to have played a notable, albeit less decisive, role in the emergence and development of the reflection on the nature and structure of language. The *Cratylus*, for instance, contains a discussion of a number of words in Greek that sound much like others in Phrygian; and in his treatise *De verborum significatione* (On the Meaning of Words), Pompeius Festus sought to show that Latin terms can closely resemble Greek ones, according to correspondences that are often regular in form.[2]

It is one thing to remark on the similarities between languages and quite another to explain them. It is true that, *de facto*, the discussion of the two questions can be joined. Enumerating the forms common to Greek and Phrygian in the Platonic dialogue, Socrates does not hesitate to derive the first from the second; and commenting in his treatise on the similarities between Greek and Latin, Festus proceeds to claim that they are the result of a phonetic alteration of the Hellenic tongue carried out by the early Romans. But no necessary logical link ties the consideration of the echoes between languages to that of their cause. The first question implies a problem of structure, the second of history. The first demands an analysis of extant phenomena; the second, by contrast, solicits an attempt to reconstruct the etiology of their correspondence. It is entirely comprehensible, in this sense, that when the eleventh-century Spanish philologist and poet Yiṣḥaq Abū Ibrāhīm Ibn Barūn composed his *Book of the Comparison Between the Hebrew and the Arabic Language*, he studied the resemblances between the two tongues with great rigor and insight without ever addressing the question of the reasons for their morphological and lexical affinities.[3] One can certainly imagine a number of positions the medieval grammarian might have held concerning the historical relations between the two languages. But they remain, in principle, extrinsic to his comparative analysis.

If today it is difficult to distinguish between these two problems, it is surely because the science of language, as it developed toward the beginning of the nineteenth century, fused the two in the elaboration of what was to become a single monumental project: to offer an account of the affinities between languages as well as their ultimate cause. In its modern origins, linguistics aimed to lay bare both the correspondences between languages and the complex heredity that united them; and its methods and aspirations, as a result, were inevitably both comparative and historical. The complex project found its first formulation in the "Discourse on the Hindus" that Sir William Jones presented to the Asiatick Society in Calcutta on February 2, 1788. Jones, who was high-court judge in Fort William, Bengal, was a classical scholar, with a knowledge of Greek, Latin, and German as well as Persian; in addition, he had begun the study of Sanskrit while in India.[4] His knowledge of the ancient Indian language seems to have been rudimentary at the time of his discourse on the Hindus, but it sufficed to inspire him with the belief that it bore more than a superficial resemblance to the classical tongues of the Greco-Roman tradition.[5] "The *Sanscrit* language," Jones declared enthusiastically:

> ... is of a wonderful structure; more perfect than the *Greek*, more copious than the *Latin*, and more exquisitely refined than either, yet bearing to both of them a stronger affinity, both in the roots of verbs and in the forms of grammar, than could possibly have been produced by accident; so strong indeed, that no philologer could examine all three, without believing them to have sprung from some common

source, which, perhaps, no longer exists: there is a similar reason, though not quite so forcible, for supposing that both the *Gothick* and the *Celtick*, though blended with a very different idiom, had the same origin with the *Sanscrit*; and the old *Persian* might be added to the same family, if this were the place for discussing any question concerning the antiquities of *Persia*.[6]

The argument of the "philologer" merits close attention. Beginning by remarking on the beauty and complexity of Sanskrit, he then affirms its "affinity" to both Greek and Latin, which, he comments, could not "possibly have been produced by accident"; and from such an exclusion of chance in the field of language, he derives the thesis that no scholar, as he presents it, could dispute. It is a claim no less forcefully presented for being qualified as a belief: all three classical languages, he reasons, must share a common heredity, which may also be that of "*Gothick*," "*Celtick*," and "old *Persian*." In the excitement of the announcement, several logical steps are thus made quickly, if not hastily. In a sentence, Jones moves from the observation of the "wonderful structure" of Sanskrit to the hypothesis of a series of correspondences between classical languages and finally to the postulate of an entire "family" of Indian and European tongues, united in their descent from a single genealogical origin: "some common source, which, perhaps, no longer exists."

Despite his passing reference to lexis ("roots of verbs") and morphology ("forms of grammar"), Jones did not provide any systematic demonstration for his claim, which may ultimately owe more to philological intuition than to scholarly research in any strict sense. Today, a good part of his argument must strike the ear as somewhat mythical in its scope. One thinks particularly of the "result" with which the third discourse concludes, in which the scholar explains that "the *Hindus* ... had an immemorial affinity with the old *Persians*, *Ethiopians*, and *Egyptians*, the *Phoenicians*, *Greeks*, and *Tuscans*, the *Scythians* or *Goths*, and *Celts*, the *Chinese*, *Japanese*, and *Peruvians*," and in which he adds, with the same tone of seeming verisimilitude, that "they all proceeded from some *central* country."[7] But in his hypothesis of a "common source" of the principal languages of modern Europe, which tied them to Sanskrit and Persian, the high-court judge of Bengal anticipated a number of the theses that would be taken as established by the science of language that developed in the nineteenth century. In less than a hundred years, a discipline of linguistic research emerged whose methods were both comparative and historical and which aimed, with increasingly scholarly rigor, to identify the complex filial relations that united many of the classical, medieval, and modern European and Indo-Iranian languages, both with respect to each other and with respect to the "same origin" from which they were all believed to have sprung.

It is difficult not to be struck, in hindsight, by the rapidity with which the nascent philological discipline advanced, both in its techniques and in its conclusions. From Friedrich Schlegel's pioneering comparative and historical essay *Über die Sprache und Weisheit der Indier* (On the Language and Wisdom of the Indians) of 1808, to Franz Bopp's early comparative study of classical verbal systems of 1816, to Jacob Grimm's *Deutsche Grammatik*, which appeared from 1819 to 1837 and was in essence a study of the history and typology of the Germanic languages, to Bopp's great *Comparative Grammar of the Sanskrit, Zend, Greek, Latin, Lithuanian, Gothic, German, and Sclavonic Languages*, published between 1833 and 1852, an entire field of scholarly research emerges and comes to maturity.[8] By 1861, when August Schleicher began publishing the monumental compendium of comparative grammar in which he offered a revision and amplification of much of the work of his predecessors, the "common source" imagined by Jones in his

103

discourse on the Hindus had acquired a scholarly name, which now extended to the new philological discipline devoted to it: "Indo-European," or, to be more exact, in the case of the German scholar himself, "Indo-German" (*indoeuropäisch* or *indogermanisch*).[9] The distant cause of the affinities between European and Indian tongues could now step forward as an idiom in its own right. It was, in Schleicher's terms, the "proto-language" (*Ursprache*) from which the "Teutonic, Lithuanian, Sclavonic, Keltic, Italian, Albanian, Greek, Eranian and Indian" languages had all once sprung, the primal—and strikingly solitary—genitor of the large and varied family of which the judge of Bengal had dreamed.[10]

Like any field of knowledge, Indo-European linguistics has its axioms. They are the fundamental principles that, strictly speaking, it cannot demonstrate but that it must presuppose for its propositions to be coherent. For the discipline that recognizes its first sketch in the eighteenth-century discourse on the Hindus, they are, as Jean-Claude Milner has shown, but two.[11] But they are hardly less decisive, or effective, for their paucity. It is presumed, first, that the resemblances between languages have a cause, and, second, that this cause is a language. On the basis of this double presupposition—which is at bottom nothing other than the presupposition of a "proto-language" as such—the comparative philologist sets out to establish concordances between many of the languages of Asia and the majority of the languages of Europe. "To be an Indo-Europeanist," Milner has written, with considerable acuity,

> is therefore (*a*) to construct a language, the language of the cause, and (*b*) to tie each of the observable languages to this cause-language (this is what one calls "etymology"). The strangeness of the concept of Indo-European comes immediately to light. It is a language in the full sense of the word, comparable in all aspects to any known

language; but it will never be attested as being spoken by subjects. In fact, if by some happenstance one discovered observable traces of it, they would have to be considered the elements of an effect-language; the long-sought-after cause-language would slip away again.[12]

The example of etymology is particularly instructive, since it illustrates the originality of the Indo-European project. With the publication of the first two volumes of August Pott's *Etymologische Forschungen auf dem Gebiete der indogermanischen Sprachen* (Etymological Researches in the Field of Indo-European Languages) in the 1830s, Indo-European philology began to develop the principles and methods of its research into the lexicon of the "proto-language." (The first volume listed 370 roots belonging to the primordial tongue, but the total set had been expanded to 2,226 roots by 1873, with the appearance of the *Wurzel-Wörtherbuch der indogermanischen Sprachen* [Root Dictionary of the Indo-European Languages].)[13] On the surface, the contributions could be viewed as a continuation of the lexicographical research of older linguistic traditions. But both the epistemology and the techniques of the new discipline were substantially novel. The new research into "root forms" was clearly unlike the etymological speculation of Antiquity and the Middle Ages, which, in the terms of Isidore of Seville, aimed, among other things, to explain the "origin" (*origo*) and "force" (*vis*) of things with reference to the formation of the words that signified them.[14] But the methods and aspirations of the Indo-European etymologists were also fundamentally distinct from those of the philologists who, during the same century, undertook such monuments of lexicography as the Bloch-Wartburg *Dictionnaire étymologique de la langue française*, the *Deutsches Wörterbuch* of the brothers Grimm, and the *Oxford English Dictionary*.[15] The dictionaries of the modern national languages provide a history of words based, to varying degrees, on the principles of textual scholarship in the traditional sense. Their entries lead, through an array of documents, from recent uses of a given term back to older ones and back, finally, to its earliest recorded mentions. Indo-European etymology, by contrast, knows few texts, and if it is to be successful, it must ultimately leave all known terms well behind. Its procedure consists in passing, according to a number of possible methods, from words attested in given languages back to the forms from which they must have sprung and for which no document, by definition, could be found. In the world of words, the proto-form is therefore quite unique. Unlike the terms in a traditional dictionary, each "reconstructed" element of the Indo-European vocabulary remains, in the necessary absence of all possible attestation, essentially a construct.

The importance of this fact is capital. It determines the epistemology of Indo-European linguistics as a science of language that is exclusively concerned with forms of speech that, by definition, have never been attested as such; it defines the philological discipline as the study of an idiom that must always already, so to speak, have been forgotten. And it is also the impetus behind the notation the new discipline developed, which was essentially unlike that of its predecessors. The scholars of Indo-European had no choice but to reform their scholarly writing, for they found themselves confronted with a problem of transcription that had never been posed before. It was simple: in the act of designating a "reconstructed" term, the Indo-European philologist inevitably risked effacing the very trait that defined it as such—namely, that it is by nature unattested. From the moment it is cited, after all, the proto-form begins to look no different from any other. Despite the best intentions of its conjurers, the undocumented datum, once named, seems to step out of the purely possible past of its hypothesis, setting foot on the firm ground of attestation. Although they did not discuss it, early scholars in the field clearly recognized the difficulty, for they quickly devised an ingenious technique to avoid it. It was typographical, and it consisted in using the asterisk, *, or, as its German masters call it, "the star" (*der Stern*).

In the first edition of his compendium, Schleicher defined the institution in a way that determined the course of the discipline. "*," he wrote in a footnote to his introduction, "designates forms that have been deduced (**bezeichnet erschlossene formen*)."[16] A "reconstructed" form would henceforth be marked at its inception by the asterisk: Schleicher's first example was *fathār*, presumed root of the Old Indic *pitā(rs)*, Greek πατήρ, and Gothic *fadar*. Once placed before the beginning of a term, the little star would distinguish it from all others. It would draw the term it announced, so to speak, out of the field of empirical attestation and secure it a safe spot in the undocumented domain of the philological postulate.

The notation met with immediate success, and since Schleicher it has continued to play a decisive, albeit largely unexamined, role in historical linguistics. Perusing works of almost two centuries, one has difficulty finding a scholarly contribution in the field that is untouched by its glimmer. The function of the mark, however, is subtle, and it is more complex than it might seem at first glance. As a typographical notation that alters the status of the value of the term to which it is attached, the asterisk recalls the quotation mark, but its force is nevertheless quite distinct. According to the complex logical structure of the quotation, to place a term in quotes is to designate a lexical unit that can also be invoked outside them. To cite a familiar conceptual distinction: to maintain that "'gerundive' is a three-syllable term" is to mention a lexeme (namely, "gerundive") that can also be used on its own ("the gerundive is a verb on horse-back").[17] But a term prefaced by an asterisk can never stand without it. It cannot be used, except insofar as it is mentioned as such. And for it to remain itself there cannot be evidence that it was ever used, except insofar as it was mentioned by a linguist (the first "attestation" of the term *fathār being, for example, Schleicher's statement that "the Gothic fadar clearly derives from *fathār"). The asterisk thus shares with the quotation mark the faculty of suspending the meaning of a linguistic form, withdrawing it from the field of ordinary reference and signification; but the manner in which it does so remains unique. It indicates that the term to which it is attached is necessary for establishing a historical series of forms and, at the same time, unattested. It points to the fact that a term is being given by the linguist, in other words, precisely to the degree to which it was never before given by any extant linguistic tradition. Hence the natural affinity of the asterisk to Indo-European studies. Nowhere does the star seem more at ease than when it joins itself to the elements of the proto-tongue, which compose less a language in the regular sense of the term than what one might term a *language.

Schleicher himself, it is worth noting, made a relatively modest use of the typographical institution. Although he employed the technique of what was later called "starring" (Besternung) to designate unattested and yet necessary terms of the individual Indo-European languages, he refrained from the practice when indicating forms of the proto-language itself. In all such cases, he explained with reserve in his introduction, "we have omitted this designation on account of its superfluity."[18] When, in a gesture of philological enthusiasm rarely equaled in the history of scholarship, Schleicher published "Eine Fabel in indogermanischer Ursprache" (A Fable in the Indo-European Proto-language) in 1868, he thus presented his work without a single star. But the sign is all the more perceptible for its absence: invisible asterisks surround each word in this imagined literary text, in which a sheep and a group of little horses, thanks to the unmatched erudition of the German scholar, converse in the primordial idiom of the Indo-Europeans.[19] Later scholars were less discriminating. After Schleicher, the asterisks of proto-forms soon came to be regularly printed despite their logical "superfluity." To judge from the fourth, and most recent, edition of Oswald Szemerényi's *Introduction to Indo-European Linguistics*, published in 1990, as a rule, maximalism, rather than minimalism, continues to predominate today. Here it is recommended that the asterisk be consistently employed "to indicate that a form is reconstructed, not attested," regardless of whether the form belongs to one of the individual Indo-European languages or the proto-tongue from which they all sprang.[20]

The asterisk seems to have been an ambiguous sign from the beginning, which extends back before even the time of Schleicher, who did so much for its rise to scholarly prominence. In a study titled "Zu Ursprung und Geschichte der Besternung in der historischen Sprachwissenschaft" (Origin and History of Starring in Historical Linguistics), E.F.K. Koerner noted that the first occurrence of the typographical sign in its modern technical sense is in the *Glossarium der gothischen Sprache* (Glossarium of the Gothic Language) published by Hans Conon von der Gabelentz and Julius Loebe in 1843.[21] Heirs to a classical philological tradition, the two authors voiced doubts about the legitimacy of adducing forms for which there was no textual evidence. They had little sympathy, for instance, for the practice of their predecessor Eberhard Gottlieb Graff, who, they write, based much of his understanding of Old High German vocabulary on "Indian models." But at times they, too, could not resist invoking unattested forms, and in those times they turned to the asterisk. In their introduction, they wrote:

We found it dubious to go back to completely imaginary roots [*ganz imaginäre Würzel*], like Graff, ... and yet, at the same time, in many cases we had no choice but to draw up basic words that are indeed lost for us but still conceivable as existing [*für uns verlorene, aber doch bestehend Stammwörter*].... We have designated such words by *.[22]

Elsewhere in their introductory remarks, the authors contrast the asterisk with the dagger (†), used in their book to signal words in Gothic that derive from Greek or Latin.[23] One can see the reason for their choice. For the grammarians, the dagger marked those terms whose origin lay in others that had been laid to rest, so to speak, long before. With perfect symmetry, the asterisk, by contrast, indicated a word that had neither died nor yet been born but was always already "lost for us," in the terms of the two philologists, "but still conceivable as existing."

In 1852, Theodor Benfey published a *Vollständige Grammatik der Sanskritsprache* (Complete Grammar of the Sanskrit Language), in which he, too, turned to the asterisk as a designation for what he called "hypothetical forms."[24] He showed no sign of being familiar with the Gothic *Glossarium* of his contemporaries. His use of the star is characterized by a certain idiosyncratic excess: when he "stars" a form, he uses not one but three symbols (***). The philological star of these years, in any case, could take several forms. In an article titled "Das Suffix *Ka* im Gothischen" (The *Ka* Suffix in Gothic) that appeared in 1857, Leo Meyer decided on a double-star system (**).[25] And in an essay published two years earlier on Gothic double consonantism, the same author proposed a triple system of starring, which could account for a range of more and less admissible forms. "We mark words by *," he wrote in a footnote, "when they appear in the context; we mark them by ** when they are deduced purely theoretically; and we mark them by *** if their existence is thoroughly improbable."[26] Here the stars of the philologist open up a world of possibilities that is truly Leibnizian and that descended, like the Palace of Destinies, from the most to the least admissible of realities. The scale of linguistic *realitas* imagined by the linguist extended from the most possible, which is actual, to the less possible, which is still conceivable, to the least possible, which approaches the impossible but remains nevertheless hypothetical.

Meyer's proposal to use one, two, and three asterisks as separate symbols appears to have been an *unicum* in the development of historical linguistics. But the sense of the asterisk was never fully fixed. The practice that became dominant, to be sure, was the one adopted by Schleicher in his compendium of 1861–62, which he appears to have acquired from Georg Bühler, who in 1859 set out to use the star to indicate an "original form" (*Grundform*).[27] Meyer's use of the star to indicate forms of varying possibilities, however, never entirely vanished from the technical notation of Indo-European philology, even where Schleicher's influence was strong. It is remarkable that in the English edition of the compendium, published in 1874, roots are designated by the mathematical square-root sign ($\sqrt{}$), whereas the asterisk is reserved, as we read in the opening table of abbreviations, for forms that "do not exist."[28] And as late as 1975, in an essay titled "The Origins of the Insular Celtic Conjunct and Absolute Verbal Endings," Warren Cowgill proposed that the asterisk be used for non-attested forms *simpliciter*, as distinguished from forms that, although not documented, were plausible and that he indicated by a section marker (§). The star, in this case, would then mark forms more impossible than possible.[29] Such uses of the asterisk could well be complemented by still others. In addition to recommending its use for all reconstructed forms, Szemerényi, for example, employed the star in a purely bibliographical sense. "In a few cases," he wrote in the preface to the English edition of his *Introduction to Indo-European Linguistics*, before beginning his exposition of the techniques of philological reconstruction, "it has seemed desirable to mention works which I have not seen: these are identified by an asterisk."[30]

Since its emergence on the horizon of philology in the mid-nineteenth century, the little star has clearly meant different things to different scholars, and one may safely surmise that it will continue to do so for some time. But it has never retreated from sight, and the light it has cast has remained constant in at least one sense: the astral sign has continued to illuminate the limitless field of imagined forms that scholars must summon whenever they wish to explain the links that bind and separate languages. And as such, it has opened the door to the material without which the work of comparative and historical linguistic reconstruction could hardly be accomplished. As the Indo-European philology of two centuries shows well, the asterisked form is no less decisive for marking what is, in all empirical terms, purely hypothetical. It is no less effective, in allowing for the demonstration of forms of filiation and divergence, for indicating phenomena unattested in fact. Effaced from the sources of the past, the starry speech furnishes a key to explaining the historical development of and affinities between languages; and it shows every sign of doing so, however paradoxical it may seem, on account of its very efface-ment. The historiography of languages is in this sense no different from the biography of individuals. In the end, it is the blank page that explains the rest, and if one wants to establish beyond doubt that shared traits are the results of a common heredity, there is no better way than to invent the influential relations who must have lived, although they did not. No family album can be complete until it contains the images of the unremembered past, and in the time line of languages one gets nowhere without pausing, if only for a moment, to draw out a speech forgotten long before.

CHAPTER TWELVE

The Glimmer Returns

A child of the nineteenth century, Indo-European philology eventually ceded its place at the forefront of linguistic research to
the great current in the study of language that followed it in
the twentieth century, structuralism.[1] However one wishes to
define the many methods and aspirations of the various scholars
of language who, in one way or another, followed in the wake of
Saussure's famous *Course in General Linguistics*, their primary aims
were neither historical nor comparative. They sought above all to
establish the semiotic, grammatical, and phonological traits that
constituted the linguistic system as such, not to specify the filiation that united a set of tongues in a single historical heredity.
Structuralist linguists, for this reason, could have little interest
in the nineteenth-century project of "reconstructing" the Indo-
European protolanguage; and at times they contested the possibility of justifying such an enterprise at all. The most famous case
was perhaps Trubetskoi, who, in a brief article on what he significantly called "the Indo-European problem," argued in 1939 that
there was no scientific reason, be it historical or methodological,
to assume that the many Indo-European languages all descended
from "a so-called protolanguage." "This supposition," he pointed
out, "is contradicted by the fact that, no matter how far back we

peer into history, we always find a multitude of Indo-European speaking peoples." Hence his conclusion, which he formulated with some equanimity: "The idea of an Indo-European proto-language is not absurd, but it is not necessary, and we can do very well without it."[2]

The publication of Noam Chomsky's *Syntactic Structures* in 1957 ushered in a new chapter in the history of the study of language, which departed even further from the philological discipline of the nineteenth century. At the opening of his brief but enormously influential book, Chomsky described linguistics as "concerned with the problem of determining the fundamental underlying properties of successful grammars."[3] In its invocation of the classical term "grammar," the proposition could seem traditional, recalling an object of study older than that of the structuralists. "Grammar," however, was in this case equivocal, and the discipline announced by *Syntactic Structures* was in truth essentially different from the philological and linguistic forms of knowledge that preceded it. The reason was simple: unlike all earlier forms of the study of language, the study of "grammar" defined by Chomsky aimed to be a science in the modern sense of the term, which is to say, strictly empirical. Its epistemology, as a result, was essentially novel. The new science of language sought to account for what is considered grammatical and ungrammatical in a single language through exclusively empirical propositions, which could be refuted by other empirical propositions. Concerning itself solely with an object that realized itself in space and time, it therefore now developed procedures of falsification. Like any other Galilean science, it had to be able to test its propositions, predictions, and descriptions against the reality of its object.[4]

Without ever acknowledging it explicitly, the new science, however, admitted a refugee from another linguistic age, which harked back to the time of the Indo-European philologists. It was,

114

of course, the asterisk. In the more modern discipline, the symbol serves a function that is quite distinct from the one it occupied in Indo-European studies, but every bit as decisive: it marks an unacceptable or ungrammatical form, that is, a linguistic element that cannot be realized within the bounds of a single language. It is thus the cipher of the function of falsification that distinguished the new science of language from those that preceded it. Chomsky himself did not use the asterisk in this new sense in *Syntactic Structures* or *Aspects of the Theory of Syntax*, which followed in 1965, but in both works the function it represented was clearly present.[5] His examples included a number of ungrammatical as well as grammatical sentences, and they did so of necessity: such invented phrases alone allowed the linguist to test the validity of the syntactic rules he proposed. In *Syntactic Structures*, Chomsky verified the validity of the transformational-question rule he had formulated, for example, by showing that it allowed for the grammatical form "does John read books?" but not the ungrammatical form "reads John books?"[6] And in *Aspects of the Theory of Syntax*, he identified a specific syntactic feature by illustrating how it gave rise to such possible English sentences as "A very frightening person suddenly appeared" but did not permit such sentences as "A very hitting person appeared."[7] The new use of the asterisk followed almost immediately. Linguists working with Chomsky's methods began to mark all such impossible phrases by an asterisk, and the star quickly became an established symbol in the formal notation of generative-transformational linguistics; and since the 1950s, it has been a standard feature of synchronic studies of languages.

The old star of linguistic "reconstruction," however, remains alive and well in historical linguistics, and today one can easily encounter either of the two asterisks in the scholarly literature on language. They are typographically indistinguishable, and one must often know to which linguistic paradigm a scholar belongs to be sure of the true identity of the symbol. It is a delicate but important matter, since the functions of the two asterisks do not coincide. In a sense, the two uses of the sign can even be opposed, although there seems little indication that the specialists themselves, for comprehensible reasons, would wish to do so. In diachronic linguistics, the star marks a form as necessary yet unattested in extant sources; in synchronic linguistics, it marks a form as impossible yet given by the scholar for reasons of scientific method.

The two stars seem united, however, in the obscurity of their sense. In the uses of the synchronic asterisk, as in those of its diachronic double, ambiguities are legion. What exactly does it mean to designate a sentence as "unacceptable"? As everyone is well aware, impossibility knows no limit, and the forms of ungrammatical utterances cannot easily be numbered. Barely a year after the publication of Chomsky's *Syntactic Structures*, F.W. Householder began to use the asterisk in its more modern sense in his courses at the Michigan Linguistic Institute, so as not to "beguile" his students into mistaking ungrammatical utterances for anything else. In 1973, fifteen years later, he remarked that the usage had become an essential part of what he called "the favored, well-nigh universal format for articles in linguistics." Feeling "somehow responsible for the spread of this notation," he devoted a paper to considering its functions. Householder commented that "the device has been used on the most odd and implausible sorts of sentences." An asterisk attached to a phrase, he observed, can mean at least three different things. If one abbreviates the phrase in question as *X*, *X can signify "'I would never say *X*' (except possibly as a horrible example), and hence, by implication, 'I have never said anything which resembles *X* with respect to the point under discussion'"; or, alternately, "'I have never seen or heard a sentence of the type of *X* and hereby wager you can't find an example (unless it's a slip, repudiated by the speaker)'"; or, finally, "'This is quite comprehensible, and I have heard people say it, but they were all K's (i.e., southerners, New York Jews, etc., etc.); in *my* dialect we would say *Y* instead.'"[8] One star would then mark degrees of grammatical "unacceptability," from the absolutely impossible and inconceivable to the unintentional but conceivable (the "slip") and, finally, to the regrettable but all too possible formulation of the aberrant group. Here we are close, at over a hundred years' remove, to the intensive possibilities and impossibilities of language distinguished by Leo Meyer in his proposition to employ a single, double, and triple asterisk (*, **, ***).

The ambiguities of the syntactic symbol are undeniable. But to the modern discipline of grammar, they remain, for reasons of method, immaterial. An empirical science of language can recognize only two values for the functional star: grammaticality and ungrammaticality.[9] For falsifying a proposition in the field, any other determination is quite superfluous. It is certainly true that in itself grammaticality, as Chomsky commented in *Aspects of the Theory of Syntax*, "is no doubt a matter of degree"; given a set of ungrammatical utterances, a scholar of speech could propose a typology that would account for the various forms of their linguistic deviance.[10] The point is that, strictly speaking, such distinctions cannot play a role in the procedures of verification that define the Galilean science. These procedures seek to do no more, and no less, than determine the truth or falsity of a proposition that predicts an empirical occurrence: an utterance that, at a certain point in space and time, can be considered grammatical. Whether such an utterance is "more or less" grammatical is of no importance from such a perspective. The one and only thing the scientist must know is whether the event predicted by the rule has taken place or not; the differential judgment alone carries weight.

There is, however, a caveat whose importance cannot be over-estimated: the fundamental distinction on which all linguistic proof must rest cannot itself be verified. No criterion exists, be it logical, historical, or sociological, by which the linguist can demonstrate that a single phrase is grammatical or ungrammatical in a given language. As Chomsky himself indicated early, when testing the value of an utterance within a grammar, one must rely in the final analysis on the "linguistic intuition of the native speaker," that is, on a phenomenon that "is neither presented for direct observation nor extractable from data by inductive procedures of any sort."[11] The Galilean science, too, has its axiom. One must presuppose, to put it simply, that there are certain things that "one does not say." For the purposes of scientific demonstration, it is assumed that one can oppose what can be uttered in a particular tongue to what cannot be uttered in it, distinguishing, with necessary certitude, between what is possible in a language and what is impossible in it. It is presumed that such an opposition can be made in principle, but in fact the distinction cannot be verified. It is in this absence of verification that empirical linguistics carries out its science, defining a language by presupposing—through the asterisk—that which it is not.

Transposed from one scientific paradigm to another, the asterisk thus retains its force. In the notation of the resolutely empirical science, as in that of Indo-European reconstruction, the little star continues to clear the way for a necessary figment of knowledge. Prefixed to phrases the linguist alone may write, it still delimits the terrain of the most scientific of wonderlands, which is filled with the fictions scholars must invent whenever they wish to come close to the reality of speech. The march of knowledge, however, is not in vain, and contemporary specialists in speech employ the forms they fashion in a manner quite unlike that of their philological predecessors. In the modern science of syntax, the asterisked phrase confirms, by its own falsity, the protocol of properly empirical verification. As a strictly impossible utterance, it assists in establishing the principles that govern a grammar by necessity. But the scholarly imperative remains the same: in the end, one must turn to an inexistent form of speech if one wishes to explain idioms that do exist. The glimmer returns: it seems that if one wishes to view a language with precision, one must do so in the light of another, whose forms—whether immemorial or inconceivable—one can only invent oneself. The little star alone allows one to navigate with certainty through the seas of a single tongue. A point of orientation no less illuminating for being imaginary, the asterisk shines its light on the shadows that encroach on a language from every side and without which none would be itself.

Chapter Thirteen

The Writing Cow

There was once a nymph who became a cow. It happened in the first book of Ovid's *Metamorphoses*, soon after Jupiter caught sight of the fair daughter of the river god Inachus, Io, and took her, against her will, to be his lover. Wishing to conceal his adulterous activities from his wife, the father of the gods shrouded the area surrounding the scene of the crime with heavy mists. But before long, Juno noticed the unusual weather and, growing suspicious of the sudden darkness in broad daylight, cleared away the obscurity her husband had produced, descending to the earth to investigate matters for herself. As Ovid tells it, Jupiter then had little choice: wanting to hide his lover from his wife, he was obliged to transform the fluvial demigoddess into a cow, albeit a beautiful one, "as white as milk." Naturally, this deception, too, did not go unnoticed; and without making any explicit accusations, Juno began to pose pointed questions to her husband concerning the birth and breeding of the striking animal, who, one supposes, stood startled and alone on the ground beside the Olympian king. On learning from her husband that the bovine beast had simply emerged, as it were, from nowhere and nothing, "bred out of the ground" and so belonging to no one, Juno asked her spouse for the animal as a gift. What was Jupiter then to do? The prospect of agreeing to the request must have been a most unpleasant one for the god, but to refuse, he quickly realized, would only make matters worse. In the words of Arthur Golding's 1567 translation of the poem, which Ezra Pound judged "the most beautiful book in the language," "Jove ... feared if he should denie a gift so light, / As was a Cow to hir that was his sister and his wyfe, / Might make hir thinke it was no Cow, and breede perchaunce some strife."[1]

It was thus that the contested cow was delivered over to the most jealous of mistresses, who placed her in the safe custody of the hundred-eyed Argus. Io could henceforth roam and graze freely by day, but by night she must return to her vigilant keeper, who would bind her by the neck and feed her only "croppes of trees and bitter weeds," compelling the erstwhile nymph, with studied cruelty, now "to drinke of muddie pitts." At times, Ovid tells us, Io sought to beg for mercy, but it was in vain: "when she did devise / to Argus for to lift hir handes in meeke and humble wise, / she sawe she had no handes at all: and when she did assay / To make complaint, she lowed out, which did hir so affray, / That oft she started at the noyse, and would have runne away."[2] One day, however, the forlorn cow found her way back to her native riverbanks, where, although still without the help of human hands and tongue, she succeeded in communication of a sort, alerting her unwitting father of the alteration she had undergone:

> She as she kyst and lickt his handes did shed forth dreerie tears.
> And had she had hir speech at will to utter forth hir thought,
> She would have tolde hir name and chaunce and him of helpe
> besought.
> But for because she could not speake, she printed in the sande,
> Two letters with hir foote, whereby was given to understande
> The sorrowful chaunging of hir shape. Which seene straight
> cryed out

Hir father Inach, Wo is me, and clasping hir about
Hir white and seemely Heifers necke and christal hornes both
    twaine,
He shriked out full piteously: Now wo is me, again.
Alas art thou my daughter deare, whome through the worlde
    I sought
And could not finde, and now by chaunce are to my presence
    brought?[3]

Unable to make a signifying sound or even an intelligible gesture, Io found her way, by means of her hoof, to the art of writing. In the sand by Inachus's river, the mute animal now traced "letters in the place of words," or, in Golding's terms, "printed in the sande, / Two letters with hir foote" (*littera pro verbis quam pes in puluere duxit*). It is a good thing the creature previously bore the name she did: how would the animal have fared, one cannot help wondering, had she once been called not Io but Alyxothoe, like the daughter of the river Granicus, or Psamathe, like the mother of Phocus, or even Menippe and Metiokhe, like the daughters of the Giant Orion? In this case, two alphabetic figures, *I* and *O*, sufficed to tell the whole tale of the "sorrowful chaunging," and the river god was the first to read it.

The scene is memorable in its details, but it is hardly without parallel in the world of Ovidian changes. In its structure, the drawing of the hoof-script can even be considered exemplary, and the tale of the writing cow can be read as an allegory of metamorphosis as such. It is a matter of principle that concerns the nature of the "shapes transformde to bodies straunge" explored by the poem as a whole. For a metamorphosis to be complete, one body must pass in its entirety into another. Anything else would amount to a modification, however decisive, but not a transformation. The nymph, in this case, must thus become a perfect cow, an animal bearing none of the characteristics of the anthropomorphic deity born to Inachus. But the literary mutation cannot end there. For if the transformation is to be perceptible as such, something must indicate that it has taken place, something in the new form must mark the occurrence of the change. Precisely for the metamorphosis to be without residue, it must paradoxically admit of a remainder that bears witness to the event of the mutation: an element both foreign to the new body and still contained within it, an exceptional trait in the body "strange" that harks back to the earlier shape it once possessed. In the case of the cow, the remainder is the written name of the vanished nymph, whose inscription marks the transformation of the creature it designates. *I* and *O*, the two letters drawn in the sand by the banks of the river, at once bear witness to the change and belie it. They are, in every sense of the word, what *betray* the metamorphosis.

The bovine letters are more complex than they might seem, and they have attracted the attention of a number of exegetes since the time they were first traced in the sand. Among those who lent particular weight to the script of the cow was the learned artist, grammarian, bookseller, and typographer Geoffroy Tory, who in 1529 published what was to become one of the most influential books of the French Renaissance, *Champfleury: Art et science de la vraie proportion des lettres*. Tory devoted several folios at the start of his book to the plight of the mythic cow, which he recounted in meticulous detail. He then proposed an allegorical interpretation of the tale, which assigned to Io a central position in the development of knowledge. "The beautiful daughter of Inachus," he explained, "we take to be science [or knowledge, *science*], which is banished by Juno, whom we take to be wealth."[4] Defined as the sole product of the spirit of knowledge, the graphemes traced by the hoof in the sand acquired a new sense. The letters of the nymph's name, the typographer pointed out, have a unique position in the alphabet: *I* and *O*, quite simply, "are the two letters from which all the other Attic letters are made and shaped."[5] What is the *A*, Tory asked, if not the composition of two (or perhaps two and a half) *I*s, and what is a *B*, if not an *I* bound to an *O*, which is "broken" at its center? "In the same way," the humanist wrote, "all the other [letters of the alphabet] are made of one of the two aforementioned letters, or of both together."[6] The *C* is an *O* slightly opened on its right side; the *D* is an *I* joined to half of an *O*; the *E*, one *I* joined to three separated segments of another.... Alone, with neither hands nor voice, the metamorphosed nymph did much more than print her name at the banks of her father. She inscribed for the first time the two elements of human writing and thereby invented, albeit *in nuce*, the totality of human script. Writing, in short, is the creation of the cow: the remainder produced in the definitive disappearance of the voice.

Here everything depends on how one understands the nature of the remainder, for speech can persist in several ways. One is that of languages deliberately maintained by those who could easily let them go, like the German tongue that Hannah Arendt knew in her youth and subsequently did not lose. Asked by Günter Gaus in an interview broadcast on West German television in 1967 about "what remained" for her "of the Europe of the pre-Hitler period," the political theorist gave the following famous answer: "What remains? The language remains (*Was ist geblieben? Geblieben ist die Sprache*)." "I have always consciously refused to lose my mother tongue [*Ich habe immer bewusst abgelehnt, die Muttersprache zu verlieren*]," she then explained.[7] And she added, a little later: "The German language is the essential thing that has remained and that I have always consciously preserved" (*Die deutsche Sprache jedenfalls ist das Wesentliche, was geblieben ist, und was ich auch bewusst immer gehalten habe*).[8] It is not difficult to measure the distance between the remaining mother tongue of which Arendt spoke and the written remnant drawn in the sand by the mute and metamorphosed Io. The mythological figure, unlike the historical individual, clearly could not have "consciously refused to lose" her tongue. In distinction to the thinker, who retained her relation to the German language despite the nation-state that claimed to represent its speakers, the fabled creature could not have conserved her speech, since the transformation she underwent, as Ovid makes clear, left nothing of her original form intact. This is why that which persists of the nymph after the mutation could only be a thing she never before possessed, to which she came in destitution and despair: writing. In the case of the nymph turned cow, the "remainder" first emerges, so to speak, in the process of remaining, and it remains, for this reason, utterly unlike that to which it bears witness.

Joseph Brodsky also once invoked a remaining language, but in terms closer, if one may say so, to the writing cow than to the political theorist. "The poet," Brodsky wrote in his Nobel Prize lecture of 1987, citing part of a verse from W. H. Auden's "In Memory of W. B. Yeats," "is language's means for existence — or, as my beloved Auden said, he is the one by whom it lives. I who write these lines will cease to be; so will you who read them. But the language in which they are written and in which you read them will remain, not merely because language is a more lasting thing than man, but because it is more capable of mutation."[9] Here language remains, but not by virtue of the will of an individual or even a community; no one "consciously" retains or releases speech. But if the determination and decision of speakers seem, in Brodsky's formulation, to have lost their force, it is not because the being they would grasp maintains itself independently of them. If language is now said to persist in the eventual absence of its speakers, it is not because it ignores them but because it has always already changed itself by means of them, being by nature "more capable of mutation" than those who would use it. At once with and without its speakers, language, over time, thus remains, but it does not remain itself. It may last, but only as another. The claim lends a final sense to the Ovidian fable: metamorphosis would be the medium of all speech, and every word, in the end, would be made of letters traced in the sand by the hoof of the nymph who no longer was.

CHAPTER FOURTEEN

The Lesser Animal

Human beings can do many things, but their actions pale, on a number of counts, when compared with those of other living creatures. With characteristic probity, Spinoza remarked on the fact in a famous scholium of the third book of the *Ethics*. "There is much to be seen in animals," he commented simply and in passing, "that far surpasses human sagacity" (*in Brutis plura observentur, quae humanem sagacitatem longe superant*).[1] Al-Jāḥiẓ, one of the greatest figures of the classical Arabic literary tradition, considered the matter with considerable acuity in a passage of his large and labyrinthine *Book of Living Things* (كتاب الحيوان), which he completed sometime toward the middle of the eighth century A.D. In his compendium, the Iraqi writer gathered, ordered, and commented on much of the medical, zoological, juridical, philosophical, and philological learning of classical Antiquity and the medieval Arabo-Islamic world. In a chapter a modern editor of the text has aptly titled "The Debilities of Man with Respect to the Powers of Animals," he made no attempt to conceal his boundless admiration for the abilities of beasts. "God," al-Jāḥiẓ stated at the outset, "placed all sorts of knowledge in animals other than man."[2] "He bestowed an extraordinary ease upon them," he wrote, "both in their technique and in their know-how; by giving them beaks or

129

paws, he opened for them a whole field of knowledge suited to the tools with which he has equipped them, and he created in many species highly developed sensory organs that make them capable of carrying out wondrous works [الصنعة البديعة]."[3] Al-Jāḥiẓ had little trouble finding examples to illustrate his point. "Behold the spider," he wrote, "or the termite, with the gifts that each has received; or take the bee and the knowledge that was imparted to it; or, better yet, the weaverbird [تنوط] and its extraordinary apti-tude, its marvelous ability to execute masterworks; and there are still more."[4] It is as if the animals other than man were united in their flawlessness. "In most of the acts they accomplish," al-Jāḥiẓ went on to explain, "God imposed on these species no deficien-cies whatsoever: from the winged insects to the little birds and the tiniest insects, they all have the most extraordinary aptitudes."[5]

The capacities proper to humankind seemed to al-Jāḥiẓ of a different order. "God made of man," he wrote, "a being gifted with reason, mastery, the ability to act, sovereignty, responsibil-ity, experience, the spirit of reconciliation, rivalry, the desire to understand, to enter into the game of emulation, and also to consider, with lucidity, the consequences of his actions."[6] Al-Jāḥiẓ believed such endowments to be far from insignificant. But he had no illusions about their limitations, at least with respect to the gifts of insects and other animals. The erudite writer knew well that man can learn: study and practice, built on a strong natural aptitude, are sure to improve his performance. But, al-Jāḥiẓ wrote, even "a man gifted with a keen sensibility, possessing all the intel-lectual qualities, trained in a great number of disciplines, excelling in many domains of knowledge, is incapable of accomplishing spontaneously most of the actions completed by animals."[7] Dis-cipline, for all its use, cannot hope to bring man within reach of the animal's wisdom, which flowers naturally in the absence of academies, schools, and education. "Without having been trained and without being educated, without being schooled and without ever having been apprenticed, and without having done either repeated or methodical exercises," the scholar commented with some astonishment, "these animal species, thanks to their natural faculties, are spontaneously capable of performing actions quickly and suddenly that the most well-informed of men, the most erudite of all philosophers could not carry out, even if they had very agile hands or if they used tools."[8] No matter how rigorous his training, how great his dedication, and how elaborate his instruments, man, the Arabic polymath insisted, remains the lesser animal among living beings.

To do less, however, is not to do nothing, and in the *Book of Living Things* the relative debility of the human species turned out to shelter a curious ability bestowed on none but it. Having described the perfection denied to humankind, al-Jāḥiẓ explained that the excellence of the inhuman species, by definition, must exclude at least one practice, whose terrain coincides with the natural province of man: failure or, to put it more delicately, doing less. "Man is made in such a way," al-Jāḥiẓ wrote, "that when he accomplishes an act that is difficult to carry out, he has the ability to do one that is less difficult" (متى أحسن شئًا كان كل شيئٍ دونه فى الغموض عليه أسهل).[9] It is an ability given to no other creature. "God created man capable of such a performance," we read, "but he did not give this power to the other animal species; although each of them knows how to accomplish certain actions that even the most skillful of men, carrying out feats of excellence, cannot equal, the other animals nevertheless cannot perform other, easier actions."[10] Take, for example, the birds the Arabic author admired so. They sing with unfailing melodic and metrical exactitude, pouring forth sounds that seem as if "prepared for modulation and harmony, obeying prosodic and rhythmic laws."[11] They cannot do otherwise. If human beings, by contrast, can sing any song at all, they can, according to al-Jāḥiẓ, always also sing an easier, simpler, and lesser one. They can also sing out of tune and out of time, distorting the composition they aim to execute; and, finally, they can always also fail to sing altogether. Al-Jāḥiẓ suggested that the essence of human action lies in this possibility of reduction; however small or great, a human act owes its consistency to its capacity to be less than itself. It follows that one cannot understand any work of man on its own. To grasp a human action as such, one must look to the shadows of the more minor acts it inevitably projects around it: to those unaccomplished acts that are less than it and that could always have been performed in its stead, or, alternately, to those unaccomplished acts with respect to which it itself is less than it could have been.

There is perhaps no better example than speech. More than once, scholars of language have found that they could learn the most about their object by exploring the varying forms of its possible failure: its distortion, omission, and disappearance among those who would otherwise seem its masters. In the field of modern linguistics, Roman Jakobson is the most brilliant case. He turned twice in his life to the simplification of language to explain its complexity, seeking to locate in the collapse of the ability to speak the key to its accomplishment. In his 1941 study *Child Language, Aphasia, and Phonological Universals*, he traced the emergence and the decay of speech, from infants who could not yet speak to those adults who could no longer speak, in an attempt to lay bare the stratified structure underlying the sound system of every tongue. And twenty years later, he returned to the analysis of aphasic disorders to define the double axes that, according to him, characterized all fully realized speech patterns: the axis of selection (or contiguity) and that of combination (or similarity), which he identified with the respective rhetorical operations of metonymy and metaphor.[12] Each of these contributions was motivated, in its own way, by the conviction that to grasp its object, the science of language had to pay close attention to those moments in which speaking beings did something other—and, more exactly, something less—than speak.

The founder of psychoanalysis also once turned to the analysis of speech disorders to define the structure of what he termed the "language apparatus" (*Sprachapparat*). The investigation marked the inception of Freud's literary production: his first book, published in Vienna in 1891, was the neurological essay *Zur Auffassung der Aphasien: Eine kritische Studie* (On the Conception of Aphasia: A Critical Study, published in English as *On Aphasia*).[13] The author seems to have held the book in high esteem, at least at first. Commenting on "the incongruity between one's own and other people's estimation of one's intellectual work" in a letter to Wilhelm Fliess of 1894, Freud singled out his study of aphasia as one of the "really good things" he had contributed to scholarship.[14] Ultimately, however, he decided against including it in the first collected edition of his works, and it came to be excluded, as a result, from the standard edition published after his death.[15] Since then, the small book has received relatively little treatment by scholars of psychoanalysis. This is no doubt in part a consequence of the modesty with which Freud presented his inquiry. At the opening of his book, he defined its goals in the technical terms of nineteenth-century neuropathology. "I shall endeavor to demonstrate," we read on the first page of *On Aphasia*, "that the theory of aphasia ... contains two assumptions which might profitably be revised," the first being that of "the differentiation between aphasias caused by *destruction of centres* and aphasias caused by *destruction of pathways*," the second "concerned with the topographical relationship between the individual speech centres."[16]

Both "revisions" pitted Freud against the bulk of the neurological doctrines that emerged in the wake of the famous findings revealed to the scientific community by Paul Broca in 1861. In a paper delivered to the Société Anatomique of Paris, Broca demonstrated on the basis of a postmortem examination that articulatory or "motor" aphasia was directly linked to damage to the third convolution of the left hemisphere of the brain (a convolution later termed, for this reason, "Broca's area").[17] Subsequent neurological research consisted largely of attempts to determine more precise and far-reaching correlations between speech disorders and cerebral sites. Carl Wernicke and Ludwig Lichtheim, to name two of the principal targets of Freud's study, aimed, in particular, to illustrate a series of such correlations through elaborate diagrams of the brain. Calling into question the assumption of the difference between aphasias caused by the destruction of cortical centers and aphasias caused by the destruction of conduits, and rejecting the received topography of the speech centers, *On Aphasia* clearly broke with such attempts to explain speech disorders by direct reference to cerebral localization. It repeatedly invoked, to this end, a principle stressed by the British neurologist John Hughlings Jackson: that the psychological cannot be reduced to the physiological; that, as Freud's predecessor had written, "in all our studies of diseases of the nervous system we must be on our guard against the fallacy that what are physical states in lower centres fine away into psychical states in higher centres; that for example, vibrations of sensory nerves become sensations, or that somehow or another an idea produces a movement."[18]

Against all attempts to reduce diverse speech functions to distinct regions of the brain, Freud consistently argued that the "language apparatus" had to be understood as essentially unitary: "a *continuous cortical region* between the terminations of the optic and acoustic nerves and of the areas of the cranial and certain peripheral motor nerves in the left hemisphere."[19] Freud believed cortical centers and conduits played a role in the activity that defined this region, but he maintained that it was only a pre-liminary one. He argued that when an idea comes to conscious-ness, a process in the brain begins that "starts at a specific point in the cortex and from there spreads over the whole cortex and along certain pathways."[20] As an example, Freud evoked the physi-ological process enabling the emergence of a visual image. A fiber departs from the optic nerve, conveying a retinal impression to another region ("the anterior quadrigemmial body"); from there, another fiber, moving through the "grey masses" that make up the brain, passes to another region ("from the ganglion to the occipi-tal cortex").[21] "It is extremely likely," Freud wrote, "that the new fibre ... no longer conveys a retinal stimulus, but the association of one or more such impressions with kinaesthetic impressions."[22] "We can only presume," he concluded, "that the fibre tracts, which reach the cerebral cortex after their passage through other grey masses, have maintained some relationship to the periphery of the body, but no longer reflect a topographically exact image of it."[23] The fibers would therefore contain the perception of the eye, but they would do so neither clearly nor distinctly. They would repre-sent it in a distorted form, scrambled, as it were, like the letters of an anagram secretly containing the elements of a different phrase. Freud's figure to designate the optic nerves was highly literary, and more precisely literal: in the end, the fiber tracts, he wrote, "contain the body periphery in the same way as—to borrow an example from the subject with which we are concerned here—a poem contains the alphabet, in a re-arrangement serving other purposes, in manifold associations of the individual elements, whereby some may be represented several times, others not at all" (*Sie enthalten die Körperperipherie, wie—um ein Beispiel dem uns hier beschäftigen Gegenstande zu entlehnen—ein Gedicht das Alphabet enthält, in einer Umordung, die anderen Zwecken dient, in mannig-facher Verknüpfung der einzelnen topischen Elemente, wobei die einen davon merhfachen, die anderen gar nicht vertreten sein mögen).*[24]

Freud suggested that the parts and pathways of the "language apparatus" were structurally the same as those of vision, only more complex. He maintained that in the processes that define the capacities of speech, a single set of elements (or "letters") can be combined and subsequently recombined "in a re-arrangement serving other purposes." The neurologist himself did not claim to know the details of all such "re-arrangements" (*Umordnungen*), but he suggested that they reflected the distinct domains, or "functions," of the speech apparatus. "If it were possible to follow in detail the re-arrangement [*Umordnung*] which takes place between the spinal projection and the cerebral cortex," he wrote, "one would probably find that the underlying principle is purely functional, and that the topographical relations are maintained only as long as they fit in with the claims of function."[25] Function was also the key, Freud argued, to the decomposition of speech. When the elements of utterances are not so much rearranged as "de-arranged," the "language apparatus" disintegrates, he claimed, according to a form that reflects the stratified levels of linguistic competence. The capacities of linguistic expression fall away in an order indicating their importance, from the most trivial to the most fundamental. Here, too, Freud found his "guiding principle" in the writings of Hughlings Jackson, who had argued that speech disorders constitute "instances of the *functional retrogression* ('disinvolution') of a highly organized apparatus, and therefore correspond to earlier states of its functional development."[26] "Under all circumstances," Freud explained, "an arrangement of associations which, having been acquired later, belongs to a higher level of functioning, will be lost, while an earlier and simpler one will be preserved."[27] As he wrote elsewhere in his study, "Aphasias simply reproduce a state which existed in the course of the normal process of learning to speak."[28]

Several aphasic phenomena could then be explained in a new way. Drawing on cases of speech disorders reported by his predecessors and even antagonists, Freud gave some examples of the stratified structure of the "language apparatus." The ability to speak a foreign language, for example, can vanish, "while the mother tongue is preserved." The lexicon may also shrink to the point of including "only 'yes' and 'no,' and other words in use since the beginning of speech development."[29] "Frequently practiced associations" may remain, while others disappear: thus the cases of "agraphia," in which patients are reduced to illiterates, capable of writing their own names but nothing else.[30] Series, too, may remain at the command of the aphasic, while their members slip away: here Freud cited one of his adversaries in the field, Hubert E. Grashey, whose patient "was unable to state a certain number directly, but ... got round the difficulty by counting from the beginning until he arrived at the requested number."[31] And in those cases of physiological aphasia and "asymbolia," in which patients fail to recall the meaning of terms, Freud wrote, "it is obvious that the words most likely to be lost are those with the most specific meaning, i.e., those which can be elicited by only a few and definite associations": proper names, first of all, but more generally nouns, then adjectives, and, still later, verbs.[32]

It is in this sense that Freud interpreted those cases in which individuals lost the ability to express themselves but still uttered certain formulas that bore witness to their earlier capacity to speak. Such phenomena clearly posed a problem to the neurologists who wished to explain aphasias solely in terms of the localization of cerebral lesions. If the inability to speak could indeed be attributed to damage to a particular cortical center or conduit, then how, one could ask, could some aphasics continue to produce, and to repeat, certain phrases long after they could otherwise not speak? To Freud such cases posed no difficulty at all, since to his mind they furnished clear evidence of the necessity of a functional account of speech disorders. "A *rare* product of speech," he wrote, "may prove highly resistant if it had acquired great force by being associated with great *intensity*."[33] Drawing again on Hughlings Jackson's case studies in "affections of speech from disease of the brain," Freud devoted several pages to the analysis of these singular "products." The English neurologist had divided them into two classes: "recurring" and "occasional" utterances. Freud, however, coined his own term for them, which he then employed as a running head in the original edition of the book. He named them "language remains," or "speech remnants" (*Sprachresten*).[34]

Freud considered such "remnants" morsels of language, as it were, left behind in the impoverished idiom of the aphasic from when he had still been able to speak. As the neurologist presented them, they could take several forms and could refer in different ways to the full discourses from which they were drawn. There were, first, those patients who, although unable to speak coherently, could still say yes or no. And there were also those aphasics who, like the hysterics to whom Freud turned soon after his book on aphasia, remained capable of uttering only "a vigorous curse": as examples, Freud cited two foreign expressions, "sacré nom de Dieu" and "Goddam."[35] But "speech remnants" could also be more extensive, as well as more specific. They could represent segments of particular conversations, declarations, and exclamations that played a decisive role in the lives of the patients before they fell nearly silent. "For instance," Freud recounted, "a man who could say only 'I want protection' owed his aphasia to a fight in which he had been knocked unconscious by a blow on the head."[36] The case of a copyist silenced at the end of his work is at least as pathetic: having had "a stroke after he had laboriously completed a catalogue," the only thing he could subsequently say was "List complete."[37] "Such instances suggest," Freud wrote, "that these utterances are the last words produced by the language apparatus before injury, or even at a time when there already existed an awareness of the impending disability. I am inclined to explain the persistence of these last modifications by their intensity if they happen at a moment of great inner excitement."[38]

It is difficult not to be struck at this point by the sudden appearance of the first-person pronoun in the otherwise-neutral discourse of the "critical study." "*I*," we now read, "am inclined to explain the persistence of these last modifications by their intensity if they happen at a moment of great inner excitement." The momentary intrusion announces a revelation drawn from the life of the author himself: probably the most arresting example cited in the work as a whole, suggesting that the neurologist's interest in his subject matter was not exclusively academic. "I remember having twice been in danger in my life," Freud added at this point, by way of conclusion to his discussion of "speech remnants,"

> and each time the awareness of the danger occurred to me quite suddenly. On both occasions I thought to myself: "Now you're gone," and while otherwise my inner language proceeds with only indistinct sound images and slight lip movements, in this danger I heard these words as if somebody were shouting them into my ears; and at the same time, I saw them as if they were printed on a piece of paper floating in the air [*In beiden Fällen dachte ich mir:"Jetzt ist's aus mit dir,"und während mein inneres Sprechen sonst nur mit ganz undeutlichen Klangbildern und kaum intensiveren Lippengefühlen vor sich geht, hörte ich in der Gefahr diese Worte, als ob man sie mir ins Ohr rufen würde, und sah sie gleichzeitig wie gedruckt auf einem flatternden Zettel*].[39]

The longest and most detailed of the "speech remnants" cited by Freud, this final example merits some attention. Unlike the others, the last is a purely imagined "remnant," to which none but the neurologist-patient himself can bear witness. It is at once an acoustic and a visual hallucination, which anticipates the false "presentiments" Freud later related in an apparently autobiographical passage of *The Psychopathology of Everyday Life* of 1901.[40] The temporal structure of the last example is equally singular. Whereas the other recurring utterances cited by Freud refer back to a time when those who repeat them could still speak normally, the imagined phrase refers forward to the fantasy of a time when he will have fallen silent; it constitutes a "remnant," so to speak, of the future, a memorial for a loss still to come. In its simultaneously aural and graphic dimensions, it thus marked the event that every linguistic remainder sealed: the irreparable point after which the "letters" of the apparatus of speech could not be rearranged again and after which the speaking being would forevermore do less than speak.

As an account of the functions and dysfunctions of the "language apparatus" in explicitly textual terms, *On Aphasia* anticipated many of Freud's most far-reaching psychoanalytic investigations, from *The Interpretation of Dreams* (1900) to *Beyond the Pleasure Principle* (1920) and "Note on the Magic Writing-Pad" (1925), all of which cast the conscious and unconscious processes of the psyche, in different ways, as forms of inscription. Most immediately, however, the neurological essay of 1891 announced the provocative sketch of the genesis of consciousness that Freud drafted in his famous letter to Wilhelm Fliess of December 6, 1896. Here Freud declared that he envisaged "a new psychology," which he could not yet fully "describe" but for which "some material" was already "at hand."[41] Its theoretical foundation lay nowhere other than in the theory of "re-arrangement" (*Umordnung*) that Freud had proposed five years earlier in his account of the unity of the "language apparatus." "As you know," he wrote to his older friend,

I am working on the assumption that our psychic mechanism has come into being by a process of stratification [*Aufeinanderschichtung*], according to which material present in the form of memory traces is subjected, from time to time, to a *rearrangement* [*Umordnung*] in accordance with fresh circumstances, to a *re-transcription* [*Umschrift*]. The essential novelty of my theory is thus the assertion that memory is present not once but several times, that it is laid down in various kinds of signs [*in verschiedenen Arten von Zeichen niedergelegt*]. I postulated a similar rearrangement [*Umordnung*] some time ago (*Aphasia*) for the paths from the periphery [of the body to the cortex]. I do not know how many of these registrations [*Niederschriften*] there are. At least three, probably more. This is shown in the following schematic picture, which assumes that the different registrations are also separated (not necessarily topographically) according to neurons which are their vehicles. This assumption may not be necessary, but it is the simplest and it is provisionally admissible.

W [*Wahrnehmungen*, perceptions] are neurons in which *perceptions* originate, to which consciousness attaches, but which in themselves retain no trace of what has happened. For *consciousness and memory are mutually exclusive* [*Denn Bewusstsein und Gedächnis schliessen sich nähmlich aus*].

Wz [*Wahrnehmungszeichen*, sign of perception] is the first registration [*Niederschrift*] of the perceptions; it is quite incapable of consciousness and is arranged according to associations by simultaneity [*nach Gleichzeitigkeitsassoziationen*].

Ub [*Unbewusstsein*, unconsciousness] is the second registration [*Niederschrift*], arranged according to other, perhaps casual, relations.

Ub traces would perhaps correspond to conceptual memories [*Begriffserinnerungen*]; equally inaccessible to consciousness.

Vb [*Vorbewusstsein*, preconsciousness] is the third transcription, attached to word presentation and corresponding to our official ego. The cathexes proceeding from this *Vb* become conscious according to certain rules; and this secondary *thought consciousness* [*Denkbewusstsein*] is subsequent in time and is probably linked to the hallucinatory activation of word presentations, so that the neurons of consciousness would once again be perceptual neurons and in themselves without memory.[42]

In the letter to Fliess, the terms of *On Aphasia* become psychological as the form attributed to brain fibers in the neurological study comes to characterize the structure of the mind as a whole. Consciousness emerges, much like the Freudian theory itself, as the product of a gradual process of writing and rewriting: the final result of the multiple "re-arrangements" and "re-transcriptions" (*Umschriften*) by which "signs" (*Zeichen*) bearing witness to "perceptions" (*Wahrnehmungen*) are "laid down," revised, and reproduced in the course of "at least" three distinct "registrations" (*Niederschriften*).

Freud went on to explain to his friend that each of the psychic "transcripts" represents a distinct period of time and that between any two "registrations" there necessarily lie gaps, which can be bridged, if not effaced, by further forms of writing: "translations" (or "transpositions," *Übersetzungen*). Such "renditions," to be exact, serve a vital function in the psychic mechanism. When a "translation" fails to mend the breaks between registrations, Freud argued, "anachronisms" (*Anachronismen*) develop. Invoking the Spanish juridical term for outdated laws that persist in certain provinces, Freud wrote that in such cases "*fueros* are still in force." "Psycho-neuroses" (*Psychoneurosen*) then emerge, and "repression" (*Verdrängung*) inevitably ensues:

I should like to emphasize the fact that the successive registrations represent the psychic achievement of successive epochs of life [*Lebensepochen*]. At the boundary between two such epochs a translation of the psychic material must take place [*An der Grenze von zwei solchen Epochen muss die Übersetzung des psychischen Materials folgen*]. I explain the peculiarities of the psycho-neuroses by supposing that this translation has not taken place in the case of some of the material, which has certain consequences. For we hold firmly to a belief in a tendency towards quantitative adjustment. Every later transcript inhibits its predecessor and drains the excitatory process from it. If a later transcript is lacking, the excitation is dealt with in accordance with psychological laws in force in the earlier psychic period and along the paths open at that time. Thus an anachronism persists. In a particular province, *fueros* are still in force; we are in the presence of "survivals" [*es kommen "Überlebsel" zustande*].

A failure of translation [*Die Versagung der Übersetzung*] — this is what is known clinically as "repression." The motive for it is always a release of the displeasure [*Unlustentbindung*] that would be generated by a translation; it is as though this displeasure provoked a disturbance of thought that did not permit the work of translation [*als ob diese Denkstörung hervorreife, die die Übersetzungsarbeit nicht gestattet*].[43]

The role of "translation" in this model of the psyche is clearly decisive. But the process invoked by Freud seems to have strangely little in common with the literary activity usually denoted by the same term. At the stage of psychic development in question in the letter, each element that defines the practice of inter-linguistic transposition appears to be lacking. Who, first of all, could be said to translate in this case? It is difficult to see how there could be a translator, in any ordinary sense, when consciousness has not yet emerged. In a field in which the first "signs" (*Zeichen*) follow on the heels of "perceptions" that "exclude" all memory, moreover, there cannot be any "original text" to be translated. Strictly speaking, there can be only renditions (and renditions of renditions) that point to an event that is in itself irreducible to notation. And it is far from clear, finally, how one could speak, in such a field, of any "languages" of translation. At a point so prior to the emergence of a speaking subject, from what idiom would one render a set of signs, and into what idiom would one transpose them? Preceding the one who would translate it, preceding the text with which it would be identified, and preceding the idioms whose passage it would ultimately articulate, the "translation" of which Freud writes seems to lie before all the terms to which it is generally bound. But this much is clear: the "psychic mechanism," as Freud presents it, issues from precisely such a "transposition." The mind continues to operate as long as "translation" lasts; and it stalls, in "repression," whenever one "registration" of its perceptions fails to be rendered into another.

The final, fantasized "speech remnant" of *On Aphasia* is perhaps best read in the light of this theory of "re-arrangement" and successive "re-transcription." A reading of the letter to Fliess of 1896 makes it clear that the words the young neurologist both heard and saw, "Now you're gone" (*Jetzt ist's aus mit dir*), announced the imminent ruin of his "psychic mechanism" not only in their semantic content, which was certainly threatening, but also in their form. By virtue of their fixity, the words "printed on a piece of paper floating in the air" spelled the end of speech. Self-sufficient and immediately intelligible to the one who perceived it, the phrase needed no commentary. Out of the hands of the writer and the reader, its letters could not be "re-arranged" and "re-transcribed," and for this reason they marked a limit point in the process of continual rewriting that defines the "psychic mechanism" as a whole. It is significant, in this sense, that Freud describes the "speech remnant" he saw and heard not as sketched, scrawled, or scribbled but as "printed" (*gedruckt*). The imprimatur withdraws it definitively from the field of drafts, rendering it resistant to all revision. It marks it as inalterable and untranslatable, the unforgettable text and testament of a linguistic capacity now gone.

Defined in such terms, the "remnant," however, implies a further and more startling claim about the nature of the order and disorders of speech, which remains implicit in a number of Freud's early analyses of the "language apparatus." It is that aphasia, contrary to the common conception, constitutes not a type of forgetfulness but exactly the reverse: an aggravated form of recollection, in which individuals, unwilling or unable to "re-arrange" or "re-transcribe" the "signs" of their perceptions, remember, so to speak, too much, condemned to the perpetual recurrence of one utterance at the expense of all others. In this sense, one might define the near-speechless characters of the neurological essay with the terms that Freud and Breuer used to characterize the protagonists of their clinical work of two years later. Like the variously deranged figures of the 1893 *Studies on Hysteria*, Freud's aphasics do less than they could because they "suffer mainly from reminiscences."[44] They show all the signs of being haunted by what they once perceived and may once have uttered; they seem bound, in their sad silence, to a past that admits of no "translationheir muteness bespeaks their impotence before the most merciless of memories: those that cannot be rewritten in time.

Freud was not alone in his awareness of the dangers of an excessive faculty of recollection. Among the posthumously published papers of his younger Austro-Hungarian contemporary Franz Kafka, one finds an untitled aphorism that presents the problem of remembering more and doing less in an abbreviated and exemplary form. It reads as follows:

I can swim just like the others. Only I have a better memory [*ein besseres Gedächtnis*] than the others. I have not forgotten the former inability to swim [literally, "the former being-able-not-to-swim," *das einstige Nicht-schwimmen-können*]. But since I have not forgotten it, being able to swim is of no help to me; and so, after all, I cannot swim.[45]

The unnamed speaker of this brief text stands in the same position with respect to swimming that the Freudian aphasics occupy with respect to language. One could say, in the terms of Kafka's lines, that they can—or could—speak "just like the others": their recurring "remnants" are the proof. Only a detail remains to be added, which at once clarifies and transforms the sense of their faculties: their memory is better. The aphasics "have not forgotten" the "signs" once printed on a "transcript" of their psyche. But since they have not forgotten them, being able to speak is of no help to them; and so they ultimately cannot speak.

One might go still further in the reading of Kafka's prose. It would be another variation on the theme. One could imagine that aphasics are those who could "speak just like the others." Only, one would then add, "they have a better memory": they have "not forgotten the former inability to speak" (or "the former being-able-not-to-speak"). Their memory would then be much better than good. For it would extend to the age of infant babble in which every individual life begins. It would reach back to the "epoch of life" to which no "sign"—other than the blankness of the unmarked "transcript" itself—would be adequate. Silent, the aphasic would obstinately bear witness to what was never written and what could not be said. One would then be obliged to conclude that at times, remembrance can be as destructive as oblivion can be productive: in this case, the end of memory would lie in muteness, and forgetting would lead to speech. There is no doubt that achievement, in these terms, grows difficult to measure. It could be rash to propose any summary judgment of the relative accomplishments of those speaking beings who can and who cannot speak. Who does more, and who does less—the one who can remember but cannot talk, or the one who forgets and can thus speak? Among lesser animals, the possibilities are many; privation bears more than a single mask.

CHAPTER FIFTEEN

Aglossostomography

The year 1630 saw the publication of a slim volume bearing the striking title *Aglossostomographie; ou, Description d'une bouche sans langue, laquelle parle et faict naturellement toutes les autres fonctions* (Aglossostomography; or, Description of a Mouth Without a Tongue, Which Speaks and Naturally Performs All Other Functions). The frontispiece of the book identified its author as one "Monsieur Jacques Roland, Sire of Belebat, Surgeon of Monsignor the Prince, Lieutenant of the First Surgeon Barber of the King, and Assistant of His Primary Physician." Monsieur Roland prefaced his medical treatise with compositions in verse that left little doubt as to his own estimation of the significance of the phenomenon it described, as well as the analysis he had dedicated to it. "This case is marvelous," he wrote in the first quatrain of a sonnet placed before the inception of the essay proper, "this miracle is very great, / But it is surpassed still by the writing of Roland, / Which will live forever over the earth and the sea." The "case" in question was that of Pierre Durard, "son of André Durard and Marguerite Salé, Laborers in the Village of la Rangezière, Parish near Monsaigne in Lower Poitou," who had been stricken with smallpox in his sixth or seventh year and subsequently contracted a particularly violent infection of the mouth. Monsieur Roland recounted that when Pierre's tongue began to decay and decompose, the child naturally sought to remove the gangrenous organ from his mouth; and so he began to "spit it out, piece by piece." According to the physician's account, the boy's assiduous efforts to rid himself of his tongue were soon successful. Before long, the physician reports, "absolutely nothing of it remained" in the mouth that once housed it.

The "miracle" announced by the author, however, did not concern the loss of the tongue, which, albeit a drastic occurrence for the "young Boy of Poitou," could hardly have struck the physician as remarkable on its own. The startling phenomenon arose after the loss of the organ was quite complete. It consisted of the unexpected fact that all the capacities generally thought to belong to the tongue seemed to survive the organ. "Today," Roland wrote, the boy "barely encounters any difficulties at all in performing the five functions attributed to this part that he thus lost, namely ... Speaking, Tasting, Spitting, Gathering in the mouth, and Swallowing."[1] In the end, the "alingual mouth" proved every bit as serviceable as a regular one, and, according to the doctor, it was a good deal more able than many. "A tongueless mouth," Roland commented in deliberately provocative terms, "can, without artifice, do everything that the tongue does in the mouth, and it can do so with so little discomfort that stutterers have a harder time making themselves understood ... than this child who has [no tongue] at all."[2] As the author presented it, Pierre was lucky, in a sense, that the infection was so grave and that it brought about the disappearance of all, not just a part, of his tongue. According to the physician, had the child lost only the tip of the tongue and retained the rest, like many before him, he would have had to go to the greatest of lengths to make an intelligible sound; left with the unwieldy bulk of the remaining organ, the boy, like all those in such a sad state, would have had to resort to all sorts of artificial devices to communicate.[3] In this case, the child's gums, palate, throat, and teeth could adjust themselves to the absence of the organ, compensating for its functions accordingly. The tongue of the child thus profited, as it were, from the rigor with which it vanished: his mouth fully freed from the organ of speech as well as whatever cumbersome morsels it might have left behind, Pierre Durard could finally talk with ease.

On January 15, 1718, less than a century after the publication of *Aglossostomographie*, there appeared in the *Mémoires de l'Académie Royale des Sciences* a brief medical and linguistic study that, recalling the case of the "young Boy of Poitou," adduced further evidence for the veracity of Monsieur Roland's claims. This time the child in question was a girl, not a boy, and not of Poitou but of Portugal. But the tongue was still missing, and once again speech persisted, apparently undaunted by the absence of the organ. The modest but pointed essay bore the title "Sur la manière dont une fille sans langue s'acquitte des fonctions qui dépendent de cet organe" (On the Manner in Which a Girl Without a Tongue Acquits Herself of the Functions That Depend upon this Organ), and from its opening pages its author drew the startling conclusion that the phenomenon clearly implied. "This singularity of a Mouth that speaks without a Tongue," the eighteenth-century scholar wrote, "must be enough to persuade us that one may not conclude that the Tongue is an organ essential to speech, for there are others in the Mouth that compete for this title, and others that make up for its absence."[4] Antoine de Jussieu, the author of the medical study, had encountered his subject while on a trip to Lisbon, at a time when the "girl without a tongue" was fifteen years old. "The daughter of poor parents in a village of Allenteïo," the child had been "presented at the approximate age of nine to his Eminence the Count of Ericeira, a Lord as distinguished by his nobility as by his Letters," who in turn sent her to the capital, where she later encountered the French physician.[5]

De Jussieu was informed that the girl had been born with no tongue. But she was nonetheless able to speak, and in her first meeting with the doctor she effortlessly answered all the questions put to her about "her state and the manner with which she made up for the absence of this part." De Jussieu, a man of no excessive credulity, then resolved to meet the patient "during the light of day," and the second, and last, time he saw her, he made sure "to have the Mouth opened." "In the place that the tongue usually occupies," he reported,

> I noted only a small elevation in the shape of a nipple, which rose, in the middle of the Mouth, to a height of about three or four lines. This elevation would have been almost imperceptible had I not assured myself by touching that which barely made itself visible to the eye. By means of the pressure of my finger, I felt a kind of movement of contraction and dilatation, which informed me that although the organ of the Tongue could be lacking, the muscles that shape it and that are meant for its movement were nevertheless present, since I saw no emptiness underneath her chin, and I could only attribute the alternating movement of this elevation to muscles.[6]

The discovery of the "small elevation in the shape of a nipple" seems to have been something of a consolation to the doctor, since it furnished him with evidence of the absence he could not otherwise have perceived: the vanished organ had left a minuscule mound, which, if effectively invisible, could still be reached by the physician's prodding finger. Without it, the "aglossostomography" might have remained too incredible, for as de Jussieu commented with some astonishment, "one could easily think the organ of speech was not lacking, were one not warned in advance."[7]

The French physicians were perhaps the first to note the survival of speech after the loss of the tongue, but they were hardly the last. Referring in passing to the seventeenth- and eighteenth-century works in the six lectures on sound and sense he gave at the École Libre des Hautes Études in New York between 1942 and 1943, Roman Jakobson commented that the "curious facts" the treatises made known "have since been confirmed many times."[8] In a pioneering study titled *Des Kindes Sprache und Sprachfehler* (The Child's Speech and Speech Defects), published in Leipzig in 1894, Hermann Gutzmann, for instance, observed, in Jakobson's words, that "although one uses the same term, *tongue*, to designate a part of the mouth and the linguistic phenomenon, the second meaning can do without the first, and almost all the sounds that we emit could in principle be produced in an entirely different manner, without any modification of acoustic facts."[9] The German child psychologist believed there were exceptions to the rule and that, in particular, fricatives (such as *z*, *s*, and the corresponding affricates) could not be properly produced without teeth. But he seems to have been mistaken. "Further research," Jakobson wrote, "has conclusively demonstrated that even these exceptions are imaginary. The director of the Viennese clinic for speech disturbances, Godfrey E. Arnold, showed in the *Archiv für gesamte Phonetik* III (1939) that even after the loss of incisives, the proper pronunciation of sibilants remains intact, as long as the subject's hearing is normal."[10]

Jakobson observed that the question admitted of several possible formulations and that the issue broached by the early-modern physicians and linguists far exceeded the terrain circumscribed by specialists in the scientific study of the human phonetic apparatus. In the preface to his *De formatione loquelae* of 1781, Christoph Hellwag, the inventor of the vocalic triangle, presented the problem in theological form. If speech were truly dependent on the human tongue, Hellwag reflected, how could the serpent of Eden ever

have conversed with Eve? "This curious question," Jakobson commented, "can be replaced by another, which is fundamentally equivalent to it but empirical. Phonetics wishes to deduce the sounds of
our language [or 'tongue': the linguist's term here is *langue*] from
the diverse forms of contact with the palate, the teeth, the lips, and
so on. But if these diverse points of articulation were in themselves
so essential and decisive, how could the parrot reproduce so many
sounds of our language [or 'tongue'] so effectively, even though it
has a vocal apparatus that so little resembles ours?"[11] The representation of the production of human speech seems, in each case,
to conceal an unstated and unsolved difficulty, one inscribed in the
very form of the term "language," which, like all the corresponding terms in other Indo-European languages, recalls the organ of
the mouth, *lingua*, with whose movements speech cannot simply
be identified. It is as if the very word "tongue" were a catachresis:
a name for something unnameable, an improper figure for a being
that could not be assigned any proper place and that could not, for
this reason, ever fully be represented.

One of Edgar Allan Poe's last short stories, "The Facts in the
Case of M. Valdemar," presents the problem in exemplary, if chilling, terms. The nineteenth-century text can be read as a precise
pendant to the earlier medical treatises, for it tells the tale not of
a "Mouth without a Tongue, which Speaks" but of a tongue, as it
were, without a mouth, which, beyond the end of the living body,
continues to talk in the absence of the being to whom it once
belonged. The narrator of the short story, a certain "P——," identi-
fies himself as a physician whose "attention," for the three years
preceding the events related in the tale, "had been repeatedly
drawn to the subject of Mesmerism" and who has become captivated, more recently still, by a single thought: "that, in the series
of experiments made hitherto, there had been a very remarkable and most unaccountable omission:—no person had as yet

been mesmerized *in articulo mortis*."[12] "It remained to be seen,"
the narrator explains in programmatic terms, "first, whether, in
such condition, there existed in the patient any susceptibility to
the magnetic influence; secondly, whether, if any existed, it was
impaired or increased by the condition; thirdly, to what extent,
or for how long a period, the encroachment of Death might be
arrested by the process."[13] P— then finds a suitable subject for
his experiment in the form of "M. Ernest Valdemar, the well-
known compiler of the 'Biblioteca Forensica,' and author (under
the *nom de plume* of Issachar Marx) of the Polish versions of 'Wal-
lenstein' and 'Gargantua.'"[14] Declared "in a confirmed phthisis"
by his physicians, M. Valdemar turns to P— in his final hours,
expressly stating his wish to be mesmerized. And a little more
than twenty-four hours before the time of decease announced
by the patient's regular physicians, the narrator thus arrives at
his bedside. P— encounters little difficulty in mesmerizing M.
Valdemar. The moribund patient, he recalls, quickly enters into
"an unusually perfect mesmeric trance."[15]

Several hours later, P— relates, the state of the patient seems
unchanged. Determining "to hazard a few words of conversation," the mesmerist asks M. Valdemar if he has slept. At first the
bedridden man says nothing; and when the physician repeats his
query, the patient still does not answer. Uttered a third time, however, the question provokes a response: "The lips moved sluggishly,
and from between them, in a barely audible whisper, issued the
words: 'Yes;—asleep now. Do not wake me!—let me die so!'"[16]
So those present wait, certain of M. Valdemar's imminent death.
But the narrator, aware that the death of the patient "must now
take place within a few minutes," still wishes to learn more while
time permits; and so he once again poses his previous question.
The long-awaited decease seems to occur at the moment of the
doctor's speech. The narrator recounts:

While I spoke, there came a marked change over the countenance of the sleep-walker. The eyes rolled themselves slowly open, the pupils disappearing upwardly; the skin generally assumed a cadaverous hue, resembling not so much parchment as white paper; and the circular hectic spots which, hitherto, had been strongly defined in the centre of each cheek, *went out* at once. I use this expression, because the suddenness of their departure put me in mind of nothing so much as the extinguishment of a candle by a puff of the breath. The upper lip, at the same time, writhed itself away from the teeth, which it had previously covered completely; while the lower jaw fell with an audible jerk, leaving the mouth widely extended, and disclosing in full view the swollen and blackened tongue.[17]

The occurrence, P— comments, is without doubt a "death-bed horror," and those present at this point retreat, startled and not a little disgusted, from "the region of the bed."

The most astonishing of the "facts in the case of M. Valdemar," however, takes place later, in the moments following the apparent death of the patient. "There was no longer the faintest sign of vitality in M. Valdemar," P— recalls,

and concluding him to be dead, we were consigning him to the charge of the nurses, when a strong vibratory motion was observable in the tongue. This continued for perhaps a minute. At the expiration of this period, there issued from the distended and motionless jaws a voice—such as it would be madness in me to attempt describing. There are, indeed, two or three epithets which might be considered as applicable to it in part; I might say, for example, that the sound was harsh, and broken and hollow; but the hideous whole is indescribable, for the simple reason that no similar sounds have ever jarred upon the ear of humanity. There were two particulars, nevertheless, which I thought then, and still think, might fairly be stated as characteristic of the intonation—as well adapted to convey some idea of its unearthly peculiarity. In the first place, the voice seemed to reach our ears—at least mine—from a vast distance, or from some deep cavern within the earth. In the second place, it impressed me (I fear, indeed, that it will be impossible to make myself comprehended) as gelatinous or glutinous matters impress the sense of touch.

I have spoken both of "sound" and of "voice." I mean to say that the sound was one of distinct—of even wonderfully, thrillingly distinct—syllabification. M. Valdemar *spoke*—obviously in reply to the question I had propounded to him a few minutes before. I had asked him, it will be remembered, if he still slept. He now said:

"Yes; —no; —I *have been* sleeping—and now—now—*I am dead*."[18]

Here it is not the speaking body that survives the demise of the tongue, as in the work of the physicians; precisely to the contrary, the tongue now lives on after the decease of the body of which it would have seemed to be a part. Sounding as if "from a vast distance," beneath the "distended and motionless jaws" and beyond the individual to which it once belonged, the organ now moves—itself—with consummate artistry, producing a noise for which the physician can find only the most metrical of terms: "the sound ... of distinct—of even wonderfully, thrillingly distinct—syllabification."

M. Valdemar's last words recall those he uttered shortly before the time of his apparent "death," but his final sentence is a good deal more perplexing than the one he has earlier uttered "in a barely audible whisper." Before, the patient has certainly assented to a question to which it is not obvious one may assent, affirming that he is indeed "asleep now." On the surface, the statement is not easy to comprehend: the transparency of its form seems to belie its content, since, to be true, the claim would have to be formulated by a subject lost in unconscious slumber. But the complexity of the final utterance reported in the tale is of a different order, for, to be true, the words "Yes;—no;—I *have been* sleeping—and now—now—*I am dead*" would have to be spoken by a subject who, *stricto sensu*, is none at all. Who or what, if not a tongue without a body, could formulate such a phrase? As Roland Barthes has noted in a close reading of the tale, "We have here a veritable *hapax* of narrative grammar, staged by *an utterance that is impossible insofar as it is an utterance: I am dead.*"[19] Barthes showed that the phrase that issues from the "strong vibratory motion ... in the tongue" is remarkable for a number of reasons, which may be enumerated as follows: first, the sentence speaks solely of the origin of its own utterance, which remains curiously resistant to analysis; second, although unprecedented and unutterable in discourse, the phrase is in fact simply the literalization of a common metaphor employed by a great many speakers ("I am dead"); third, in the set of all possible utterances, "the composition of the first person 'I' and the attribute 'dead' is precisely what is radically impossible—the empty point, the blind spot of language"; and, finally, on the semantic level the sentence "simultaneously asserts two contraries ('Life, Death') and thus gives shape to a unique enantioseme, neither an affirmation ('I am dead') nor a negation ('I am not dead') but an affirmation-negation: 'I am dead and not dead,'" which marks the emergence of a linguistic form in which "*true-false, yes-no,* and *death-life* are conceived as an indivisible *whole.*"[20]

The final phrase of the unruly tongue, therefore, seems not only an "incredible" statement, as the narrator of the tale himself repeatedly insists, but even an inconceivable one. And it is clearly for this reason that the critic characterizes it as nothing less than a "radically impossible utterance": a statement that, by definition, cannot be strictly true at the time of its perception.[21] But the limits of speech are not those of language, and in this case the sentence that cannot truthfully be proffered can still be formulated, albeit in a domain of expression that is not that of the utterance: writing. The literary text itself suggests as much, since the event of decease sets the stage for the entrance into the story of the unmistakable elements of graphic composition. Here the moment of death is the one in which the skin of the body assumes "a cadaverous hue, resembling not so much parchment as white paper," and in which the tongue, in turn, steps forward, on its own, "blackened" as never before: decease, as it is described at this point, turns the body into paper and pen. The unutterable phrase "I am dead" is the product of this transformation of life into writing. Rising out of the disappearance of the animate word, it is the sole text and testimony of the death of the Polish patient: a funerary inscription made audible, so to speak, by the erstwhile organ of the body that no longer lives.

It is all the more significant, from this perspective, that the tongue that affirms the death of the body speaks in the tale for itself. The "strong vibratory motion" could clearly also have resulted in a statement in the voice of a third person, of the kind the narrator might have offered the reader: "*He is dead.*" M. Valdemar's tongue, however, has an "I," which lends it its unspeakable sense and places it in a singular and unexamined relation with the history of the forms of writing. It is worth noting that the curious declaration of decease ("I am dead"), although unprecedented in narrative, is in itself not unique in the literary tradition. It constitutes, on the contrary, a precise repetition of the oldest documents of the Western tradition, with which it is not impossible that Poe was familiar: the funeral inscriptions of archaic Greece. It is well known that the earliest surviving alphabetic texts of classical Antiquity consist not of literary works or economic inscriptions in the strict sense (such as inventories and records of transactions) but of graffiti and funeral inscriptions commemorating and recalling the dead.[22] It is perhaps less well known that the form of these commemorative texts is quite unlike that of their modern equivalents. As a rule, the ancient objects bearing commemorative texts speak, exactly like the tongue of the dead M. Valdemar, for themselves, using a first-person-singular pronoun. On a Theban object from the eighth century B.C., for instance, one finds an inscription that reads, "I am the kylix of Korakos";[23] and on memorials from the same period, one encounters such phrases as "Eumares built me as a monument," or, more striking still, "I am the commemoration [μνῆμα] of Glaukos."[24]

It is worth pausing to consider the precise form of these inscriptions, which bears more than a superficial resemblance to the words articulated by the tongue of the defunct M. Valdemar. In an important study of the practices of reading and writing in ancient Greece, Jesper Svenbro considered these archaic texts at length, offering an illuminating account of the first-person formula they regularly employed. "These inscriptions," he commented in *Phrasikleia*, "are not transcriptions of something that could have been said in an oral situation and subsequently transcribed upon the object.... Quite to the contrary: these statements are in some sense characteristic of writing, which allows written objects to designate themselves by the first-person pronoun, even though they are *objects* and not living, thinking beings gifted with speech."[25] The first person of the memorial object, from this perspective, appears as a purely written phenomenon. It constitutes the sign not of a living being but of its absence, and only as such can it mark the decease of the one it commemorates. Svenbro recalled, in this context, the etymological account of the first-person pronoun once proposed by Karl Brugmann, according to which the Greek term *ego*, as well as its Indo-European relations, derives from a neuter noun (*eg[h]om*), meaning simply "here-ness" (*Hierheit*): originally, "I" would signify the insubstantial being of whatever can be indicated as "here," be it animate or

160

inanimate, human or inhuman, its expression spoken or written.[26] So, too, the "I" of the funeral object, Svenbro argued, is to be understood as the cipher of the substanceless presence of writing. "As long as one can read the inscription," the classicist wrote, "the object will be there. No one can better lay claim to the 'here-ness' of written enunciation than the object."[27] The commemorated human being, by definition, is absent; and the engraver vanishes with the completion of his work, becoming "a third person by the fact of writing."[28] The inscribed "I" alone remains.

The bodiless tongue of the mesmerized translator is a being of this funerary and graphic order. Its "strong vibratory motion" announces, for those who can hear it, the most astounding of the "facts in the case of M. Valdemar": that language persists in the disappearance of its speaker, that the tongue remains, like the "blackened" surface of "white paper," to bear witness to the vanishing of that which it would seem to represent. "Aglossostomography," in the literary work, thus turns into what one might call, with an equally strange term, "asomaglossography": in the place of the medical account of a "Mouth without a Tongue, which Speaks," the tale offers us the sketch of a "Tongue without a Body, which Writes." The two "graphies" coincide, however, in telling the tale of a single noncoincidence: whether the speaking mouth outlives the tongue or, by contrast, the tongue survives the speaking body, language, loosened from that to which it would seem to belong, lives on, sounding "from a vast distance, or from some deep cavern within the earth" that cannot easily be identified. More or less than one, the "tongue" in this way passes away and still persists. It stretches, in each case, beyond the body and the speaker, surviving in the oblivion of that from which it appeared to come and that for which it seemed to live. What we call a "language," one might conclude, is nothing other than that: a being which outlasts itself.

CHAPTER SIXTEEN

Hudba

To lose one's tongue is certainly a troubling thing, but to acquire another is also not without its difficulties, even if they can hardly be called uncommon. Sooner or later, one is confronted by an idiom one cannot call one's own, before which one must either adapt one's own speech or fall silent. It is in this moment that speaking beings grow conscious that they have learned no more, and no less, than one language among others. Considered as an object of science, such a tongue certainly varies from place to place and from time to time: for one speaker, it may be Tamil; for another, Amharic; or, to choose yet another, equally arbitrary example, Bulgarian. But as a phenomenon common to the experience of all speaking beings, such a language also bears a single name, which was coined in the later Middle Ages and has never fallen out of use: the "mother tongue" (*materna lingua*).[1] Dante, who considered himself the first to have reflected on the subject as such, argued that the difference between the speaking being's original and subsequent forms of speech was one not only of number but also of nature. "Our first language [or 'primary' language, *prima locutio*]," he wrote in the famous opening paragraphs of *De vulgari eloquentia*, "we acquire from those around us," "imitating our nurses without any rules" (*sine regula nutricem imitantem accipimus*). Our "second" (or "secondary") tongue, by contrast, we learn deliberately and methodically as we master the system of principles that the medieval poet-philosopher, in accordance with the practice of his time, designated by the richly equivocal term "grammar" (*gramatica*).[2] Dante's perspective on the matter, of course, was decidedly medieval. To his eyes, there could be only one such "second language," and it was Latin, the language of the schools. But for better or worse, something of his conception of the diversity of languages remains in force today, for few would doubt that one learns one's mother tongue in a manner fundamentally unlike that in which one acquires those that follow it.

The gulf that separates "first" and "second" languages is clear, at least as far as their acquisition is concerned, and it cannot but raise questions about the nature and possibility of the transition between the two types of idioms. How, one might wonder, could one ever start to learn a "language" through study, if until then one had only ever begun to speak by "imitating ... without any rules"? And if one did succeed in learning a "second" language through the mastery of the principles of grammar, would such an acquisition not have consequences for the one that preceded it? It is not certain that after having taken up residence in the ordered system of a foreign grammar, speaking beings can ever fully return to the unruly medium of their "first speech." But such queries are not limited to the passage between the mother tongue and the "secondary" ones that follow it. They may arise even with respect to the "first" language itself; they make themselves felt at a moment prior to the acquisition of any language that can be opposed to the "primary speech" of which Dante offered the first philosophical formulation. For there are those—however few they may be—who have more, or less, than a single "mother tongue": those who, even before they study a foreign language, have already begun to lose the one they once learned "without any rules," and to acquire another simply by "imitating [their] nurses."

Elias Canetti is an exemplary case. Born in Bulgaria in 1905 to a Sephardic Jewish family, he first learned the Judeo-Spanish idiom of the Jews who lived in Spain until their exile in 1492, Ladino. To be sure, a number of languages were spoken during Canetti's childhood in Rustchuk, the city of his birth. "On one day," he recalled in the first volume of his autobiography, *The Tongue Set Free* (*Die gerettete Zunge*), "one could hear seven or eight languages," for the city was home not only to Spanish Jews but also to many Bulgarians, Turks, Greeks, Albanians, and Gypsies, in addition to some Romanians and Russians, "here and there."[3] As Canetti presented it, the largely medieval Spanish of the Sephardim was his first tongue; it was the language of his family and their friends, as well as of his first nursery songs and the romances he learned as a child. But the future writer was already exposed to another tongue in his house as a child. Although his parents always spoke Spanish to their children and to their friends, they had between themselves a different language, German, "the language of their happy schooldays in Vienna."[4] It was perhaps only natural for their eldest child, Elias, to become fascinated with the foreign tongue at an early age, and when his mother and father spoke to each other in it, he was immediately captivated. "I would listen with utter intensity and then ask them what this or that meant," he wrote. "They laughed, saying it was too early for me, those were things I would understand only later. It was already a big deal for them to give in on the word 'Vienna,' the only one they revealed to me. I believed they were talking about wondrous things that could be spoken of only in that language. After begging and begging to no avail, I ran away angrily into another room, which was seldom used, and I repeated to myself the sentences I had heard from them, in their precise intonation, like magic formulas."[5]

In 1911, Canetti's parents moved with their children to England, seeking to extricate themselves from a dominating father and the oppressive conditions of their native city. Two of Elias's uncles already lived in Manchester, where they had started a flourishing business; they now offered Elias's father a partnership in the enterprise. The English period of the son's youth, however, was cut short. A little more than a year after the family arrived, Elias's father died suddenly, at the age of thirty-one; and barely a year later, his widow resolved to move the family again, this time to Vienna. Their journey brought them through London, Paris, and finally Lausanne, where Canetti's mother rented "an apartment at the top of the city, with a radiant view of the lake and the sailboats sailing on it."[6] It was ostensibly a summer holiday; but Elias soon learned there were other grounds for their stop by the lake of Geneva on the way to Vienna. "The real reason" for the Lausannois summer stay, Canetti explained, "was that I had to learn German first. I was eight years old, I was to attend school in Vienna, and my age would put me in the third grade of elementary school. My mother could not bear the thought of my perhaps not being accepted in this grade because of my ignorance of the language, and she was determined to teach me German as quickly as possible."[7]

After well over half a century, Canetti seemed to have forgotten close to nothing of the methods by which his mother put her decision into practice. "We sat in the kitchen," he recalled, "at a big table, I on the smaller side, with the view of the lake and sails," his mother on the left side, making sure to hold her German-language textbook in such a way that her son could not see what its pages contained. To Canetti's mother, it was a matter of pedagogical principle. The language learning, if it was to succeed, had to do without books and written study. She was convinced, Canetti tells us, that "books are bad for learning languages; that one must learn them orally, and that a book is harmless only when

166

one knows something of a language."[8] Holding her precious possession "always far" from her son, Señora Canetti would thus read him a sentence in German. Elias was then to repeat it, syllable for syllable, word for word, clause for clause; he was to try over and over again until his pronunciation finally struck his mother, if not as good, then at least as "bearable." "Only then," Canetti recalled,

> did she tell me what the sentence meant in English. But this she never repeated, I had to master it instantly and for all time. Then she quickly went on to the next sentence and followed the same procedure; as soon as I pronounced it correctly, she translated it; eyed me imperiously to make me note it, and was already on the next sentence. I don't know how many sentences she expected to drill me in the first time; let us conservatively say it was few; I fear it was many. She let me go, saying, "Repeat it to yourself. You must not forget a single sentence. Not a single one. Tomorrow, we shall continue." She kept her book, and I was left to myself, perplexed.[9]

The following day, Elias's performance was mixed. Questioned on the meaning of one of the sentences he had repeated and learned the day before, the child succeeded in summoning the correct English equivalent. "But then," Canetti wrote, "came the catastrophe," for he could not recall the sense of any of the other German phrases he had learned, and when asked to give their meaning after repeating them in the new language, he could only "falter and fall silent."[10] The child then found that his initial success could also be turned against him. "You remembered the first one," his mother charged, "so you must be able to do it right. You don't want to. You want to remain in Lausanne. I'll leave you alone in Lausanne. I'm going to Vienna ... you can stay here in Lausanne, by yourself."[11] But abandonment was not the worst of what Canetti's mother could threaten him with in such situations. When he could not recall the sense of any of the sentences he was to commit to memory, Elias was forced to face the maternal affect he feared most: contempt. "When she became particularly impatient," Canetti wrote, "she threw up her hands over her head and shouted: 'My son's an idiot! I didn't realize that my son's an idiot!' Or: 'Your father knew German too, what would your father say!'"[12]

So began the terrible time in which the young Canetti, alone in French Switzerland, having left England after Bulgaria, acquired the German language his mother had resolved to impart to him without reading and writing. The child's life now changed as the anxiety of not forgetting the tongue he did not yet know filled his days and his nights, imposing itself on him both when he was with his mother and when he was without her. "I now lived in terror of her derision," he recalled, "and during the day, wherever I was, I kept repeating the sentences. On walks with the governess, I was sullen and untalkative. I no longer felt the wind, I didn't hear the music, I always had my German sentences and their English meanings in my head."[13] The boy had fallen under the spell of his mother's tongue, and he could barely speak—or, in the terms of the autobiography, he had been hypnotized, and he could not come to without the consent of the one who had so "trapped" him: "My mother had trapped me in a dreadful hypnosis, and she was the only one who could release me."[14] Relief, however, came from the assistance of the child's English governess, who, after a period of indeterminate length Canetti thinks may have lasted a month, convinced the principled and hitherto-merciless pedagogue to allow her son access to the precious script in which his new sentences were sealed. Elias now received the book that until then had been withheld from him, and, albeit still unaided by his mother, he now learned to read the "boxy letters" of the Gothic typeface in which German texts of the time were largely printed. "The worst suffering," Canetti wrote, "was now past."[15]

His mother continued to believe in the pernicious properties of books for language learning, and during their lessons the
child was still to memorize his sentences without recourse to the
printed page. But Elias could now consult the textbook on his
own, and after and between lessons he could "strengthen through
reading" whatever he had previously learned purely by speaking.
The supplement of writing proved decisive: the boy learned more
quickly and better, and his mother, as he later reported, "now had
no more opportunities to call me an 'idiot.'"[16] It was the beginning, Canetti recalls, of a "sublime" period in the life of the child
and his mother, in which they could converse freely in their new
language during the lessons and outside them. For the widow, the
fact was of the greatest importance, as the son fully realized only
later. "She herself had a profound need to use German with me,"
Canetti wrote, "it was the language of her trust":

> The most terrible wound in her life, when, at twenty-seven, she lost
> my father, was expressed most sensitively for her in the fact that their
> long conversations in German were stopped. Her true marriage had
> taken place in that language. She didn't know what to do, she felt
> lost without him, and she tried as fast as possible to put me in his
> place.[17]

For the child, the acquisition of the new tongue was perhaps even
more momentous. As the autobiographical narrator presents it, the
terrible training furnished him not, as one might have expected,
with a foreign language, but with a far more startling thing: "a
mother tongue implanted belatedly, and in true pain" (*eine spät
und unter wahrhaftigen Schmerzen eingepflanzte Muttersprache*).[18]
It was to become the language of his lifework, and for the adult
Canetti its acquisition was the equivalent of a second birth, which
gave him an existence he would otherwise never have known:

We spent three months in Lausanne, and I sometimes think that no other time in my life has been as momentous. But one often thinks that when focusing seriously on a period, and it is possible that each period is the most important and contains everything. Nevertheless, in Lausanne, where I heard French around me, picking it up casually and without dramatic complications, I was reborn under my mother's influence to the German language, and the spasm of that birth produced that passion tying me to both, the language and my mother. Without these two, which are fundamentally one and the same, the future course of my life would have been senseless and incomprehensible.[19]

There is still more, however, to the story of Canetti's mother tongues. Ladino and German were not the only languages the author learned by imitation as a child. Yet another idiom could lay claim to the title of the "speech" the boy "received," in the terms of Dante's definition of the *prima locutio*, "without any rules, from those around [him]," when he first learned "to distinguish sounds."[20] It was the language of the peasant girls who lived and worked in the Canetti household in Rustchuk, with whom Elias spent so many of his first years: Bulgarian. The mature Canetti could not recall exactly how and when he acquired the tongue, yet he appeared to be certain of the central role it played in his childhood; and with the secure distance of hindsight, he seemed every bit as certain that he later lost the Slavic language altogether. "To each other," Canetti wrote, explaining the linguistic situation of his family, "my parents spoke German, which I was not allowed to understand. To us children and to all relatives they spoke Ladino. That was the true vernacular, albeit an ancient Spanish, and I often heard it later on and never forgot it."[21] But Judeo-Spanish was hardly the only "vernacular" in the household, as Canetti subsequently made clear: "The peasant girls at home knew only Bulgarian, and I must have learned it with them. But since I never went to a Bulgarian school, leaving Rustchuk at the age of six, I very soon forgot Bulgarian completely."[22]

Although he claimed he remembered nothing of the Bulgarian language, Canetti had no doubts that he nevertheless retained many memories of the events that had taken place in the Balkan tongue of his first years. They remained, but not as they were. At a point the mature Canetti could neither date nor place with precision, what he had once experienced and remembered passed, in its entirety, into German. "All events of those first years," he wrote,

> were in Ladino or Bulgarian. It wasn't until much later that most of them rendered themselves into German for me [*Sie haben sich mir später zum grössten Teil ins Deutsche übersetzt*]. Only especially dramatic events, murder and manslaughter so to speak, and the worst horrors have been retained by me in their Ladino wording, and very precisely and indestructibly at that. Everything else, that is most things, and especially anything Bulgarian, like the fairy tales, I carry around in German. I couldn't say exactly how this happened. I don't know at what point in time, on what occasion, this or that translated itself [*Ich weiss nicht, zu welchem Zeitpunkt, bei welcher Gelegenheit dies oder jenes sich übersetzt hat*]. I never probed into this matter; perhaps I was too afraid to destroy my most precious memories with a methodical investigation based on rigorous principles. I can only say one thing with certainty: the events of those years are present to me in all their strength and freshness (I've fed on them for over sixty years), but the vast majority are tied to words that I did not know at that time. It seems natural to me to write them down now; I don't have the feeling that I am changing or warping anything. It is not like the literary translation of a book from one language to another, it is a translation that happened of its own accord in my unconscious, and since I normally avoid this word like the plague, a word that has

become meaningless from overuse, I apologize for employing it in this one and only case.[23]

It is worth pausing to consider the fate of Canetti's Bulgarian, which differs considerably from that of the two other languages of childhood he discusses in his autobiography, Ladino and English. It certainly does not meet the end of the English that Elias spoke in Manchester, for which he willfully and painfully sought to substitute German during the months preceding his "rebirth" into his belatedly implanted mother tongue by the lake of Geneva. But it also does not follow the course of his Ladino, which passes, without his ever seeming to notice it, into German while still leaving behind particularly memorable segments of speech: the testimonies of "dramatic events, murder and manslaughter so to speak, and [of] the worst horrors," whose original Spanish wording even the adult writer could never forget. Canetti's childhood Bulgarian, by contrast, would seem to have vanished altogether, imperceptible in its passing and utterly irretrievable after its disappearance. The narrator does not appear to believe he had much, if anything, to do with it. According to the letter of the text, it was not he who "translated" or "transposed" (*übersetzt*) his experiences from one tongue into another but they themselves which "rendered themselves" into a new idiom, in a process of translation without translator that altogether effaced the original in transposing it, "of its own accord," into a form it never before possessed. "Completely forgotten," the Bulgarian of the child thus transformed itself into the German of the adult as the experiences of the young Elias, "tied to words" of much later times, gave rise to the conscious recollections of Canetti the writer: memories of things that, strictly speaking, could never have happened as such, and whose proper place was nowhere if not in the imagined past of the German writer.

On the whole, it seems that foreign tongues for Canetti were creatures of childhood, like the mother tongue for most. One might well wonder whether, for the Bulgarian German writer of Judeo-Spanish extraction, the two types of tongues could even be distinguished at all. But there is one exception that casts significant light on the languages of the author's youth and reveals a great deal, in particular, about the one tongue he so unequivocally claimed to have "completely forgotten." In May 1937, Canetti traveled from Vienna to Prague. Shortly before, he had seen the large exhibit of Oskar Kokoschka's works that had been organized at the Kunstgewerbemuseum in Vienna in honor of the painter's fiftieth birthday. Greatly impressed by the works he had discovered there, the young writer resolved to visit the artist, with whom he shared a good friend, to tell him of the enthusiasm with which the exhibit had been greeted by the Viennese public. Predictably, the meeting with the older artist was for Canetti a memorable event, and in the third volume of his autobiography, *The Play of the Eyes* (*Das Augenspiel*), he gave a detailed account of it. But he seems to have been at least as struck on his trip to Prague by the unfamiliar Czech language he heard around him. "It seemed to me," he wrote, "to be a fighting language, since all the words were strongly accented on the first syllable; in every discussion that one heard, one could perceive a succession of small blows, which continued to repeat as long as the conversation lasted."[24]

For Canetti, the peculiar power of the central European tongue was nowhere as evident as in its striking word for music: *hudba*. "As far as I knew," he recalled, "in the European languages there was only ever one and the same word for it: *music*, a beautiful, melodious word, whose pronunciation in German gives the impression of soaring upward together with it," and which, when accented on the first syllable (as in English or Spanish), "remained hovering for a short while, before fading away."[25] Years before, the young writer had reflected on the apparent universality of the appellation and wondered if it truly did justice to the diversity of the phenomena it designated. He had once even gone so far as to pose the question to Alban Berg. "Ought there not to be other *words* for music?" he courageously—or rashly—asked the disciple of Schoenberg. "Is the intractable obstinacy of the Viennese with respect to everything new not bound to the fact that they have become perfectly sure of their *representations* of the word, so perfectly sure that they cannot tolerate the possibility of the word's changing meaning?"[26] Naturally, Berg would not hear of such an idea; the dodecaphonist was perfectly convinced that he composed music no less than his predecessors in the tradition, and Canetti never again spoke of the matter. But when he discovered the word *hudba* on his trip to Prague, he recalls, he could not avoid the conclusion it imposed on him. "This," he wrote, "was the word for Stravinsky's *Rite*, for Bartók, for Janáček, and for much more."[27]

The music of the Czech language, however, was not altogether without resonances with the other idioms that Canetti knew and had once known. The only explanation he could find for the force with which the Slavic sounds impressed themselves on him was that they somehow recalled the tongue he could no longer clearly remember, Bulgarian. "I wandered as if spellbound," Canetti wrote,

> from one courtyard to another. What I perceived as a challenge was perhaps mere communication, but if so, it was *more furious* and contained more of the speaker than we are used to consigning to our communications. Perhaps the force with which the Czech words entered into me was due to memories of the Bulgarian of my early childhood. But I never thought of this, since I had completely forgotten Bulgarian, and I am not in a position to determine how much of forgotten languages is nevertheless left over inside one. It is certain, in any case, that something in those Prague days brought me back to things that had played themselves out in separate periods of my life.

174

I took in Slavic sounds as parts of a language that, in an inexplicable way, affected me deeply.[28]

Here it becomes clear that the fate of the Slavic language of Canetti's early years is a good deal more complex than it may seem at first glance and, perhaps, than the autobiographical narrator himself may have wished to acknowledge. On the surface, to be sure, the account of the infant tongue offered at this point remains identical with that proposed in the first volume of the author's memoirs: just as Canetti earlier wrote that Bulgarian was the one childhood language he "forgot ... completely," he now informs the reader that he had "completely forgotten Bulgarian."[29] But it is difficult to avoid the impression that the near-perfect repetition conceals a disavowal ("I never thought of this"), which obstinately bears witness to the reality of the phenomenon it expressly denies. At the least, one may surmise that the Slavic language did not pass, as the narrator earlier claimed, entirely into German, leaving behind—in distinction, notably, to Ladino—no residue whatsoever. A good two decades after his departure from Rustchuk, the ostensibly forgotten tongue continued to affect the individual who once spoke it without hesitation, allowing him to "take in" the sounds of the related Slavic tongue as he would otherwise have not. In its vanishing, Bulgarian had cleared the way for the indistinct but undeniable "memories" Canetti would not, but must, recognize: the "memories" of a "completely forgotten" tongue, which remained, "in an inexplicable way," "left over inside" him.

What did Elias Canetti hear in the *hudba* of the Czech language? Obviously, it was not—or not merely—the idiom of the inhabitants of Prague, since, as he makes clear, he could understand close to nothing of that tongue at all. But it would be equally inadequate to conclude that the writer simply perceived in it Bulgarian. Even had Canetti retained his knowledge of the Balkan language, despite his repeated statements to the contrary, he could hardly have discovered it again within Czech. The typological affinities between the southern Slavic and the western Slavic tongues do not suffice for one to assert that each can be found within the other. It would be more precise to maintain that in Prague, Canetti heard not a language but an echo: the sound within one tongue of another that had been forgotten. It is no accident that the scene of the echo lies at the end of the autobiographical trilogy published in his lifetime and, more exactly, immediately before the last chapter of the work as a whole, which bears the unambiguous title "Mother's Death." The music of Czech, as Canetti perceived it, summoned the one childhood tongue that was not bound to his mother, which not only preceded the German he learned from her in Lausanne but also was independent of the Ladino in which she spoke to him before his father's death. Recalling to him a tongue that could not be characterized as in any sense maternal, the "furious" communication of the inhabitants of Prague simultaneously announced the irretrievable loss with which the autobiography ends. This may well be the secret sealed in the word *hudba*, which the tale of Canetti's life ultimately exposes: no matter what language one speaks, and no matter how many one may learn and one may forget, there is none that does not open onto another, there is none that can be fully "native." In this sense, no tongue is truly a "mother tongue," not even one's mother's.

At the start of a letter to Rainer Maria Rilke dated July 6, 1926, Marina Tsvetaeva composed the following sentences about the mother tongue, which she formulated not in Russian but in German, while living in exile in France:

> Goethe says somewhere that one cannot permit oneself anything meaningful in a foreign language—and to me that always sounded

wrong. (Goethe as a whole always sounds right, but only as a *summa*; so I'm doing him an injustice now.) To compose is already to translate, out of the mother tongue—into another, whether it's French or German has no importance. No tongue is [the] mother tongue [*Keine Sprache ist Muttersprache*]. To compose is to compose after [*Dichten ist nachdichten*]. That is why I don't understand when people speak of French poets, Russian poets, and so on. A poet can write French; he cannot be a French poet. That is risible.[30]

There are good reasons to understand Tsvetaeva's statement that "no tongue is [the] mother tongue" in the most apparent sense: no language may justly lay claim to the title of being a "first" language, acquired purely by imitation and so untouched and untouchable by rules and writing, schools and grammatical consciousness; every language, in the terms of Dante's treatise, is "first" and "second" at once. But the poet's claim also means more. It can be understood in the paradoxically positive sense implied by its undeniably affirmative logical form. For "no tongue is [the] mother tongue" (*Keine Sprache ist Muttersprache*) suggests not only that "there is no mother tongue." It also implies, quite literally, that "no tongue *is* [the] mother tongue," that there is, in other words, a mother tongue, but that it is not one, in the way a particular language ("whether it's French or German has no importance") may be one. It may well be the tongue in which the poet—and not only she—crafts her work: a simultaneously single yet multiple idiom in which writing and translating, "compos[ing]" and "compos[ing] after," production and reproduction, cannot be told apart. A language that is none, such a "mother tongue" may be the ultimate medium of all speech: the element in which every language, moved by a music that resonates beyond its borders, translates itself "of its own accord" and passes "into another, whether it's French or German has no importance."

CHAPTER SEVENTEEN

Schizophonetics

Louis Wolfson seems never to have had any doubts about the identity of his mother tongue—or, for that matter, about the fact that he could not bear a single sound of it. In a book published in 1970, he alluded to the difficulties he had encountered when, as a child, he first learned to speak, read, and write it; and he recorded in vivid detail the lengths to which he later went, as a young adult, to forget it. The composition of the book appears to have played no insignificant part in the author's efforts to free himself from the language he could hardly avoid. Shunning the sole idiom of his home and his schooling, English, the author consigned the entire tale of his battle with the mother tongue to the benignly foreign idiom he knew best, French, publishing the book not in the country of his birth, the United States, but in Paris, where it appeared, accompanied by a preface by Gilles Deleuze, in a series of psychoanalytic works directed by J.-B. Pontalis. It is impossible for anyone who has read the book not to imagine the discomfort with which its author might greet its translation, even in part, into the language of his mother. Yet if one wishes to speak of the singular work without adopting the methods of its author, one has little choice in the matter. One must risk restituting the book to the tongue against which it represents something of a monument, starting with its very title, which, with translatorly audacity, one may render as follows: *The Schizo and Languages; or, Phonetics of a Psycho (Sketches by a Schizophrenic Student of Languages).*[1]

In his book, the author refers to himself exclusively in the third person, designating himself by a series of related epithets: "the young schizophrenic," "the psychotic," the "alienated" or "mentally disturbed young man," or, as in the final syntagma of the title, "a schizophrenic student of languages." One may surmise from a number of remarks in the book that the schizophrenic's systematic efforts to liberate himself from the domination of English began in early adulthood and, more precisely, some time after his college years and before he turned twenty-six, when he describes his organized struggle with the mother tongue as having been well under way for some time. It was after "fleeing" one of the psychiatric hospitals to whose control his mother had delivered him, Wolfson recounted, that he "decided more or less definitively to perfect his competences" in the two foreign tongues he had studied in high school and university, French and German, and "later to extend his language studies to include a Semitic language and a Slavic one, not to mention still others."[2] "Pursuing these studies with true mania," we read toward the beginning of *The Schizo and Languages*, the mentally ill young man "systematically sought not to listen to his mother tongue,"

which was exclusively used by all those around him, and which is spoken by more people than any other language, except for Chinese, whose preponderant zenith is in fact something of an optical illusion, which is to say, insomuch as it consists of a commonly understandable writing (which, however, indicates pronunciation only very incompletely, and relatively, and inexactly, and frequently), as opposed to a more or less equally phonetic phenomenon, since the various Chinese dialects display significant variations in sounds and are not mutually intelligible. Nevertheless, since it was hardly possible not to listen to his mother tongue at all, he tried to develop ways to convert words almost instantly (especially those he found most troublesome) into foreign words each time, after they had penetrated his consciousness despite his efforts not to perceive them. So that he could somehow imagine that he was not being spoken to in that damned tongue, his mother tongue, English. Indeed, he experienced reactions that were at times acute and that made it even painful for him to hear the language without being able to convert the terms into words that were foreign to him, or without being able to destroy constructively, in his mind, the terms that he just heard in that bloody language, English![3]

The schizophrenic, as the author presents him here, came to his battle methods only at the moment he fully recognized the extent of his enemy's force. Only when he accepted the unparalleled ubiquity of his mother tongue could he devise a strategy to master it. There was nothing he could do: it was "hardly possible" for him to avoid the sound and sense of "that bloody language." But he could alter his field of perception so that when confronted with the bothersome and even dolorous idiom, he could "convert" its elements into "words that were foreign to him." Naturally, he would still have heard the mother tongue; more exactly, he would have to have heard it to be able to transform it into another. Hence the need for an ever-increased speed of operation: the alienated young man would seek to put his strategies of defense in practice "almost instantly," so as "to destroy constructively" the language he could not avoid as quickly as possible.

The fundamental principle of the schizophrenic's strategy, as Deleuze made clear in his preface, can thus be easily formulated: "Any maternal sentence whatsoever is to be analyzed in its phonetic elements and movements so as to be converted *as quickly as possible* into a sentence in one or several foreign languages, which resemble it not only in sense but in sound."[4] Often, however, the object of the young man's concern was not a sentence but a sentence fragment, or even merely a single word. Although the schizophrenic student of languages could not completely shut out the detestable tongue spoken everywhere around him, he could certainly do his best to ward off a good part of it. When his mother would address him in the terrible idiom, "as if decided to strike her son simultaneously with the tongue of her mouth and of the English people every time she spoke to him," there were, after all, small gestures the alienated young man could make to protect himself.[5] He could immediately plug his ears with his fingers, or cover them with the headphones of his handy transistor radio, for example, so as to perceive only the opening syllables of whatever sentence had been put to him. Then he had to "convert" not sentences but their dismembered and isolated parts; and if he could banish them from his mind, he reckoned, he would be safe from the assault of whatever discourse they had inaugurated.

When his mother wished to tell him, as she often did, of her certainty of a given fact, the alienated young man would quickly move to stop up his ears with whatever he could find around him, but the defense could not be complete: he would still hear, as a rule, the characteristic first two words of her declaration, and despite his best efforts he would still find himself "penetrated by English words."[6] As she "repeated almost incessantly and at the top of her lungs to her interlocutor—twenty, thirty, even forty times, it seemed—the words 'I know!,'" her alienated son would immediately begin to "convert" them out of their native idiom into foreign expressions of similar phonetic and semantic properties.[7] He would transform the two-syllable phrase into the French *connais*, whose first *c* reminded him of the initial *k* of "know," "although the latter letter is silent," or, more often, he would turn the English "I know" into the Russian *ya znayou* (as я знаю appears in the author's naturally French transliteration of the expression), which retained the opening semivowel first-person pronoun ("I," *ya*) and whose second and third syllables (*znayou*) would perhaps remind him of the final diphthong of the hated maternal expression.[8]

The words the mentally ill young man found himself obliged to convert were sometimes isolated lexical elements that reached him from conversations and discussions whose sound he could not tolerate. Hearing the word "sore," he would quickly think of a number of foreign terms into which he could transform it, such as "the following German terms (all of the same meaning as the English 'sore'): *schmerzhaft, schmerzlich, schmerzvoll*, all accented on the first syllable, which is pronounced *chmèrts*, whereas, concerning the suffixes of these three German adjectives, the *h* and the *t* of the first are perceptible, the *i* of the second is open and hence short and the *ch* is soft (for it follows an *i*), and, finally, the *v* of the third is pronounced as if it were an *f*."[9] The conversion of a single word could then furnish him with strategies for the phonetic alteration of his mother tongue and allow him to reflect on the fundamental relations between the phonological systems of different languages. In this case, for example, he would find justification for what he realized was his "strong habit, or perhaps more precisely an almost irresistible need, immediately to transform the *s* of many English words into *sch* (pronounced *ch*) of their German etymological cognates."[10] The young schizophrenic student of languages would then be led to still other languages and language groups in which the *s* and *sh* phonemes (*s* and *ʃ*) bore a structural relation: from the fact that "the symbols for the *ch* sound in the International Phonetic Alphabet and in English (and in Swahili) are respectively a kind of capital *S* (the same sign as the one for integral in mathematics) and the orthographic group *sh*," to the link between the Hebrew and the Arabic letters *sin* (ש, س) and *shin* (ש, ش), to "the Russian letter *c* (termed *ès* and generally pronounced as a voiceless *s*, never as *k*, but voiceless or voiced according to whether the following consonant [continuous or instantaneous, except for *v*] is voiced or voiceless: regressive assimilation)," and, further still, to the Slavic sound *tch* (ч) and its related functions, phonetic realizations, and points of articulation, in a flight from the mother tongue that seemed to take him ever further from the English term with which he began.[11]

At times, the young psychotic converted the words of his mother tongue into foreign expressions by the slightest of phonetic operations. In some cases, an English word could be almost instantly transformed into several foreign lexemes at once simply through the repetition of a given term that substituted in it a voiced consonant for an unvoiced one or, inversely, an unvoiced consonant for a voiced one. A good example is the word "bed," which, as the author explains to his French readership in characteristically painstaking detail, "is pronounced *bèd* and means 'bed'":

> The schizophrenic student would imagine that one had to articulate the last letter as if the word were German (or Dutch, or Afrikaans, among Germanic languages), or Russian (or Polish, or Bulgarian, or Czech, among Slavic languages), that is, by pronouncing the *d* (a voiced consonant) as if it were a *t* (the corresponding unvoiced consonant) and in particular as an aspirated *t*. As a consequence, in his imagination this English word immediately became identical in pronunciation with its German etymological relative *Bett*, of the same meaning, and concerning which he would then recall that, although neuter, this word takes as a mark of the plural the ending *-en*, which is in general that of feminine nouns in the plural, or, to state things more grammatically, he would then think that this noun belonged to the declension that is said to be "mixed," which in the plural follows

the declension said to be strong and in the singular follows that said to be weak.[12]

Here the young schizophrenic accomplishes his goal by a single phonetic alteration that, from a structuralist perspective, constitutes the simplest of linguistic operations: he merely substitutes an unmarked phoneme (the unvoiced final dental of the German word *Bett*) for a marked one (the voiced final dental of the English word "bed"). With a lucid consciousness of the phonological structure of the lexeme he could not bear, the alienated young man thus succeeds in "converting" the term through the manipulation of its most minimal constituent, the phoneme, and its most elementary graphic representative, the letter. Decomposing the word he heard into its phonological properties and the signs of their written notation, the New York psychotic could alter one of the atoms, so to speak, of its sound shape and carry the entire term out of the terrible language of its original utterance and into another (or, to be exact, into several others).

In the tale of the alienated young man's battle with the mother tongue, the "bed" conversion constitutes a limit case. As such, it lays bare the single institution on which all the conversion techniques of the schizophrenic student of languages ultimately rest: phonetic transcription or, more simply, writing. Had the mentally ill man been unable to write and rewrite the painful terms that penetrated his consciousness, he could not have converted any of them. He could not have divided them into their phonetic constituents, analyzed them, and transposed as much of them as possible, as quickly as possible, into semantically related terms in the foreign languages he had studied (of which at least two, Russian and Hebrew, are written in a script that can be converted into the Latin alphabet only by phonetic transcription). The mentally disturbed young man had no choice: he had to write to save himself from the language that so assaulted him, since only by transcribing his mother tongue could he dissolve it into another. It is significant, in this sense, that each time the schizophrenic student cited an English expression, he immediately presented it in its graphic phonetic form, which he then generally glossed in turn: "'vegetable oil,' which is pronounced *vèdjtebel oïl* (the second and third *e*'s are schwas, the *o* is open and short, and the *i* is open and fleeting, forming a falling diphthong)."[13] The psychotic young man knew better than anyone that if he was truly to cherish a hope of not remembering his mother tongue, he must be able to dismember it thoroughly in writing.

Transcription, however, is by nature ambiguous, and the text of the schizophrenic student of languages is no exception to the rule. The phonetic forms offered by the alienated young man in the place of their common English spelling, the foreign linguistic expressions to which they gave rise, and, more generally, the pages of *The Schizo and Languages* as a whole, can all be understood only as long as they are referred back to the mother tongue from which they were to liberate the mentally disturbed student of languages. It is inevitable: the more the young schizophrenic wrote, the more he continued to write out the letters—however decomposed, however scrambled—of the one language he could not bear. Transcription guarded the memory of the tongue it aimed to extinguish; writing, in this case, obstinately bore witness to the willful oblivion in whose service it was yoked. With his customary clear-sightedness, the deranged young man was the first to take stock of the paradox, which posed an unavoidable difficulty to his enterprise: forcing himself never to forget to forget his mother tongue, he obliged himself always to remember to remember it. It was only natural for the schizophrenic student of languages to wonder, for this reason, whether his project could possibly succeed on its own terms. "Have I truly forgotten English," he asked himself at one point, "or is this perhaps all some kind of brain defect?"[14]

At times, oblivion seems so deliberate that one may wonder whether its object has indeed been forgotten and not, on the contrary, willfully preserved in its apparent effacement. Such a phenomenon was once analyzed with acuity by the critic and satirist Karl Kraus in the pages of the Viennese periodical to whose widely read issues he was the principal and often sole contributor, *Die Fackel* (The Torch). Kraus, whom Walter Benjamin once likened to a modern-day Hārūn al-Rashīd, "roaming incognito by night among the sentence constructions of the newspaper and behind the petrified facades of phrases ... to discover the violation, the martyrdom of words," was the author of a series of commentaries on linguistic anomalies in the speech of his time: neologisms, solecisms, and barbarisms that might otherwise have passed unnoticed and whose analysis the writer took to belong to the general field of the "doctrine of language" (*Sprachlehre*).[15] Among such formations (or malformations) of speech was a curious expression for forgetting that seems to have been in vogue in the first decades of the last century, and to which Kraus dedicated a short article in the edition of *Die Fackel* published on June 23, 1921. The peculiar idiom, which certainly strikes the German ear today as odd, may be translated into English, without too great a distortion, as "to forget on" (*daran vergessen*). Kraus began his article by explaining:

> One should not think that the expression is in every case false, since there is nothing false in language that language cannot correct. The science of language is the indispensable condition for knowing how one may treat it properly. A sentence could be composed of glaring mistakes and still be correct. And this is not only so for sentences that are clearly modeled on a certain linguistic usage. Rules are certainly derived from a feeling for language [*Sprachgefühl*]; but a higher

feeling could still arise from their dissolution. "To forget on" would be an extreme example of this; and for the sake of a fundamental presentation of such a possibility, one can therefore take it into consideration. The expression is related to "to remember" [*sich daran erinnern*, the German expression for "to remember," means literally "to remember oneself on"] and "to reflect on" [*denken daran*], forms whose negation is not thought through to the end, such that the positive dimension of the term "on" persists, when it should in principle disappear completely, together with all "remembrance." Such an expression can imply that a "forgetting," however strongly it may be emphasized, remains fettered "to" or grafted "onto" an object, as if with the deliberate intention of not *wanting* to remember it. It would be as if one forgot the very thing that one remembered all too well, carrying out this inversion after the object of remembrance was safely posited, in such a way that the "forgetting" could be properly concerned "with" it and turn "on" it.... One could say of an unreliable witness who could not remember something which he did not want to remember that he had really "forgotten on it"; and one would have done no injustice to his psychological state. For language is capable of transforming even a false linguistic usage into a correct one.[16]

In this case, the critic had little need to demonstrate the peculiarity of the object of his "language doctrine." By the standards of correct German, "to forget on" was and remains an incorrect expression (even if it is one that wandered out of the streets of Vienna and into the pages of at least one of its great writers, Sigmund Freud).[17] One may well "remember on" (*daran erinnern*) and "reflect on" (*daran denken*) something, but the common verb for the act of oblivion admits of no preposition: when one "forgets" in the Teutonic tongue, one does it simply and directly, without the intervention of the term that ties remembrance and thought to a determinate object. But, Kraus insists, the phrase is hardly meaningless; and there are times when it may be the only expression adequate to a "psychological state" whose complexity defies common grammar. The "unreliable witness who could not remember something which he did not want to remember" makes the point perfectly clear. Such a figure cannot be said to have simply forgotten what he cannot recall, for his oblivion, albeit real, remains obstinately bound to the object of its apparent loss. He may not have reflected on it himself, but he has already, for one reason or another, forgotten "on" that which he will not remember.

The psychotic phonetician is the perfect example, and his written work is its matchless record. The schizophrenic student of languages does nothing if not "forg[e]t the very thing that [he] remember[s] all too well, carrying out this inversion after the object of remembrance was safely posited, in such a way that the 'forgetting' could be properly concerned 'with' it and turn 'on' it"; and however systematic it may appear, his forgetting remains forever "fettered 'to' or grafted 'onto' an object, as if with the deliberate intention of not *wanting* to remember it." Between the unbearable possibility of reflecting on his mother tongue and the equally unimaginable possibility of not reflecting on it, the deranged young man thus clears a third path, which he follows with delirious determination throughout the pages of his book: he "forgets on" the "bloody language," resolutely committing himself to the activity of the entirely "unreliable witness who could not remember something which he did not want to remember." The record of this simultaneous recollection and oblivion, as a result, cannot but be an ambiguous being, monument and memorial to an impassioned invocation and an implacable banishment at once. "No doubt a monstrosity," in the terms of its creator, and certainly "a Tower of Babble" (*une Tour de Babil*), the book, in its chapters, may well delimit the multiple chambers in which the "echomania-cal or more exactly echolalical brain" of the young schizophrenic recapitulates, without healing, the wounds inflicted on him by the sounds of the tongue that is like no other.[18] But they may also allow him "one day" to enter into a new relation to the language he can neither recall nor forget, a relation that the last lines of *The Schizo and Languages* announce in terms no less serious for the unmistakable irony of their "hope":

> It seemed, in any case, happily, that as the alienated young man grad-ually pursued his linguistic games based on resemblances in sound and sense between English words and foreign words, his mother tongue, that of those around him, became more and more bearable to him. And there was even the hope that after all—but this could be the case only when, among other things, he became truly bored with such games (and it seemed more or less that he would become bored with them)—the mentally ill young man would one day be capable once again of using normally this language, the famous Eng-lish language.[19]

CHAPTER EIGHTEEN

A Tale of Abū Nuwās

Abū Nuwās, perhaps the most brilliant figure of the classical Arabic literary tradition, was not always a great poet. He had to become one, and if one believes the classical sources dedicated to the life and works of the eighth-century Arabo-Persian writer, the training he undertook to that end could not have been more arduous. In his *Tales of Abū Nuwās* (أخبار أبي نواس), the medieval biographer Ibn Manẓūr relates that before beginning to compose his own verse, the young poet turned for advice and assistance, as tradition would have it, to an authority in the field, Khalaf al-Aḥmar. Khalaf obliged, but not without demanding of his pupil a feat of which few would be capable. Ibn Manẓūr writes:

> Abū Nuwās asked Khalaf for permission to compose poetry, and Khalaf said: "I refuse to let you make a poem until you memorize a thousand passages of ancient poetry, including chants, odes, and occasional lines." So Abū Nuwās disappeared; and after a good long while, he came back and said, "I've done it."
>
> "Recite them," said Khalaf.
>
> So Abū Nuwās began, and got through the bulk of the verses over a period of several days. Then he asked again for permission to compose poetry. Said Khalaf, "I refuse, unless you forget all one thousand lines as completely as if you had never learned them."

"That's too difficult," said Abū Nuwās. "I've memorized them quite thoroughly!"

"I refuse to let you compose until you forget them," said Khalaf.

So Abū Nuwās disappeared into a monastery and remained in solitude for a period of time until he forgot the lines. He went back to Khalaf and said, "I've forgotten them so thoroughly that it's as if I never memorized anything at all."

Khalaf then said, "Now go compose!"[1]

As a pedagogical exercise, the practice demanded by Khalaf is certainly not without its difficulties for the teacher and the pupil alike. Committing a poem to memory, after all, is a relatively straightforward task, whose success or failure can be measured without much trouble. But what of committing a poem, so to speak, to oblivion? As Abdelfattah Kilito has observed in a reading of the anecdote, the forgetting of verse with which the poetic training culminates would seem to pose an insurmountable challenge both to Abū Nuwās and to Khalaf. "A student can train his memory," Kilito comments, "strengthen his powers of recall, dominate the ebb and flow of his consciousness, and establish mental points of reference—but how can he consciously forget something imprinted in his memory? How could one ask or demand that someone forget something—that one erase or cancel out every syllable of a thousand poems? How, moreover, can the teacher who checks to make sure the student has memorized his poems ever check to make sure he has forgotten them?"[2]

The task demanded of Abū Nuwās may well have been close to impossible, and Khalaf al-Ahmar may have been incapable of ever ascertaining that his disciple had truly accomplished it. And even if it could be proved that the young poet had in fact forgotten the thousand passages of ancient poetry he had learned, one could still wonder whether it was indeed a case of simple oblivion and not of exacerbated and intensified recollection: for how, after all, could the poet truly forget all the passages he had learned by heart if he did not continue to remember to do so? It is all the more significant, for this reason, that Ibn Manẓūr seems certain that Abū Nuwās did what was asked of him and that Khalaf, in turn, clearly recognized it. It is as if in the eyes of the classical biographer, the peerless art of the poet's verse could be fully explained only as the product of such a practice of simultaneous composition and decomposition. It is as if for him the sole place of poetry were in an indistinct region of speech in which memory and oblivion, writing and its effacement, could not clearly be told apart.

193

CHAPTER NINETEEN

"Persian"

In 1937, a young Italian writer, Tommaso Landolfi, published his first book of short stories. Its title, *Dialogo dei massimi sistemi* (Dialogue of the Greatest Systems), was also that of the collection's third story, which seems for this reason to be exemplary of the work as a whole. The tale itself could not be more clearly about the nature of art. But the account of the writing of literature it offers is perplexing at best. In this story the mastery of technique seems to coincide with its undoing, and the perfection of a literary language comes perilously close to its forgetting.

It all begins with the unannounced arrival one morning of one of the narrator's acquaintances, a "shy and unassuming fellow dedicated to strange studies carried out as rites in solitude and mystery."[1] This day, however, the acquaintance, who bears the name Y., seems quite beside himself, agitated as the narrator has never seen him. Y. clearly wishes to talk about something, but he refuses to begin until he receives the assurance that he will not be interrupted before he has finished. The narrator is quick to oblige, and Y. agrees to tell his tale. "Long ago," he explains, "I dedicated myself to a patient and meticulous study of the constitutive elements of the artwork. This is how I came to the precise and incontrovertible conclusion that for an artist, having rich and varied means of expression at one's disposal is anything but a good thing. For example, I think it is far better to write in a language of which one has an imperfect knowledge than in one which one knows completely."[2] Lacking a full grasp of the vocabulary of a language, for example, a writer is forced to arrive at new ways to say what he means; he is more likely to avoid the commonplaces that regularly inhibit "the birth of the artwork" as he finds new and often circuitous ways to carry out his ideas. It was in the period in which Y. first came to this belief in the aesthetic virtues of unknown languages (or at least partially unknown languages) that, while dining one evening in a restaurant, he met an English captain who had spent many years in the Orient and claimed to speak a number of foreign tongues. When the captain, no doubt sensing the attraction such languages held for his new friend, offered to teach him the foreign tongue he knew best, Persian, Y. found himself immediately drawn to the idea. It seemed the perfect way to put his theory into practice. Now he could train himself systematically to express himself, as he explains to the narrator, "without always calling things by their proper names."[3]

So began weeks and then months of assiduous language learning, in which the two new friends resolved to speak and write only Persian whenever they were together. "During our strolls," Y. explains, "we spoke only that language, and when we became too tired to walk any more, we would sit in a café, where before our eyes white sheets of paper would fill up with strange and tiny signs."[4] The teacher could not but be highly satisfied with the progress of his pupil. The captain, Y. recalls, not without a trace of pride, "did not tire of giving me great praise for the ease with which I had benefited from his instruction." After a little more than a year the lessons came to an end, for the captain, as he explained to Y., had to leave for Scotland. But by this point, neither teacher nor pupil had any doubt that language learning could be effectively continued independently. As ambitious as always, Y. now continued his studies, as he explains to the narrator, "with the greatest possible ardor," resolving henceforth to write his own poetry exclusively in Persian (for Y. is himself a writer). After much time spent writing and revising under these linguistic and literary constraints, he finished three poems, hardly an insignificant amount of writing for Y., who was not "a very prolific poet."[5] But at a certain point it seemed to Y. that his skills in writing would profit from his reading Persian poetry in the original; it was at last time, he decided, to expose himself to the literature of the language directly. Convinced that "there is never any danger of learning a language too well by reading a poet," Y. resolved to procure for himself the edition of the works of an Iranian author, and he soon found what he was seeking. "Apprehensive about this first encounter," he recalls, "I scurried home, turned on the lights, lit a cigarette, adjusted the lamp so that it would cast its light in the right way on the precious book, made myself comfortable, and opened the wrapper."[6] An unfortunate surprise, however, awaited him. Y. could not read any of the words in the book; he could not even make out any of its letters. Was the book, Y. asked himself, not in Persian after all? He quickly confirmed, much to his consternation, that it was. "Then I began to wonder," Y. recounts, "if the captain, albeit forgetting the characters, had still taught me the language, even if it was with an imaginary system of writing; but this hope, too, was soon dashed." In the absence of his teacher, Y. began to make a series of inquiries, to examine literary anthologies and grammars, to consult experts, and even "sought and found two authentic Iranians"; but the startling conclusion could not be avoided. "In the end," Y. tells the narrator, "the terrible reality showed itself to me in all its horror: *the captain had not taught me Persian!* There's no point telling you that I tried desperately to find out whether that language was at least Jakutic, or an Ainu language, or Hottentot; I got in touch with the most famous linguists in Europe. It was all useless, useless: *a language like this one does not exist and has never existed!*"[7]

What language had Y. spent so long learning, and in what tongue had he written his three poems? Eventually Y. had no choice but to turn to the captain himself, who, shortly before leaving for Scotland, had given him his address, in case his former pupil "should for any reason have further queries." But the teacher was of little help. In response to the letter Y. sent him demanding some explanation for the so-called Persian he had learned from him, the Englishman responded in polite but unequivocal terms: "Despite my considerable linguistic experience," the Captain wrote,

> I have never heard of a language remotely like the one to which you refer; the expressions you cite are completely unknown to me and seem to me—please believe me when I say this—a product of your own fervid imagination. As to the bizarre signs that you have had the courtesy to append to the letter in a note, they resemble, on the one hand, Aramaic characters and, on the other, Tibetan characters, but make no mistake: they are neither the one nor the other. Regarding the episode of our pleasant time together ... to which you refer, I shall respond in all sincerity. It is possible that in teaching you Persian, I failed to recall a particular rule or word, after not having spoken it for such a long time; but I see that as no reason for worry, as there will be no lack of occasions for you to rectify whatever inaccuracies ... I may have imparted to you. Please be sure to keep me informed about how you are doing.[8]

It takes the narrator a few moments to grasp the full dimensions of Y.'s predicament. At first he tries to console him by telling him it is simply a matter of lost time and effort: "Well, Y., what

happened to you is certainly unfortunate; but all things considered, aside from the energy you wasted on it, what's so bad about
it all?" But Y. will have none of it. "So that's how you reason!" he
exclaims, growing more aggressive. "'So you haven't understood
the worst part, the terrible point of the whole story? You haven't
understood what it's all about? And my three poems,' he added,
getting more worked up, 'in which I put the best of myself! My
three poems, what are they then? They're written in no language,
and so it's as if they weren't written at all! So what do you have
to say about *that*, about my three poems?'"[9] Suddenly the narrator sees what he had failed to grasp. His friend is not simply
concerned that he dedicated himself to learning an imaginary language, an idiom nowhere truly spoken or written, a tongue that
is not Persian but instead, as Y. thinks, merely what the captain
"retained of real Persian, his own 'personal Persian,' so to speak."[10]
It is a question of a real and written literary language—which
seems, however, never to have existed: the language of his three
poems. "It is a terrifyingly original aesthetic problem," the narrator comments sagely.[11]

Seeking the advice of an expert, Y. and the narrator pay a
visit a few days later to the house of a great literary critic, "one
of those men," the narrator notes, "before whom aesthetics has
no secrets and on whose shoulders rests the spiritual life of an
entire nation."[12] But here, too, they find few real answers. The
critic seeks to convince his guests that Y.'s poems should simply be
considered works written in a dead language of which few traces
remain. "As you know," he explains to them in didactic tones,
"there are languages for which we possess only a few inscriptions and hence an extremely small number of words, yet these
languages are nevertheless quite real. I will even go one step further: even those languages whose existence is attested to solely
by indecipherable—and I mean in-de-ci-pher-able—inscriptions

have a right to our aesthetic respect."[13] Both the narrator and Y. immediately see the flaw in the critic's reasoning. Testimonials of dead languages, after all, still refer back to a historical and social reality, "without which they would be absolutely indistinguishable from any old mark on any old stone." "But what past do you want these poems to have," the narrator asks pointedly, "and from what can they draw their sense?"[14]

The problem is that the language of Y.'s poems is not only "dead" in the sense that, with the exception of Y., no one speaks (or writes) it anymore. It is not at all clear that the language was ever spoken (or written), and it may well be that the idiom in which his poems are written was in this sense always already, so to speak, dead. Y. himself, to be sure, believes that he learned a language that was alive, if only briefly. He is convinced that during the time they spent together, he and the Englishman regularly communicated in the strange tongue of his poems. The captain's later bewilderment, the disgruntled pupil maintains, is merely the result of forgetfulness. The man who once presented himself as a master of the language was in fact, Y. claims, an "improviser," who, "in the fluttering of his thoughts and the illusion of perhaps trying to recover a lost knowledge, invented the horrible tongue" while pretending to teach it, only to "forget his invention" later and to be "genuinely startled" that Y. had truly learnt it.[15] But can one be sure? Perhaps it is not the master but the student who forgot the language and, in complete isolation after the departure of his teacher, gradually developed an idiom of his own that hardly resembled the one he had been taught. The possibilities, in any case, hardly rule each other out. It could be that one oblivion followed another as the tongue of an entire people led to an isogloss of two and finally to a "language" that can barely be called one at all, utterly singular and already obsolete at the moment it first emerged from the pen of its author. *Dialogo dei massimi sistemi*

200

would then be the story of the layers of a single oblivion: the captain forgot the Persian he once knew, Y. forgot the Persian he once learned, and both forgot the fact that they ever forgot.

One thing, in any case, is certain: in the story, the witness to the forgetting of language is poetry. The final critical pronouncement in the tale, which breaks off in an unmistakably ironic ellipsis, suggests that such literature, incomprehensible by nature, could have more than a little to say about the nature of art as such: "'Art,' interrupted the great critic, still amiable but by now impatient, 'everyone knows what art is...'"[16] Everyone, it could be added, knows what it provokes. It suffices to recall the words of the poet driven mad by the tongue he cannot know: "This damned language, which I don't even know what to call, is beautiful, beautiful, beautiful ... and I adore it."[17]

CHAPTER TWENTY

Poets in Paradise

Sometime close to the year 1033, the great Syrian poet and critic Abū al-'Alā' al-Ma'arrī received a letter from his slightly older contemporary, the Aleppine writer and grammarian 'Ali ibn Ibn Manṣūr, who was known by the title Ibn al-Qāriḥ. The two were well-known writers with distinguished literary careers behind them. Al-Ma'arrī had spent many years in the 'Abbasid capital, Baghdad, where he had earned a place of undisputed authority in the Arabic literary world, notably through the composition of verse of unprecedented formal complexity. Ibn al-Qāriḥ had risen to prominence through the public protection he had received from Abū' l-Ḥasan al-Maghribī, the secretary of state of the Hamadani court in Aleppo and, later, the Fatimid dynasty in Cairo. It would seem, however, that at the time the letter was sent, the two poets were not well acquainted, for in his missive Ibn al-Qāriḥ presented his correspondent with a summary sketch of his life until then. Adopting a tone of unmistakable penitence, he explained that he had left their native Syria many years before for reasons that, if comprehensible, could hardly be commended. "I traveled to Egypt," he wrote, "and indulged my soul in its animal inclinations and its yearnings for sinful pride; I wanted to allow my soul to taste the sweetness of life."[1] Today it is not entirely clear why Ibn

al-Qāriḥ turned to al-Maʿarrī to denounce his previous activities;
but it is evident that his epistle was, among other things, a request
for support, which may well have been financial. The letter was
perhaps meant to cast new light on the undeniable biographical
facts of which al-Maʿarrī was surely well aware: namely that, after
having spent many years in the secure protection of Abū' l-Ḥasan
al-Maghribī, Ibn al-Qāriḥ had openly turned against him when
the secretary fell into disfavor with the Fatimid authorities he had
served. The unpleasant tale had been recorded by Ibn al-Qāriḥ's
own hand, since after the erstwhile secretary of state found himself and his family living, for complicated political reasons, under
threat of death, the poet, fearing for himself, composed a poem
that derided his former protector in no uncertain terms. "I sus-
pect," Ibn al-Qāriḥ confessed in his letter to Al-Maʿarrī, "that you
think my character to be of a lowly sort and that you imagine me
to be one of those over whom ingratitude, rather than gratitude,
prevails."[2]

Al-Maʿarrī responded to the poet in a "letter" of some three
hundred pages, which, clearly outstripping the epistolary form
it ostensibly invoked, was one day to number among the mas-
terpieces of classical Arabic literature: *The Epistle of Forgiveness*
(رسالة الغفران).[3] He opened his reply by praising, with unmistakable irony, the force with which the penitent poet had denounced
his life of vice and by recalling the points mentioned by his correspondent in the account of his former sinful existence; he went on
to suggest that, having turned from such vice to virtue, the penitent sinner might well, after death, be admitted into the blessed
garden of Paradise. Here al-Maʿarrī began the sketch of a fantastic
journey that constitutes the first half of his *Epistle of Forgiveness* and that, as historians of literature have often noted, bears
more than a superficial resemblance to that work of the European
Middle Ages that would later be drafted by the Italian poet and

philosopher with the highest esteem for the achievements of classical Arabic culture, Dante Alighieri. Three centuries before the
Commedia, al-Ma'arrī imagined Ibn al-Qāriḥ as he travels from
this life into the next, visits both Heaven and Hell, and converses
with many of their illustrious inhabitants.[4] The dramatis personae
of the medieval Arabic comedy, however, remain decidedly more
limited than those of the Florentine's. Dante's poet-protagonist
meets characters of the most varied sorts: statesmen and sci-
entists, poets, philosophers, and figures drawn from scriptural,
classical, and medieval sources. Ibn al-Qāriḥ's interlocutors, by
contrast, share a single trait: they all number among the set of
those personages known to classical Arabic culture as "the people
of language" (أهل اللغة). It is perhaps only natural, as a result, that
they have little interest in politics and history, as well as science
and theology, and that they have little worldly or even speculative
information to impart to the poet. Grammarians, philologists,
lexicographers, and writers, the figures who inhabit the Heaven
and Hell of al-Ma'arrī's *Epistle of Forgiveness* offer the poet enlightenment on the fate of the single being to which they all once
dedicated themselves. They converse with him about language at
the end of time.

Ibn al-Qāriḥ's journey, unlike Dante's, begins after death, at
the point when he passes definitively from this world to the next.
The sincere repentance he expressed in his letter to al-Ma'arrī
allows him entry into Paradise, but the passage is not easy. At the
gates of the afterlife, an angel confronts him, like all men, with the
written book containing the list of his earthly sins, which is in his
case, one imagines, especially long and detailed. Only on its last
page does it contain the summary report of the poet's penitence;
but the few lines suffice to efface the memory of his sins. Having patiently waited through the extended reading of the catalog
of his crimes, the poet receives, with understandable relief, the

official document that bears witness to the judgment: a certificate of divine forgiveness written in the angelic hand whose script none could forge. Soon thereafter, however, Ibn al-Qāriḥ finds himself distracted by the unexpected appearance of an eminent tenth-century grammarian, Abū' l-'Alī al-Fārisī. Understandably excited at the possibility of conversing with him, he rushes up to the authoritative figure to ask him about a number of technical points in Arabic linguistics. Only at the end of the discussion does the penitent poet realize what such haste has cost him: he discovers, much to his dismay, that he has misplaced the precious administrative document he procured only shortly before. The consequences of the loss of the certificate threaten to be severe. As Ibn al-Qāriḥ and the reader soon learn, the angelic guardian of the gate to Paradise, Riḍwān, admits no one whose papers are not in order. But after six months of waiting in the square before Paradise, Ibn al-Qāriḥ has a change of luck. He catches sight of an Islamic judge, and, enlisting the benevolent legal authority in his struggle to cross the gate to the afterlife, he enters the promised world.

It is natural, therefore, that once he finally reaches Paradise, Ibn al-Qāriḥ has no intention of leaving. When the protagonist of *The Epistle of Forgiveness* does discover the world of the damned, he does so by a feat of which few others might be capable: he explores it without ever setting foot in it. Unlike Dante, the Arabic poet always observes Hell from a significant distance, safely perched in the "outermost region of Paradise, from which one can look over into Hell."[5] His attention is first drawn to the observation point by an alluring lady whom he sees looking out beyond the limits of the land of the blessed. She turns out to be none other than the greatest woman poet of the first age of Islam, who acquired a central place in the Arabic literary tradition through her elegies for her two brothers. "I am al-Khansā' of the tribe of Sulaim," she tells Ibn al-Qāriḥ, and I wanted to see my brother Ṣakhr. I looked over [into Hell], and there he was, like a tall mountain; blazing fire rained down upon him. He spoke to me and said, "What you said about me was right!" He was thinking of my verses: "May the rulers take Ṣakhr as an example! / For he is like an elevation over whose peak fire rains down."[6]

It is from this paradisiacal observation point that the Syrian poet sees all of Hell; and it is from here, too, that he converses with its inhabitants, who cannot touch him. Predictably, the first figure he addresses is Satan, perhaps the only figure in *The Epistle of Forgiveness* with little respect for the profession of its protagonist. "What an occupation!" the king of the damned exclaims. "It is truly a slippery territory, on which one's foot can easily go astray."[7] He assures the poet that many of his kind have found their way into the land of the damned, and he courteously points them out to Ibn al-Qāriḥ by name.

The protagonist's encounters with his damned colleagues provide him with literary enlightenment of various kinds. As a rule, Ibn al-Qāriḥ is indifferent to the sufferings of his interlocutors, and as the most inhuman of punishments are meted out to them, he calmly asks them to explain their work to him in its most minute details. When, for example, the poet addresses Imru' al-Qays, perhaps the greatest of the pre-Islamic poets, he confronts him with philological questions about the transmission of his most famous ode, whose text, according to tradition, was so prized by the ancients as to be hung on the Kaaba in Mecca.[8] Three verses of the poem, Ibn al-Qāriḥ comments, are transmitted in two forms; in most versions the lines begin without the conjunction "and," but in their Iraqi recension they include it. Hence the vexed question that the editor and scholar could not avoid but that the author alone could resolve: which is the correct reading? "May God blot out the scholars of Baghdad!" Imru' al-Qays responds. "They have corrupted the transmission [of the text]. If one reads the verse in such a way, what is left of the distinction between poetry and prose? Anyone who can do such a thing lacks the slightest sense of poetry and understands nothing of meter."[9]

Ibn al-Qāriḥ seems satisfied with the answer, but his queries to the poet of Hell are not complete. He proceeds to ask him about the authenticity of an irregular geminated consonant recorded in a later verse of the same poem, as well as about a song of doubtful attribution said by many to have been composed by the great pre-Islamic poet. And so Ibn al-Qāriḥ carries on with each of the damned writers he encounters from his paradisiacal point of observation. He will not be dissuaded from his philological research by the walls of smoke that often separate him from his interlocutors; and in each case, he finds clear answers to the various textual, grammatical, lexical, and metrical questions he puts to the classical authors who appear before him.

Hell, in this sense, has much to offer the scholar, at least from the perspective of redemption. But Paradise also contains its treasures for the poet, which are at least as unexpected and often cast new light on the literature with which he believes himself to be familiar. Ibn al-Qāriḥ comes to realize this with particular force when, turning his gaze away from the inhabitants of Hell, he mounts one of the countless riding animals placed at his disposal in the land of the saved, rides away, and finds himself in "cities that are unlike the [other] cities of Paradise," that are not "bathed in shining light" but rather "filled with caves and fertile valleys."[10] He has found his way, as an angel informs him, to "the Paradise of those spirits who believed in Muhammad (may God bless him and protect him!)." Here Ibn al-Qāriḥ encounters al-Khaita'ūr, a pious spirit who inhabited the world long before the creation of Adam. The poet, ever curious about his art, immediately asks the polite creature, who bears the form of an old man, for instruction in the one field of knowledge he can offer him: "the poetry of the spirits," a body of literature to which classical Arabic authors often allude.

Ibn al-Qāriḥ soon learns that he knows less about the subject than he thinks. When he cites the fabled work of al-Marzubānī, an Iraqi scholar of the tenth century who wrote *The Poetry of the Spirits*, al-Khaita'ūr's previous courteousness toward him suddenly turns to contempt. "That's all nonsense!" he answers, brimming with the pride of his people and overflowing with scorn for humanity. "What do men know about poetry? About as much as the brute beast knows of astronomy and land surveying. Human beings know of fifteen meters, and their poets rarely ever go beyond this set. We, on the other hand, have thousands of meters that are completely unknown to men."[11] To the spirit, even the greatest of human compositions in verse seems hardly remarkable. "Rumors have reached my ears," al-Khaita'ūr tells Ibn al-Qāriḥ,

> that human beings are completely sold on the ode by Imru' al-Qays which begins "Stop, let us weep at the memory of a loved one and her dwelling at the place where the sands twist to an end between al-Dukhūl and Hawmal," and that schoolboys are even taught to commit it to memory. If you want, I can dictate to you thousands of words in this same meter that all rhyme in *lī* [like the ode by Imru' al-Qays], as well as thousands that rhyme in *lū*, and thousands that rhyme in *luh*, and thousands that rhyme in *lih*. They are all the work of one of our poets who died an unbeliever and is now burning in the circles of Hell.[12]

At first the poet thinks he cannot resist the gift offered him. "Can you truly dictate to me something of these poems?" he asks the spirit.[13] But when al-Khaita'ūr assures him that he can recite "more verse than a camel can carry and than can be copied onto all the leaves in the world," the poet grows less certain that this is as attractive a prospect as he initially thought. "In the earthly world," Ibn al-Qāriḥ recalls,

> I did my best to write, but it did me little good. I dedicated myself to writing to win the favor of the mighty; but in doing so, I merely milked the milk of a milk-poor camel, struggling with the teats of a dromedary who gave milk only with the greatest reluctance. I will have gained nothing if I abandon the pleasures of Paradise now to busy myself copying out works by spirits.[14]

Confronted with the unimaginable wealth of the literature promised him in Paradise, the penitent poet thus ultimately chooses to put an end to his art. He renounces the unknown verse he could transcribe and, setting aside the pen by which he once lived, resolves, once redeemed, to write no more.

In the blessed afterlife imagined by al-Maʿarrī, Ibn al-Qāriḥ proves himself less exceptional than one might think. For the poets the protagonist encounters in Paradise seem, in one way or another, to have left their poetry behind; and although they respond to the sound of the names they bore on earth, the saved poets appear to have little, if any, remembrance of the literary works for which they were once well known. The pre-Islamic poet al-Nābigha al-Jaʿada is the first to make this strange fact known to the protagonist of *The Epistle of Forgiveness*. Ibn al-Qāriḥ, rather predictably, asks him about the famous work in which the mythic poet related the tale of his "brief visit to the humid, but soon abandoned meadow." Al-Nābigha answers him in unequivocal terms: "I have no memory of ever having visited any such meadow."[15] The near-homonymous poet who happens to be standing beside him at this point, Nābigha Banū Dhubyān, tries to resolve the problem by suggesting that it is simply a matter of faulty attribution. The "meadow" poem, he explains, is in fact the work of another poet, a member of the tribe of Thaʻalaba ibn ʻUkāma whose name he does not recall, but with whom he once traveled to al-Ḥīrah, and from whom he heard the "meadow" poem on earth. But when Ibn al-Qāriḥ subsequently turns to the second Nābigha, asking him to clarify several passages in his own great ode that rhymes in the letter *shīn*, the author is of decidedly less assistance to the inquisitive scholar. "I never wrote any ode rhyming in the letter *shīn*," Nābigha Banū Dhubyān declares after listening to Ibn al-Qāriḥ recite the poem by memory. "And in this poem there are a number of expressions that I have never heard before, such as, for instance, its words for 'green,' 'table,' and 'little gazelle.'"[16]

It is but the beginning of a series of troubling encounters, which eventually lead Ibn al-Qāriḥ to the most distressing of conclusions: the great poets of antiquity seem all to have been struck in Paradise by an apparently irreparable case of literary and linguistic amnesia. When the newly saved poet meets al-Shammākh ibn Dirār and explains his delight at being finally able to confront the author with a set of pressing philological queries, in particular concerning his "ode which rhymes in the letter *zāy*" and his "poem in *jīm*," the protagonist receives an honest, if peremptory, answer. "My eternal beatitude," al-Shammākh replies, "has allowed me to forget all of these poems, and I no longer remember a single line of them" (لقد شغلنى عنهما النعيم الدائم فما أذكر منهما بيتا وحدا).[17] But the older poet clearly has no wish to make things particularly difficult for his studious colleague, and when Ibn al-Qāriḥ offers to recite him a few of the texts he has in mind to jog his memory, al-Shammākh obliges. "Recite them for me," he enjoins him, "and may God's mercy be bestowed upon you plentifully." But it is to no avail. "Our sheikh," as al-Maʻarrī calls his protagonist, not without a touch of irony, "soon found that the poet knew absolutely nothing about his ode. So he asked him about other matters; but

he had to conclude that al-Shammākh had no knowledge whatsoever of any of them. Al-Shammākh said: 'The joys of immortality
have dissuaded me from considering all these reprehensible things'
(شغلتنى لذائذ الخلود عن تعهد هذه المنكرات)."[18]

Ibn al-Qāriḥ is certainly discouraged by his failure to procure
the philological information he seeks, but he remains undaunted.
When he catches sight of Tamīm ibn Ubai, another great pre-
Islamic poet, he does not hesitate to tell him what is on his mind.
After verifying that he is truly in the presence of the mythic liter-
ary figure, the medieval scholar says:

> So explain to me this verse of yours: "O dwelling places of Salmā!
> Since they are deserted, I shall now place the burden on al-Mazāna
> alone, until it [or 'she'] becomes weary of it." What exactly did you
> mean by "al-Mazāna"? Some say you were thinking of the name of a
> woman. But others are of the opinion that it is in fact the name of a
> camel; and still others maintain that it signifies "habit."[19]

But in this case, too, the protagonist receives only a frustrating,
albeit earnest, reply. "By God," Tamīm responds, "once I passed
through the gates of Paradise, not a single word of all my odes and
poetry remained in my recollection."[20] Ḥumaid ibn Thaur, a poet
of the early age of Islam, is of just as little assistance, but he is a
good deal less polite. When Ibn al-Qāriḥ tries to spur him on to a
discussion about his famous "ode which rhymes in the letter *dāl*,"
the Umayyad poet explains to him that no topic could interest
him less. "I have forgotten every single rhyming letter," he tells
him, "and now my only occupation is playing games with the well-
endowed maidens of Paradise."[21]

Perhaps no encounter, however, is as startling to the penitent
poet as his meeting with al-Khalīl ibn Aḥmad, who was not only
one of the first and greatest grammarians of classical Arabic but

also, according to tradition, the single inventor of the entire system of versification in the language. Ibn al-Qāriḥ sees him riding
on a beatific chariot, and his mind immediately turns to some
verses commonly attributed to the grammarian; as he ponders
the verses in his memory, it occurs to him that one could truly
dance to the music of their elaborate rhythm. No sooner does the
thought cross his mind than, with beatific efficiency, it comes to
pass before his very eyes:

> At that very instant, God the Almighty, in the kindness of his wisdom,
> allowed a walnut tree to emerge from the ground. The tree immedi-
> ately let its nuts ripen, and threw so many of them to the ground that
> God alone would be capable of counting them. The walnuts broke
> open, and from out of each nut there stepped four maidens, who
> inspired wonder in all those, near and far alike, who saw them. They
> danced to the verses attributed to al-Khalīl, which run as follows:

> The beloved has ridden away, so let your love sickness, too, be gone,
>   or you shall fall!
> If there were not four maidens present, as lovely as little wild ante-
>   lope calves,
> Umm ar-Rabāb, Asmāʾ and al-Baghūm and Bauzaʿ,
> Then I would say this to the one who followed behind the chariot of
>   his lady:
> "Do as you like, leave it alone or prevail upon it!"[22]

"Our sheikh," who seems by now to have grown more than a
little suspicious of the paradisiacal poets, inevitably then poses
the vexed question of authorship to al-Khalīl: "Who wrote these
verses?" The answer he receives is at least as perplexing as the
explanation that follows it:

"I don't know," replied al-Khalīl. "But in the earthly world," said Ibn al-Qāriḥ, "it is transmitted as written by you." "I can't remember a thing about it; so it may well be that it is correctly attributed to me." "Did you really forget it," the sheikh inquired, "you of all people, who in your time possessed the greatest memory of all Arabs?!" Al-Khalīl said: "The passage beyond the Bridge of Hell [into Paradise] liberated my memory from everything that had been stored in it" (عبور استودع مما الخلد ينفض السراط).[23]

The poet wanders away, and his attention is quickly distracted from the troubling explanation as he stumbles upon a marvelous "river of precious and delicious beer" at which God has benevolently assembled "all the beer-drinkers of Paradise, be they Iraqi, Syrian, or from any other countries."[24] But it is unlikely he has forgotten the forgetfulness of the philologist who once "possessed the greatest memory of all Arabs" and who, before crossing into the timeless oblivion of Paradise, dedicated his life to those rules of time and timing that constitute the doctrine of prosody.

The famous figures of classical Arabic literature are not the only ones in Paradise afflicted by what surely appears, at least to Ibn al-Qāriḥ, as a mnemonic malady of the first order. In the imaginary universe of *The Epistle of Forgiveness*, where every man is a writer, even the father of humankind appears as a forgetful poet. Toward the end of his journey through the afterlife, Ibn al-Qāriḥ encounters Adam, whom he addresses in the following terms:

O father of us all, may God bless you! It is said on earth that you composed a poem that contains the following two verses:

We are the children and inhabitants of the earth; from the earth were we created, and to the earth must we return.

> Happiness does not remain in the hands of those who possess it,
> but nights of happiness efface unhappiness.[25]

Adam shows every sign of being willing to discuss the verses with
the poet, and after hearing them, he makes it clear that he agrees
completely with the spirit expressed in them. "What is said in these
lines is true," he comments sagely, "and whoever composed them was
surely a wise man." Nevertheless, he cannot help adding a final remark
that could hardly reassure the poet who cited them. "I, however,"
Adam tells Ibn al-Qāriḥ, "have just heard them for the first time."[26]

It is a serious matter, and neither the poet nor the father of
humanity has any intention of letting the question go without
resolving it conclusively. Ibn al-Qāriḥ, for his part, seems ready
to assume that Adam has simply forgotten that he did in fact once
write the verses attributed to him on earth. "Perhaps, O father of
us all," the poet suggests respectfully and rather tentatively to the
mythical man, "you composed these verses and then forgot them.
You know well that you are very forgetful."[27] As proof of his claim,
he cites the verse of the Qur'ān: "We once made a covenant with
Adam, but he forgot, and it had no consistency."[28] The poet also
adduces philological and, more exactly, etymological grounds for
the belief in the primary man's oblivion: "A scholar has argued
that you are in fact named 'man' [إنسان] on account of your forgetfulness [نسي]."[29]

Adam's critical reasoning, however, is keener. Although somewhat wearied by the philological question put to him by the pre-
sumptuous poet, he has no trouble finding textual evidence that
resolves the question incontrovertibly. "You children are clearly
determined to disobey me and to insult me," he states; but he does
not let the discussion end there. Setting out to explain the error
in the poet's reasoning with the rigor of a trained pedagogue,
Adam reminds the scholar that he has completely overlooked the

problem of the language of the text attributed to him, namely, Arabic. The omission is decisive. "When I was in Paradise," Adam begins, I spoke Arabic. Once I fell to the earth, my language changed and became Aramaic, and up to the moment of my death I never spoke any language other than Aramaic. When the great and mighty God later allowed me to return to Paradise, I once again spoke Arabic. So when could I have drafted the poem—in the earthly world or in the next? The man who composed it must have done so in the lower one. Just think of the second hemistich of the verse, "From the earth were we created, and to the earth must we return"! How could I have said such words when my language on earth was Aramaic? Before I left Paradise, I knew nothing of death; I did not know that it was imposed upon man like doves on a necklace, and I did not know that it bows to no one's body and life. And after my return to Paradise, the words "to the earth must we return" would have been utterly meaningless to me. Such a phrase would have then been most certainly untrue: here we, the flock of those who dwell in Paradise, remain eternal, since we have attained immortality.[30]

The tongue of the poem, Adam notes, is an index of time, and in this case it points to the two, and only two, moments in which the father of humankind could have composed the verses attributed to him. Adam could have written poetry in Arabic only during the twin periods of his beatitude; but precisely then, as he explains, he would never have written them, since they would have been for him "utterly meaningless" and "most certainly untrue." As the mythic man explains, there is therefore only one thing to conclude: the composition is a forgery, a literary prank "most likely composed by some fellow in his spare time."[31]

Adam may have thus proved he is no author, but he has simultaneously conceded, albeit implicitly, that the allegations made against him by the penitent poet are not altogether false. Whether he knows it or not, the father of humanity has admitted that in the course of his errant existence, he has forgotten at least one thing, and forgotten it at least twice. It is, of course, his tongue. What else could have happened to the original Arabic the first man knew when he "fell to the earth," and what became of the Aramaic he spoke on earth "up to the moment of [his] death," after he returned to the land from which he had been banished? Once expelled from Paradise, Adam, as Kilito has noted, "forgets Arabic and speaks Aramaic; back again in Paradise, he forgets Aramaic and speaks Arabic."[32] One language inevitably effaces the other; each, after the Fall, arises in the oblivion of the one that went before it. It seems more than enough to justify the learned etymology tying the name of "man" (إنسان) to that of "oblivion" (نسيان). In the world of *The Epistle of Forgiveness*, moreover, it certainly confirms Adam's position as the model man. For those graced with permission to enter al-Ma'arrī's land of the blessed follow, as a whole, in the footsteps of their forefather. Unlike the inhabitants of Hell, who can invariably recall and comment on their work with ease, the poets of Paradise forget, although they seem hardly to know it. One might well go so far as to define the Paradise of the Arabic comedy as the terrain of their oblivion: the region in which that naturally absentminded animal, man, finds himself, at last, happily consigned to the essence of his Adamic forgetfulness.

The decisive exception, of course, is the protagonist of the work itself: Ibn al-Qāriḥ. He is the one poet who gains admission to the afterlife of the blessed without acquiring that granted to those he encounters there, for which they seem so thankful: the "salvation" of memory, which, with the greatest of divine mercies, frees the human faculty from recollection of whatever content it once possessed. The fact can be interpreted in several ways. It can certainly be read as a sharply ironic rejoinder to Ibn al-Qāriḥ the man, the final trick played by al-Ma'arrī on the hapless poet who so strenuously professed his penitence in a letter he should per-

haps never have sent. *The Epistle of Forgiveness* would then constitute a parody of the pious letter from which it departed. It would
tell the tale of the erstwhile sinner who, now furnished with his
precious document of repentance, finds his way to Paradise despite
everything, his faculties superior even to those of the greatest poets
of antiquity. But Ibn al-Qāriḥ's mnemonic prowess may also be
interpreted in another way, which is at once more literal and more
profound. His flawless memory may be the surest mark of the
redemption he cannot achieve, the telling sign that, no matter how
many and how angelic the documents of repentance, his salvation
remains, at bottom, the invention of a man of letters, a fiction in
every sense.

It would be the cruelest of ironies: the hypocrite writer would
find his way to salvation without ever having been saved, destined
to wander in Paradise with the sure and solitary consciousness of
belonging in Hell. Such a reading, to be sure, would hardly flatter
the figure of Ibn al-Qāriḥ; but it would certainly assign him an indis-
pensable role in the unfolding of the literary work. Admitted to Paradise without belonging in it, the falsely penitent poet would bear
witness to the one thing to which the happily oblivious poets could
never testify: their redemption. Only the obstinately unsaved poet,
after all, could remember what the saved had always already forgotten; only he could retain and recall the beatitude of those who,
happily delivered over to forgetfulness, no longer have any need
of recollection. And only he, the fragile figure of a resolutely unre-
deemed humanity, could therefore glimpse a relation to language
that would do justice to the empty essence of the speaking being
who forgets: a relation in which recollection and oblivion remain as
indistinguishable as the continuity and discontinuity of the time to
which they are bound, and in which the memory of speech is at last
"liberated . . . from everything that had been stored in it."

CHAPTER TWENTY-ONE

Babel

Everyone knows the tale of the Tower of Babel, that archaic monument to the folly of men. According to the eleventh chapter of Genesis, which recounts the story in the briefest of terms, the edifice did not last long; and in one sense, it did not last at all, since it was destroyed by divine decree well before it was fully built. The consequences of its demise, however, appear to have been without end. For the tower ushered in the age in which humankind has lived ever since: that of the "confusion of the language of all the earth." On this much, all can agree; to go further in the summary of the tale is to step into an obscure terrain of which one may propose a great number of accounts. It is difficult, in particular, to identify precisely why the ancient and unnamed builders undertook to construct the mythic tower; and it remains equally obscure exactly how they were then punished for their work. Everything is complicated by the fact that in the biblical account, the people who inhabit the valley of Shinar appear to undertake the architectural project to preserve themselves from the very condition that the massive building ultimately imposes on them: that of being "scattered." "Let us build a city and a tower whose top may reach into heaven," they are said to argue, before beginning to build,

and let us make us a name, lest we be *scattered* abroad upon the face
of the whole earth

(ויאמרו הבה נבנה־לנ עיר ומגדל וראשו בשמים ונעשה־לנו שם פן־נפוץ
על־פני כל־הארץ).[1]

The Bible employs the same term a few verses later when, nar-
rating the events leading up to the destruction of the edifice, it
specifies the punishment that was imposed on the people for their
act. God resolves to put an end to the building by "confounding"
the language of men, "that they may not understand one another's
speech." "The Lord," we then read,

scattered them abroad from thence upon the face of the earth: and
they left off to build the city

(ויפץ יהוה אתם משם על־פני כל־הארץ ויחדלו לבנת העיר).[2]

Despite its fame, the judgment passed on the builders of Babel
remains, for this reason, difficult to define with precision. Its
execution comes perilously close to confirming the good reasons
of the crime it would seem to punish; and as a decision, it would
seem therefore to justify the fear—if not the very act—that motivated the building it aims to level. The paradox is striking. Dis-
persed on account of their sacrilegious construction, the people of
the valley of Shinar are ultimately delivered over to the fate they
feared most and had sought to avoid, and this precisely because of
having attempted, by their city and tower, to escape from it. Did
the people, one cannot but wonder, bring on their own "scattering" precisely in seeking to flee from it? One thing, in any case, is
certain: in the Babylon of the Book of Genesis, act and judgment,
crime and retribution, grow curiously indistinct. It is as if the
ultimate danger were already contained, at least potentially, in the
gesture that aimed to distance it. It is as if retribution in some way

preceded the act to which it referred, and even provoked it.

The nature of the punishment imposed on the builders remains equally obscure. The verses of the Bible leave no doubt that the construction and destruction of the edifice brought about the diversity of human languages and, with it, the mutual incomprehension of speaking beings. Before the building began, we read, "the whole earth was of one language, and of one speech" (ויהי כל־הארץ שפה אחת ודברים אחדים). When the Lord interrupted the architectural project, "scattering" the people, he "confounded the language of all the earth" (בבל יי שפת כל־הארץ), and for what would appear to be the first time, no one "understood another's speech" (לא ישמעו איש שפת רעהו). But how was the divine judgment executed, and how exactly did the whole earth pass from one tongue to many? There is no discussion at this point of any act of divine creation. Strictly speaking, God does not produce the plurality of tongues that will henceforth divide the people of the earth: nothing, it would seem, is added to the "one speech" that precedes the tower to make it multiple. At the same time, however, the biblical account of the punishment nowhere indicates that the divine will now intervenes to withdraw a common element from the original language of humankind: nothing is subtracted from the single tongue of men to allow it to be scattered. It is perhaps in this sense that we are to understand the Hebrew verb used to characterize the divine action taken against the builders of Babel (בבל), which involves addition no more than it does subtraction. God, the Book of Genesis tells us, "confounded" the language of the earth, and the result of his act was neither creation nor destruction but, quite simply, a state of general confusion.

The first-century Alexandrian philosopher, theologian, and biblical exegete Philo Judaeus, who was to exert such a profound influence on the development of Church doctrine, considered the problem at some length, and with considerable precision, in a treatise known to the Latin literary tradition as *De confusione lin-guarum*. He took great pains to demonstrate that "to confound" or "to confuse" (the Greek term he uses is συγχέω, literally, "to pour together," "to mix by pouring," and, by extension, "to trouble" and "to violate") is neither merely to destroy nor simply to create. "To confuse," he argued, "is to destroy primitive qualities ... in view of creating a single and different substance."[3] He took his example from the field of medicine, writing:

> A case of what I am speaking of is the drug composed of four ingre-dients that is used by physicians. If I am not mistaken, wax, tallow, pitch, and resin enter into its composition. But once the synthesis has been fully realized, it is no longer possible to distinguish the various properties of the ingredients. Each of them, in fact, has disappeared; and their destruction has engendered a new substance, of which it is the only type of its kind (ἀλλ' ἑκάστε μέν αὐτῶν ἠφάνισται, πασῶν δ' ἡ φθορὰ μίαν ἑκαίρετον ἄλλην ἐγέννησε δύναμιν).[4]

"Confusion," as Philo describes it, begins as the composition of elements and ends in their mutual annihilation; but considered as such, it can be identified with neither one nor the other. In the process of being "confounded," wax, tallow, pitch, and resin, to retain the philosopher's example, are transformed into both more and less than themselves. Once they are "confused," the elements give way in their unity to "a new substance" in which "it is no longer possible to distinguish the various properties" of any one of them. The erstwhile components now subsist at a point where creation and destruction, addition and subtraction, cannot be told apart: the point, that is, of their common "con-fusion."

In a sense, the event recounted in the Book of Genesis con-stitutes a case of "confounding" that is the inverse of the one invoked by Philo. The punishment of the Babelic builders did not bring about the union and dissolution of a plurality of elements into "a new substance." It was, quite to the contrary, the occasion for the definitive vanishing of "one language, and ... one speech," and for the emergence in its place of an irreducible multiplicity of tongues. The form of the biblical occurrence, therefore, is still more complex than the example of the medicament would allow. Without the intervention of any clear act of production or destruction, without apparent addition or subtraction, the original idiom of humankind, it would seem, came to be "confounded" and so diversified, transformed at once into the seventy-two distinct tongues that, according to tradition, the people of Shinar began to speak the moment they were "scattered."[5]

What kind of confusion could lead one tongue to become many? A parenthetical remark in the first book of Dante's *De vulgari eloquentia* offers an answer to the question. Discreetly inserted in a relative clause of a secondary phrase, it could go unnoticed even by the attentive reader. After offering a cursory account of the "three branches" of the language of medieval love poetry, which philologists identify today with Old Occitan, Old French, and Italian, Dante recalls a classical metaphysical principle that he invokes at several other points in his philosophical works: "No effect, as such, can exceed its cause, since there is nothing that can produce something that does not [already] exist" (*Nullus effectus superat suam causam, in quantum effectus est, quia nil potest efficere quod non est*).[6] He then adds:

Given that, with the exception of the language created by God at the same time as the first man, each one of our languages has been reconstituted according to our liking after the confusion (which was nothing other than the forgetting of the previous language), and given that man is an extremely variable and mutable animal, our languages cannot have any duration or continuity. Like everything else that belongs to us, such as our habits and customs, our languages must necessarily vary with respect to space and time.[7]

On the surface, the claim belongs to the major and most well known theses of the medieval treatise. The statement furnishes the double cause of the essential variability that, as Dante repeatedly insists, defines the totality of human languages. On the one hand, all languages, we read, represent reconstitutions or "reparations" (*reparata*) that follow in the wake of the great "confusion" (*confusio*) that need not even be named. None may lay claim to originality in the strong sense, since each is fashioned in accordance with a particular "liking" or "will" (*sit a nostro beneplacito*) that arises after the tongues of men become multiple. At the same time, each of these forms of speech, Dante writes, bears the mark of the "extremely variable and mutable" beings who speak it. By nature, the forms of speech must therefore continue to differ, geographically and historically, both from each other and from themselves.

The sentence, however, also offers a striking characterization of the "confusion" to which it briefly alludes, which, although undeniably placed by its author in a position of syntactic subordination, may well express an intuition central to Dante's reflection on the origin and structure of human speech. The formulation can be read as a definition of sorts, which specifies the precise nature of the event recounted in the Book of Genesis: namely, that "confusion" which, the poet-philosopher writes, "was nothing other than the forgetting of the previous language" (*confusionem illam que nil aliud fuit quam prioris oblivio*). Those commentators on *De vulgari eloquentia* who have noticed the remark have not been sympathetic to it, and they have often taken it to be an example of a certain obscurity—if not downright confusion—on the part of its author. In the most recent thoroughly annotated edition of the text, for example, one finds at this point a note alerting the reader that "the passage poses delicate problems."[8] If one accepts Dante's claim, one scholar has argued, one must also believe that the original language of men disappeared entirely at Babel and that the languages spoken by humanity after the confusion were therefore created by God. But such a position, as the editor points out, would be at odds with other indications in the treatise, which suggest that the multiple idioms of men emerged on their own, so to speak, in the moment of the famous "confounding." In the end, the editor is led to a conclusion whose apologetic tone seems decidedly misplaced in a study of Dante. "Perhaps it is inappropriate," he writes, "to demand absolute consistency and systematic coherence from Dante's formulations."[9]

The author of *De vulgari eloquentia*, however, needs no excuses, and his explanation of the Babelic *confusio* may well mean exactly what it says: that the great "confounding" of Babel involved neither addition nor subtraction, neither creation nor destruction, but, instead, a loss of memory, which destined speaking beings to forget their "one language, and ... one speech" and, in their oblivion, to develop the many idioms in which they would henceforth be scattered. Interpreted as "the forgetting of the previous language [*prioris oblivio*]," the confounding would then mark the mythic inception of the diversity of languages. But the confusion would not end there. As the element from which all languages departed and by means of which they ceaselessly multiplied both temporally and geographically, "confusion" would remain inseparable from the idioms to which it gave rise. It would constitute the invariable core of the variable being we call a tongue, the inalterable kernel of every alteration of speech. Defined as the oblivion of its predecessor, each language, then, would "repair" the loss of the one in whose wake it followed and at the same time acknowledge its irreparable absence; each would constitute not only the reconstitution of the one before it but also, paradoxically, its de-constitution. By speaking, we would always already, in short, have begun to forget, even—or especially—when we did not know it.

Among the doctrines in the traditions of reflection on the destruction of Babel, the thesis implicit in Dante's remark can hardly be considered dominant. But it is not altogether unique. It finds a precise parallel in an account of the biblical tale proposed in the final pages of that sourcebook of late-ancient Judaism, the tractate *Sanhedrin* of the Babylonian Talmud. The rabbinic sages are discussing the ultimate fate of the sinners and ungodly figures who people the opening chapters of the Torah; and inevitably, they pause at a certain point to consider "the generation of the dispersion," which, according to a dictum of the Mishnah, "has no portion in the world to come" (דור הפלגה אין להם חלק לעולם הבא).[10] The Jewish legal and theological authorities do not hesitate to confront the sole question whose resolution could explain the judgment. "What," they ask simply, "did they do?" Several answers are proposed. According to Rabbi Jeremiah ben Eliezer, at the time they began the construction, the builders were already divided into three parties: "One said, 'Let us ascend and dwell there,' the second, 'Let us ascend and worship idols'; and the third said, 'Let us ascend and wage war [with God].'"[11] Three punishments, not one, were then meted out to the overweening architects. Those who would dwell in the heavens were "scattered"; those who wished to serve idols were "turned into monkeys, spirits, devils and night-demons"; and the final, bellicose third party were the ones whose hitherto unitary language was irreparably confounded.[12]

The voices of the Talmud are no less divergent in their views of Babel than on anything else, and Rabbi Jeremiah ben Eliezer's interpretation is immediately followed by rejoinders that offer different accounts of the ancient occurrences in the valley of Shinar. To the contention that the builders had three distinct goals, Rabbi Nathan responds that "they were all bent on idolatry, for it

226

is written, 'let us make us a *name*' [Genesis 11.9]; whilst elsewhere it is written, 'and make no mention of the *name* of other gods' [Exodus 23.13]; just as there idolatry is meant, so here too."[13] And Rabbi Jonathan explains that it was not the motivation for the human construction but rather its divine destruction that took a threefold form. When the Lord intervened to punish the builders and make an end to their work, he explains, he took a triple action against the monument they had erected: "One third of the tower was burnt, one third was sunk [into the earth], and one third is still standing."[14] It is worth pausing to consider his account. Certainly the most unexpected news it conveys comes at the end: a good part of the mythic tower, if one believes the rabbi, would be standing even today! But there is still more: an altogether decisive detail remains to be specified. After commenting on the persistent portion, the rabbi adds: "The air around the tower makes one lose one's memory" (אויר מגדל משכח).[15]

The startling remark, like others of its kind, seems to go without comment in the Babylonian Talmud, and after its formulation the sages soon move on to a different but closely related question, namely, the fate of the inhabitants of Sodom. But the implications of Rabbi Jonathan's statement are far-reaching, and they can hardly be avoided. They concern not only the demise of the architectural structure but also the punishment of those who inhabited it and were ultimately abandoned within it. Theirs would have been a curious fate: consigned by the air around them to a state of perpetual forgetfulness, they would have been oblivious of what had befallen them and oblivious, one presumes, of the very fact that something had befallen them at all. If one takes the Talmudic tale at its word, however, the final third cannot be overlooked. It is true that in such a field, nothing can be ruled out with certainty; but it seems unlikely that there were many, if any, who escaped the destruction of the first part of the tower by fire and

227

the burial of the second beneath the earth. It seems more likely, so to speak, that the ones who survived the punishment were those who remained within the fragmented edifice. They, the people of the third third, would have outlived the destruction by forgetting it; and left within the architectural project that had once been theirs, they would have lost all knowledge of the ruined edifice in which they continued to dwell.

Walter Benjamin once invented a concept for that which persists undaunted by the vicissitudes of the human faculties of remembrance and forgetting alike. He called it "the unforgettable" (*das Unvergessliche*). The notion appears most famously in the introductory essay that Benjamin wrote for his translation of Baudelaire's *Tableaux parisiens*, "The Task of the Translator," the bulk of which appears to have been composed in 1921.[16] At the start of his essay, Benjamin set out to define the sense in which a work may be said to be "translatable" (*übersetzbar*), and to this end he dismissed the "superficial" belief that the question could be resolved with reference to the presence or absence of an adequate translator. The philosopher instead argued, in programmatic terms, that "certain relational concepts [*Relationsbegriffe*] find their good, even their true, meaning when they are not related exclusively to human beings."[17] He then invoked "the unforgettable":

> One might speak of an unforgettable life or moment even if all human beings had forgotten it. For if, by virtue of its essence, it demanded not to be forgotten, then that predicate would correspond not to a falsehood but to a demand [*Forderung*], a demand to which human beings did not correspond. At the same time, it would refer to a realm that did correspond to it: God's remembrance [*auf ein Gedenken Gottes*]. One would then consider the translatability of linguistic creations as corresponding [*entsprechend*] even if they remained untranslatable by human beings.[18]

If one wants a fuller presentation of the same concept, one must turn to the brief essay Benjamin published on *The Idiot* in 1917, where the notion is referred not to "relational concepts" in the strict sense but to the life of Dostoyevsky's protagonist:

> Of Prince Myshkin, one may say that his person ... steps back behind his life like the flower behind its fragrance, or the star behind its glimmer. Immortal life [*das unsterbliche Leben*] is unforgettable; that is the sign by which one knows it. It is the life that without memorial and memory, and perhaps even without witness, must remain unforgotten. It cannot be forgotten. [*Es ist das Leben, das ohne Denkmal und ohne Andenken, ja vielleicht ohne Zeugnis unvergessen sein müsste. Es kann nicht vergessen werden.*] This life remains, at the same time, the abiding [*das Unvergängliche*], without container and form. And "unforgettable," by its meaning, says more than that we cannot forget it; it points to something in the essence of the unforgettable itself, by which it is unforgettable. Even the lack of memory [*Erinnerungslosigkeit*] of the prince in his later illness is a symbol of that which is unforgettable about his life, for this lies visibly submerged in the abyss of the memory of himself from which it will not rise again. The others visit him. The novel's brief concluding report stamps everyone forever with this life, of which they had a part, without knowing how. [*Die andern besuchen ihn. Der kurze Schlussbericht des Romans stempelt alle Personen für immer mit diesem Leben, an dem sie teilhatten, sie wissen nicht wie.*][19]

Perhaps the most striking trait of the "unforgettable," as it is defined in these passages, is the one on which Benjamin both times so strenuously insists—namely, that it can quite easily be forgotten by men. In the terms of the essay on the translator, the predicate "unforgettable" thus refers not to humanity but to a demand (*Forderung*) indifferent to its realization: the demand that something remain, by virtue of its essence, "unforgotten." And in the essay on

Dostoyevsky, "unforgettable life" can therefore be defined as the life "that without memorial and memory, and perhaps even without witness, must remain unforgotten." So little is the unforgettable opposed to forgetting that it may even slip the mind of the one to whom it would most exemplarily apply. Thus Myshkin, whose epileptic bouts of memory loss (*Erinnerungslosigkeit*), according to Benjamin, constitute the "symbol of that which is unforgettable about his life." Amnesia, in this sense, can guard the unforgettable; it may even be its safest refuge.

The ruined tower of the Talmudic sage may be a being of this immemorial nature. One can imagine that for those who continued to dwell within it after the punishment, it remained no less their home for being forgotten. Its floors and walls, grown imperceptible, still preserved them from a destruction that might otherwise have left no survivors. Although they did not know it, the people of the tower would still have belonged to the Babelic monument that no longer was. They would have been touched by the unforgettable, exactly as those who once knew the idiot prince, in Benjamin's terms, were "stamp[ed]" by his life, "without knowing how." And as long as they continued to move in the air transformed by divine decree, they would continue to forget and, in this way, to allow the forgotten to remain about them; they, and their children after them, would still breathe in the element of oblivion imposed on them. Might they be our true ancestors? We would all then be descended from the amnesiac inhabitants of the bit of Babel that remained. The possibility perplexes, but it is less astonishing, in a sense, than the one to which it leads. For it is not certain that we ever left the mythic tower, and there is no assurance that after the great confounding, we once again set foot on firm ground. Today many, to be sure, believe the biblical building to be long gone. But a belief is no guarantee. The surest sign of our residence in the tower could well be that we no longer know it: to dwell within the ruined edifice, after all, is nothing if not to subsist on its confusing air. Destroyed, Babel, in this case, would persist; and we, consigned without end to the confusion of tongues, would, in obstinate oblivion, persist in it.

Notes

NOTE ON TRANSLATIONS

Wherever possible, I have indicated English translations of works cited in the notes and used them in quotations. On occasion, however, I have silently modified published versions in accordance with the originals.

Unless otherwise noted, all translations are my own.

An earlier version of "Aleph" appeared as a section of "Speaking in Tongues," *Paragraph* 25, no. 2 (2002), pp. 92–115. "Aglossostomography" was published in a slightly different form in *Parallax* 10, nos. 1–2 (Jan.–March 2004), pp. 40–48.

CHAPTER ONE: THE APEX OF BABBLE

1. Jakobson, *Kindersprache, Aphasie, und allgemeine Lautgesetze*, rpt. in Jakobson, *Selected Writings*, vol. 1, *Phonological Studies*, p. 335; English in Jakobson, *Child Language, Aphasia, and Phonological Universals*, p. 21.

2. *Ibid.*

CHAPTER TWO: EXCLAMATIONS

1. Jakobson, *Kindersprache, Aphasie, und allgemeine Lautgesetze* (1940–42), rpt. in Jakobson, *Selected Writings*, vol. 1, *Phonological Studies*, p. 339; English in Jakobson, *Child Language, Aphasia, and Phonological Universals*, p. 26.

2. Trubetskoi, *Grundzüge der Phonologie*, pp. 205–206; English in Trubetskoi, *Principles of Phonology*, pp. 207–209.

3. *Ibid.*

4. *De interpretatione*, 17a6–8.

5. Trubetskoi, *Grundzüge der Phonologie*, p. 205; *Principles of Phonology*, p. 208.

6. *Ibid.*

7. Dante, *De vulgari eloquentia* 1.4.4, pp. 42–44.

CHAPTER THREE: *ALEPH*

1. Jakobson, *Kindersprache, Aphasie, und allgemeine Lautgesetze*, rpt. in Jakobson, *Selected Writings*, vol. 1, *Phonological Studies*, pp. 370–71; English in Jakobson, *Child Language, Aphasia, and Phonological Universals*, p. 63. While discussing the similarities between speech disorders in dreams and aphasic symptoms, Jakobson comments: "Not only the words actually uttered by the dreamer, but also the 'introspectively graspable non-motor speech' which is only dreamed, can be subject to certain sound mutilations. I have observed this phenomenon several times in my own dream language. The alarm clock recently interrupted my sleep, in which I dreamed of having said *seme*. As I awoke, I was positive that this stood for *zemrˇel*, 'dead' (in my dreams, I now mainly speak in Czech)."

2. Sībawayh, *Al-Kitāb*, vol. 3, p. 548. On Sībawayh's treatment of the hamza, see al-Nassir, *Sibawayh the Phonologist*, pp. 10–12.

3. Spinoza, *Compendium grammatices linguae hebraeae*, in *Opera*, vol. 1, *Korte verhandeling van God; De Mensch en deszelfs welstand; Renati Des Cartes principiorum philosophiae pars I & II; Cogitata metaphysica; Compendium grammatices linguae hebraeae*, p. 288.

4. *Ibid.*, p. 287.

5. On *aleph* in the biblical language, see Joüon, *Grammar of Biblical Hebrew*, vol. 1, *Orthography and Phonetics; Morphology*, pp. 25–26.

6. Abrams, *The Book Bahir*, p. 123, par. 13. As the notes to this edition indicate, the claim is attributed in some manuscripts to Rabbi Amoray, in others to Rabbi Rehumay.

7. *Sefer ha-Zohar* 2b. An English translation can be found in *The Zohar*,

vol. 1, p. 9. Many works, primary and secondary, could be cited on the status of letters in the kabbalistic doctrines of creation; for an overview of the problems at issue in the kabbalistic philosophy of language, see Gershom Scholem's fundamental essay, "Der Name Gottes und die Sprachtheorie der Kabbalah," in *Judaica III*, pp. 7–70; see also Sirat, "Les Lettres hebraïques."

8. *Sefer ha-Zohar* 3a; English in *Zohar*, vol. 1, p. 12.

9. *Ibid.* 3a–3b; English in *Zohar*, vol. 1, pp. 12–13 (trans. modified).

10. *Midrash rabbah* 1.10; an English translation can be found in *Midrash Rabbah*, vol. 1, *Genesis*, p. 9; cf. *Sefer ha-Bahir* 3.

11. *Eliahu rabbah* 31.

12. *Midrash rabbah*, 1.10; English in *Midrash Rabbah*, p. 9.

13. *Ibid.*, p. 43.

14. *Shir ha-shirim rabbah* 5.9.

15. *Makkot* 24a.

16. Maimonides, *Le Guide des égarés*, vol. 2, ch. 33, p. 75.

17. *Ibid.*, p. 74.

18. *Ibid.*, p. 75.

19. *Ibid.*, p. 75.

20. *Shabbat* 105a. On *notarikon* and other figures of letters in Talmudic hermeneutics, see Ouaknin, *Le Livre brûlé*, pp. 124–26.

21. Scholem, "Religious Authority and Mysticism," in *On the Kabbalah and Its Symbolism*, p. 30.

22. *The Book Bahir*, p. 149, sec. 53.

23. *Zohar* 21a; English in *Zohar*, vol. 1, p. 89.

CHAPTER FOUR: ENDANGERED PHONEMES

1. See, for example, Riegel, Pellat, and Rioul, *Grammaire méthodique du français*, p. 41.

2. *Ibid.*, p. 44.

3. *Ibid.*, p. 49.

4. Mallarmé, *Œuvres complètes*, p. 67.

5. Cornulier, *Art poëtique*, p. 249. See also, by the same author, "Le Droit de

l'*e* et la syllabilicité," and "Le Remplacement d'*e* muet par è et la morphologie des enclitiques."

6. Cornulier, *Art poëtique*, p. 250.

CHAPTER FIVE: *H* & CO.

1. On the development of Greek scripts, see Jeffery, *Local Scripts of Archaic Greece*, esp. pp. 24–25 and, on the *vau*, pp. 326–27.

2. On the continental *g*, see Pyles and Algeo, *Origins and Development of the English Language*, pp. 139–40; on English orthography more generally, see Scragg, *History of English Spelling*.

3. On the Old Church Slavonic alphabet, see, among others, Leskien and Rottmann, *Handbuch der altbulgarischen (altkirchenslavischen) Sprache*, pp. 9–19.

4. Heine, *Werke*, vol. 4, *Schriften über Deutschland*, p. 558. Heine also has the letter *h* appear in a dream to the poet Yehuda ha-Levi; see "Jehuda ben Halevy," *Hebräische Melodien*, bk. 3, in *Werke*, vol. 1, *Gedichte*, pp. 199–226.

5. See Allen, *Vox Graeca*, pp. 52–56, on which the following summary is based.

6. Allen, *Vox Latina*, p. 43. For what follows, I am indebted to Allen's economical summary, pp. 43–45.

7. *Institutio oratoria* 1.4.9; 1.5.19.

8. Priscian, *Institutionum grammaticarum*, bk. 18, 1.8.47. Also see Marius Victorinus, *Ars grammatica* 3.10, p. 68: "H quoque admittimus, sed adspirationis notam, non litteram aestimamus."

9. See Allen, *Vox Latina*, pp. 43–44.

10. *Catullus, Tibullus, Pervegilium Veneris* 84, pp. 160–62: "*Chommoda* dicebat, si quando *commode* vellet dicere, et *insidias* Arrius *hinsidias*, / et tum mirifice sperabat se esse locutum, / cum quantum poterat dixerat hinsidias" (Arrius if he wanted to say "winnings" used to say "*whinnings*," and for "ambush" "*hambush*"; and thought he had spoken wonderfully well whenever he said "*hambush*" with as much emphasis as possible).

11. *Confessions* 1, ch. 18: "Uide, domine ... quomodo diligenter a prioribus locutoribus ...; ut qui illa sonorum uetera placita teneat aut doceat, si contra

disciplinam grammaticam sine adspiratione primae syllabae *ominem* dixit, displiceat magis hominibus quam si contra tua praecepta hominem oderit." English in Augustine, *Confessions*, pp. 38–39.

12. *The Attic Nights of Aulus Gellius*, pp. 128–29.

13. See Petrus Helias, *Summa super Priscianum*, vol. 1, p. 83: "*H* littera non est, sed cum aspirationis nota propter solam figuram in abecedario scribitur intra litteras."

14. Richardson, *Trattati sull'ortografia del volgare*, p. 95.

15. Trissino, "I dubbî grammaticali," in *Scritti linguistici*, p. 110.

16. Tory, *Champfleury*, Iiij r.

17. Bovelles, "De nota aspirationis *H*," in *Sur les langues vulgaires et la variété de la langue française*, ch. 32.

18. Nebrija, *Reglas de orthografía en la lengua castellana*, pp. 139–40.

19. See Schibsbye, *Origin and Development of the English Language*, vol. 1: *Phonology*, pp. 96–97.

20. Smith, *Literary and Linguistic Works: Part III, a Critical Edition of "De recta et emendata linguae Anglicae scriptione, dialogus,"* p. 108.

21. Holder, *The Elements of Speech*, p. 68, cited in Wallis, *Grammar of the English Language*, p. 59.

22. See Hamann, "Neue Apologie des Buchstaben *H*," in *Sämtliche Werke*, vol. 3: *Schriften über Sprache, Mysterien, Vernunft, 1772–1788*, p. 91.

23. *Ibid.*, p. 91.

24. *Ibid.*, p. 92.

25. *Ibid.*

26. *Ibid.*, p. 94.

27. *Ibid.*

28. *Ibid.*, p. 105.

29. Kraus, *Schriften*, vol. 9, *Gedichte*, p. 40.

30. See Celan, né Antschel, *Der Meridian*, p. 115: "The poem: the trace of our breathing in language [or speech]" (*Das Gedicht: die Spur unseres Atems in der Sprache*).

Chapter Six: Exiles

1. The work in question is *Al-ḍarūrī fī-l-lugha al-'ibranīa*; on it, see Zafrani, *Poésie juive en Occident musulman*, pp. 226–42. On the Hebrew adaptation of Arabic meters, see Nehemia Allony's fundamental study *Torat ha-mishkalim*.

2. Baneth, *Kitāb al-radd wa'l-dalīl fī'l-dīn al-dhalil*, pp. 82–83.

3. Benavente Robles, *Tešubot de los discípulos de Menahem contra Dunaš ben Labrat*, p. 19.

4. On the loss of Hebrew in Joseph Caspi and medieval Jewish literature, see Aslanov, *Le Provençal des juifs et l'hébreu en Provence*, pp. 114–18.

5. Benavente Robles, *Tešubot*, p. 15:

ואילו לא גלינו מארצינו והיתה לשונינו כולה נמצאת בידינו כירחי קדם,
בשבתינו בטח במשכנות שאננות, אזי מצאנו כל דקדוקי לשונינו ומינו
תוצאתיה, וידענו משקלה, ועמדנו על גבולה. כי לשון עם ועם יש משקולת
ודקדוק, רק אבדה מידינו, יען כי רב העוז, ונעלמה ממנו עקב כי גדלה
האשמה, מיום אשר נפלנו בגולה. ואחרי אשר היתה רחבה נקצרה ונסתרה
ותהי נעדרת. ולולי אל מפליא פלאה, בעני עמו ראה, אבדה ונכלאה
השארית הנמצאה.

6. Brodsky, "The Condition We Call Exile," in *On Grief and Reason: Essays*, p. 32.

Chapter Seven: Dead Ends

1. Al-Harizi, *Las asambleas de los sabios (Tahkemoni)*,1, sec. 14, p. 39.

2. Horace, *Ars poetica* 60–64: "Ut silvae foliis pronos mutantur in annos / prima cadunt: ita verborum vetus interit aetas, / et iuvenum ritu florent modo nata vigentque. / debemus morti nos nostraque." See Klein, *Latein und Volgare in Italien*, p. 91.

3. Isidore of Seville, *Etymologiae sive originum*, vol. 1, 9.1.6. Cf. Klein, *Latein und Volgare in Italien*, who characterizes these four moments as veritable *Alters-stufen*.

4. Introduction to the *Commento* to his sonnets (cited in Klein, *Latein und Volgare in Italien*, p. 91): "Massime insino ad ora si può dire essere l'*adolescenzia*

238

di questa lingua (volgare) ... E potrebbe facilmente nella gioventù ed adulta età sua venire in maggiore perfezione."

5. Sperone Speroni, *Dialogo delle lingue*, pp. 183–84; see Klein, *Latein und Volgare in Italien*, p. 92.

6. Speroni, *Dialogo*, p. 185; Klein, *Latein und Volgare in Italien*, p. 92.

7. Speroni, *Dialogo*, p. 185; Klein, *Latein und Volgare in Italien*, p. 93.

8. Cited in Klein, *Latein und Volgare in Italien*, p. 94.

9. Davanzati to Baccio Valori, 1599, cited in *ibid.*, p. 96.

10. Krauss, "World's Languages in Crisis," p. 4.

11. Kincade, "Decline of Native Languages in Canada," pp. 160–63.

12. Wurm, "Methods of Language Maintenance and Revival"; a commentary can be found in Crystal, *Language Death*, p. 21. In this case, the linguist refers to human beings whose ailments mirror that of the tongue they speak; both are destined soon to pass away. Where the parallels are less exact, linguists speak in simpler metaphoric terms: "healthy speakers" will be distinguished from "terminal speakers" or "semi-speakers" where the predicate of health has a purely linguistic connotation. See Dorian, "Problem of the Semi-Speaker in Language Death."

13. Cited in Crystal, *Language Death*, p. vii.

14. Cited in *ibid.*, p. viii.

15. Sasse, "Theory of Language Death," p. 7.

16. Crystal, *Language Death*, p. ix.

17. *Ibid.*, p. 1.

18. The currency of the term "language suicide" is in large part due to Nancy C. Dorian; see her *Language Death*. "Language suicide" has been adopted by many scholars as a conceptual substitute for the earlier notion of "language murder," or "linguacide"; see Dressler, "Language Shift and Language Death," p. 5.

19. Crystal, *Language Death*, p. 142.

20. *Ibid.*, p. 145.

21. Andersen, "Burial of Ubykh," p. 3, cited in Crystal, *Language Death*, p. 2.

22. Terracini, "Come muore una lingua," p. 20.

23. *Ibid.*, p. 21.

24. Vendryes, "La Mort des langues," pp. 5–6.

25. Crystal, *Language Death*, p. 2.

26. Vendryes, "La Mort des langues," p. 6.

27. Terracini, "Come muore una lingua," p. 21.

CHAPTER EIGHT: THRESHOLDS

1. Terracini, "Come muore una lingua," p. 17.

2. Vendryes, "La Mort des langues," pp. 7–8.

3. *Ibid.*, pp. 7–8.

4. *Odyssey* 4.456–58; see Dressler, "Language Shift and Language Death."

5. Cerquiglini, *La Naissance du français*, p. 26.

6. *Ibid.*, pp. 25–42.

7. Meillet, *Linguistique historique et linguistique générale*, p. 81.

8. Cerquiglini, *La Naissance du français*, p. 42.

9. "Si ergo per eandem gentem sermo variatur, ut dictum est, successive per tempora, nec stare in ullo modo poest, necesse est ut disiunctim abmotimque morantibus varie varietur." Dante, *De vulgari eloquentia* 1.9.10, p. 78.

10. Vendryes, "La Mort des langues," pp. 5 and 14.

11. *Ibid.*, p. 15.

12. Terracini, "Come muore una lingua," p. 18.

13. Montaigne, "De la vanité," in *Essais*, 3, 9, p. 982. The entire passage reads as follows: "J'escris mon livre à peu d'hommes et à peu d'années. Si c'eust esté une matiere de durée, il l'eust fallu commettre à un langage plus ferme. Selon la variation continuelle qui a suivy le nostre jusques à cette heure, qui peut esperer que sa forme presente soit en usage, d'icy à cinquante ans? Il s'escoule tous les jours de nos mains et depuis que je vis s'est alteré de moitié. Nous disons qu'il est à cette heure parfaict. Autant en dict du sien chaque siecle. Je n'ay garde de l'en tenir là tant qu'il fuira et se difformera comme il faict."

CHAPTER NINE: STRATA

1. Emerson, "The Poet," in *Selected Essays*, p. 271.

2. Proust, *A la Recherche du temps perdu*, p. 153: "Tous ces souvenirs ajoutés les uns aux autres ne formaient plus qu'une masse, mais non sans qu'on ne pût distinguer entre eux—entre les plus anciens, et ceux plus récents, nés d'un parfum, puis ceux qui n'étaient que les souvenirs d'une autre personne de qui je les avais appris—sinon des fissures, des failles véritables, du moins ces veinures, ces bigarrures de coloration, qui dans certaines roches, dans certains marbres, révèlent des différences d'origine, d'âge, de 'formation.'" English in *Remembrance of Things Past*, p. 203.

3. On Bredsdorff and the development of the concept of the substrate, see Nielsen, "La Théorie des substrats et la linguistique structurale."

4. Fauriel, *Dante et les origines de la langue et de la littérature italiennes*; Diez, preface to *Etymologisches Wörterbuch der romanischen Sprachen*; Schuchardt, *Der Vokalismus des Vulgärlateins*, vol. 1, p. 86; Ascoli, "Una lettera glottologica."

5. Walther von Wartburg, *Zeitschrift für romanische Philologie* 56 (1932), p. 48, cited in Kontzi, introduction to *Substrate und Superstrate in den romanischen Sprachen*, p. 10 n.30.

6. The first occurrence of the term seems to be in Valkhoff, *Latijn, Romaans, Roemeens*, pp. 17 and 22, as indicated by the author in the acts of the *Cinquième Congrès International des Linguistes, 28 août–2 septembre 1939*, pp. 47–65.

7. For a summary of the debates on the subject, see Nielsen, "La Théorie des substrats et la linguistique structurale."

8. Merlo, "Lazio santia ed Etruria latina?" cited in Kontzi, *Substrate und Superstrate in den romanischen Sprachen*, p. 15.

9. See, among others, Campanile, *Problemi di sostrato nelle lingue indoeuropee*; and, more generally, Silvestri, "La teoria del sostrato."

10. See Riegel, Pellat, and Rioul, *Grammaire méthodique du français*, p. 44.

11. On the history of linguistic and philological scholarship on the subject, see the materials compiled by Jacoby, *Zur Geschichte des Wandels*, esp. pp. 1–15.

12. Koschwitz, *Überlieferung und Sprache der Chanson du Voyage de Charlemagne à Jérusalem et à Constantinople*, p. 36.

13. *Ibid.*, p. 36.

14. *Ibid.*, p. 36.

15. See Jacoby, *Zur Geschichte des Wandels*. Cf. Schuchardt, review of *Kurzge-fasste Irische Grammatik mit Lesestücken*, esp. pp. 140–54; and see Goidánich, *L'origine e le forme della dittongazione romanza*.

16. Meyer-Lübke, *Einführung in das Studium der romanischen Sprachwis-senschaft*, pp. 172ff.

17. Philipon, "L'U long latin dans le domaine rhodanien."

18. See, for example, the phonological portrait in Lambert, *La Langue gauloise,* pp. 40–43.

19. Paris, *Vie de Saint Alexis*, pp. 61ff.

20. Paris, review of *Die aeltesten franzoesischen Mundarten*, esp. pp. 129–30.

21. Rudolf Lenz, "Zur Physiologie der Geschichte der Palatalen" (diss., Bonn, 1887), cited in Jacoby, *Zur Geschichte des Wandels*, p. 5.

22. Meyer-Lübke, *Grammatik der romanischen Sprachen*, pp. 67ff. See Meyer-Lübke's later statement on the matter in his essay "Zur u-y Frage."

23. See, for example, Otto Jespersen (1925), cited in Kontzi, *Substrate und Superstrate in den romanischen Sprachen*, p. 6. Leo Weisgerber dates the end of the regular use of the Celtic language to the third century A.D., although traces of the tongue can be found as late as the fifth; see *Die Sprache der Festlandkelten*, p. 177, cited in Kontzi, introduction to *Substrate und Superstrate in den romanischen Sprachen*, p. 6.

24. Meillet, "La Notion de langue mixte," in *La Méthode comparative en lin-guistique historique*, p. 80; Merlo, "Il sostrato etnico e i dialetti italiani."

25. Becker, *Die Heiligsprechung Karls des Grossen und die damit zusammen-hängenden Fälschungen* cited in Kontzi, introduction to *Substrate und Superstrate in den romanischen Sprachen*, p. 8.

26. Pokorny, "Substrattheorie und Urheimat der Indogermanen."

27. Menéndez Pidal, "Modo de obrar el substrato lingüistico." A similar reasoning can be found in Silvestri, "La teoria del sostrato," p. 149. Cf. the larger work by Silvestri, *La teoria del sostrato.*

CHAPTER TEN: SHIFTS

1. Kafka, "Kleine Rede über den Jargon," in *Gesammelte Werke*, vol. 5, *Beschreibung eines Kampfes und andere Schriften aus dem Nachlass*, p. 152.

2. On the derivation of Latin from Greek, see Gabba, "Il latino come dialetto greco"; Opelt, "La coscienza linguistica dei Romani"; Tavoni, "On the Renaissance Idea That Latin Derives from Greek."

3. Matthias Brenzinger, *Foundation for Endangered Languages Newsletter* 1 (1995), p. 5, cited in Crystal, *Language Death*, p. 22.

4. Garbell, "Remarks on the Historical Phonology of an East Mediterranean Dialect," pp. 303–304.

5. See Werner Diem's synthesis of the matter, "Studien zur Frage des Substrats."

6. Sobhy, *Common Words in the Spoken Arabic of Egypt of Greek or Coptic Origin*, p. 3.

7. For a cautious view of the situation, see Wilson B. Bishai's three articles on the subject: "Coptic Grammatical Influence on Egyptian Arabic," "Nature and Extent of Coptic Phonological Influence on Egyptian Arabic," and "Notes on the Coptic Substratum in Egyptian Arabic." Cf. Diem, "Studien zur Frage des Substrats," pp. 50–52.

8. Fellmann, "A Sociolinguistic Perspective on the History of Hebrew," p. 33; see also Chomsky, *Ha-lashon ha-ivrit be-darkhe hitpathutah*, p. 226, cited in Wexler, *Schizoid Nature of Modern Hebrew*, p. 14.

9. Gold, "Sketch of the Linguistic Situation in Israel Today," p. 364.

10. Whereas the verbal system of biblical Hebrew is founded on the opposition between the perfect and the imperfect, the modern Israeli system is one of tense: a biblical imperfect thus has the force of a future in Ivrit, and a perfect a past. Hence the need for a new form for the present, designed by the Zionist language planners on the basis of a biblical participle.

11. See Haim B. Rosén, cited in Wexler, *Schizoid Nature of Modern Hebrew*, p. 10, n.6.

12. Bergsträsser, *Einführung in die semitischen Sprachen*, p. 47.

13. Bendavid, *Leshon mikra u-leshon hakhamim*, vol. 1, p. 253, cited in Wexler, *Schizoid Nature of Modern Hebrew*, pp. 11–12.

14. Wexler, *Schizoid Nature of Modern Hebrew*, p. 36.

CHAPTER ELEVEN: LITTLE STARS

1. On the comparison of biblical Hebrew expressions with Aramaic and Arabic terms in the Talmud and Midrash, see Cohen, "Arabisms in Rabbinic Literature." On the comparison of Hebrew with other languages in medieval Spanish philology, see Valle Rodríguez, *La escuela hebrea de Córdoba*, pp. 257–64.

2. See, in particular, *Cratylus* 410a. See Pompeius Festus, *De verborum significatione* 392, where it is remarked that the Greek ἕξ ἑπτά corresponds to the Latin *sex septum*, a fact which is said to indicate that the Latin *s* stands in the place of the Greek aspirate: "ὕλας dicunt et nos *siluas*, item ἕξ *sex* et *septa* ἑπτά."

3. The Arabic title is as follows: كتاب الموازنة بين اللغة العبرنية والعربية. On Ibn Barūn, see Pinchas Wechter's translation, introduction, and commentary in *Ibn Barūn's Arabic Works on Hebrew Grammar and Lexicography*; for the text of the treatise, see Abū Ibrāhīm Ibn Barūn, *Kitāb al-muwāzana*, ed. Pavel Konstantinovich Kokovtsov as the first volume of his *K istorii srednevekovoi evreiskoi filologii i evreiskoi-arabskoi literaturi*. Cf. the revisions in Eppenstein, *Ishak ibn Baroun et ses comparaisons de l'hébreu avec l'arabe*.

4. On Sir William Jones, see Cannon, *Life and Mind of Oriental Jones*; and on the famous discourse on the Hindus, see in particular chapter 10, "A Genetic Explanation: Indo-European (1787–1788)," pp. 241–70.

5. As Maurice Olender has observed in *Les Langues du paradis*, p. 25 n.37, Jones' letters would suggest that he only began the study of Sanskrit toward the end of 1785.

6. *Collected Works of Sir William Jones*, vol. 3, pp. 34–35.

7. *Ibid.*, pp. 45–46.

8. Bopp's 1816 study is *Über das Conjugationssystem der Sanskritsprache in Vergleichung mit jenem der griechischen, lateinischen, persischen, und germanischen Sprachen*.

9. The full German title read *Compendium der vergleichenden Grammatik der*

indogermanischen Sprachen: Kurzer Abriss einer Laut- und Formenlere der indoger-manischen Ursprache, des Altindischen, Alteranischen, Altgriechischen, Altitalischen, Altkeltischen, Altslawischen, Litauischen, und Altdeutschen. It appeared in English in 1874 as *A Compendium of the Comparative Grammar of the Indo-European, San-skrit, Greek, and Latin Languages.* Today the dominant German term for "Indo-European" remains "Indo-German" (*indogermanisch*). The term *indoeuropäisch*, however, was adopted in the second edition of Bopp's *Vergleichende Grammatik*, published between 1857 and 1861. On the origin and senses of the terms *indo-germanisch* and *indoeuropäisch*, see Koerner, *Practicing Linguistic Historiography*, pp. 149–77; cf. Bolognesi, "Sul termine 'Indo-Germanisch.'"

10. *Compendium of Comparative Grammar*, p. 8. The members of the Indo-European family are counted somewhat differently today. In Oswald J.L. Szemerényi's *Introduction to Indo-European Linguistics*, they are said to be twelve: Aryan (or "more accurately" Indo-Aryan), Armenian, Anatolian, Tocharian, Greek, Italic, Venetic, Celtic, Germanic, Baltic, Slavic, and Albanian (pp. 11–12).

11. Milner, *L'Amour de la langue*, p. 107.

12. *Ibid.*, pp. 107–108. Milner notes that this was in fact the fate of Hittite, as of Sanskrit before it: after being briefly considered, in his terms, a "cause-lan-guage," each was relegated to being but an "effect-language."

13. On Pott and the development of the discipline of Indo-European lin-guistics, see Lepschy, ed., *History of Linguistics*, vol. 4, *Nineteenth-Century Lin-guistics*, by Davies, pp. 150–89, esp. p. 152.

14. Isidore of Seville, *Etymologie sive originum*, esp. bk. 1, ch. 29. On etymol-ogy in late Antiquity and the Middle Ages, see Curtius, "Etymology as a Category of Thought," in *European Literature and the Latin Middle Ages*, pp. 495–500.

15. The derivational practices of each of these dictionaries, to be sure, are distinct; so, too, are the suppositions about the nature and function of etymol-ogy that motivate them.

16. Remarkably, the note on the asterisk is itself marked, as a note, by an asterisk. See *Compendium der vergleichenden Grammatik*, vol. 1, p. 12.

17. The sentence is Osip Mandelstam's. See Mandelstam, "Journey to Armenia," in *Collected Critical Prose and Letters*, p. 374.

18. Schleicher, *Compendium der vergleichenden Grammatik*, vol. 1, p. 12n.

19. August Schleicher, "Eine Fabel in indogermanischer Ursprache," *Beiträge der Zeitschrift für vergleichende Sprachforschung* 5 (1868), pp. 206–208. Since its publication, Schleicher's fable has been "corrected" several times: see Hirt, *Die Hauptprobleme der indogermanischen Sprachwissenschaft*; Lehmann and Zgusta, "Schleicher's Tale after a Century"; and Campanile, "Le pecore dei neo-grammatici e le pecore nostre."

20. Szemerényi, *Introduction to Indo-European Linguistics*, p. 32.

21. Koerner, "Zu Ursprung und Geschichte," pp. 185–186.

22. Gabelentz and Loebe, *Glossarium der Gothischen Sprache*, pp. vi–vii, cited in Koerner, "Zu Ursprung und Geschichte," p. 186.

23. Gabelentz and Loebe, *Glossarium der Gothischen Sprache*, p. vi, cited in Koerner, "Zu Ursprung und Geschichte," p. 186.

24. Benfey, *Vollständige Grammatik der Sanskritsprache*, p. 71 n.1, cited in Koerner, "Zu Ursprung und Geschichte," p. 186.

25. Meyer, "Das Suffix ka im Gothischen," p. 2, cited in Koerner, "Zu Ursprung und Geschichte," p. 187.

26. Meyer, "Gothische doppelconsonanz," cited in Koerner, "Zu Ursprung und Geschichte," p. 187.

27. Bühler, "Das gothische zd," p. 151, cited in Koerner, "Zu Ursprung und Geschichte," p. 188.

28. *Compendium of Comparative Grammar*, p. x.

29. Cowgill, "Origins of the Insular Celtic Conjunct and Absolute Verbal Endings," p. 58, cited in Koerner, "Zu Ursprung und Geschichte," p. 189.

30. Szemerényi, *Introduction to Indo-European Linguistics*, p. viii.

CHAPTER TWELVE: THE GLIMMER RETURNS

1. On the definition of "structuralism" in linguistics, see Milner, *Le Périple structural*.

2. Trubetskoi, "Gedanken über das Indogermanenproblem"; English in "Thoughts on the Indo-European Problem," in *Studies in General Linguistics and Language Structure*, p. 87.

3. Chomsky, *Syntactic Structures*, p. 11.

4. On the epistemology of generative-transformational linguistics, see Milner, *Introduction à une science du langage*, pp. 23–90.

5. On the "asterisk-function" and the implications of the invented linguistic example as an object of empirical science, see *ibid.*, pp. 109–26.

6. Chomsky, *Syntactic Structures*, p. 67.

7. Chomsky, *Aspects of the Theory of Syntax*, pp. 150–51.

8. Householder, "On Arguments from Asterisks," pp. 370–72.

9. The terms employed by linguists vary, for reasons often of method: some speak of grammaticality and ungrammaticality; others of acceptability and unacceptability; still others, in a more traditional vein, of correctness and incorrectness. Chomsky famously distinguished between acceptability, which he defined as belonging to performance, and grammaticality, which he defined as pertaining to competence (see *Aspects of the Theory of Syntax*, pp. 11–12). Whatever one's preferred terms, however, their value remains differential, as Milner has demonstrated (see *Introduction à une science du langage*, pp. 55–56).

10. Chomsky, *Aspects of the Theory of Syntax*, p. 11.

11. *Ibid.*, pp. 24 and 18.

CHAPTER THIRTEEN: THE WRITING COW

1. Ovid, *Metamorphoses*, bk. 1, ll. 767–70, p. 24.

2. *Ibid.*, bk. 1, ll. 786–91, p. 25.

3. *Ibid.*, bk. 1, ll. 801–11, p. 25.

4. Tory, *Champfleury*, pp. c.j.r.–c.ij.v.

5. *Ibid.*, p. c.ij.v.

6. *Ibid.*, p. c.ij.v. Tory also entertained the possibility that the *O* could be said "to be made from the I," but only in passing.

7. Gaus, "Was bleibt? Es bleibt die Muttersprache," in *Zur Person*, p. 24; English in Arendt, "What Remains? The Mother Tongue Remains," in *Essays in Understanding*, p. 12.

8. Gaus, "Was bleibt?" p. 24; Arendt, *Essays in Understanding*, p. 13.

9. Brodsky, "Uncommon Visage: The Nobel Lecture," in *On Grief and Reason*, p. 57.

CHAPTER FOURTEEN: THE LESSER ANIMAL

1. Spinoza, *Ethics* 3, scholium to prop. 2.

2. The Arabic edition on which I have relied is the seven-volume one edited by 'Abd al-Salām Muhammad Hārūn: *Al-Kitāb al-Hayawān*, vol. 1, p. 35. I have been aided in my translation of the Arabic by Lakhdar Souami's selection in French, published as *Le Cadi et la mouche*, p. 62.

3. *Al-Kitāb al-Hayawān*, vol. 1, p. 35; *Le Cadi et la mouche*, p. 63.

4. *Al-Kitāb al-Hayawān*, vol. 1, p. 36; *Le Cadi et la mouche*, p. 64.

5. *Ibid.*

6. *Ibid.*

7. *Al-Kitāb al-Hayawān*, vol. 1, pp. 35–36; *Le Cadi et la mouche*, pp. 63–64.

8. *Ibid.*

9. *Al-Kitāb al-Hayawān*, vol. 1, p. 36; *Le Cadi et la mouche*, p. 64. The Arabic passage reads as follows:

تم جعل الإنسان ذا العقل والتمكين، والاستطاعة والتصريف، وذا التكلف والتجربة، وذا التأني والمنافسة، وصاحب الفهم والمسابقة، والمتبصر شأن العقبة، متى أحسن شيئا كان كل شيء دونه في الغموض عليه أسهل، وجعل سائر الحيوان، وإن كان يحسن أحدها ما لا يحسن أحذق الناس متى أحسن شيئا عجيبا، لم يمكنه أن يحسن ما هو أقرب منه في الظن، وأسهل منه في الرأي، بل لا يحسن ما هو أقرب منه في الحقيقة .

10. *Ibid.*

11. *Al-Kitāb al-Hayawān*, p. 35; *Le Cadi et la mouche*, pp. 62–63.

12. See Jakobson, "Toward a Linguistic Typology of Aphasic Impairments," in *Selected Writings*, vol. 2, pp. 289–306; "Linguistic Types of Aphasia," in *Selected Writings*, vol. 2, pp. 307–33, and "On Aphasic Disorders from a Linguistic Angle," in *Selected Writings*, vol. 7, *Contributions to Comparative Mythology; Studies in Linguistics and Philology, 1972–1982*, pp. 128–40.

13. Freud, *Zur Auffassung der Aphasien*; the study was translated into English by E. Stengel. In subsequent notes, page references to the original German edition appear in square brackets.

14. Letter of May 21, 1894, in Sigmund Freud, *Briefe an Wilhelm Fliess*, p. 67; *The Complete Letters of Sigmund Freud to Wilhelm Fliess*, p. 74.

15. See Ernst Kris, introduction to Freud, *Origins of Psychoanalysis*, p. 18 n.19.

16. Freud, *Zur Auffassung der Aphasien*, p. 39 [1]; *On Aphasia*, p. 1. Here, as in all subsequent citations, I have preserved Freud's italicization, which Stengel did not include in his translation.

17. Broca, "Remarques sur le siege [*sic*] de la faculté du langage articulé suivies d'une observation d'aphémie (perte de la parole)."

18. Cited in Freud, *Zur Auffassung der Aphasien*, p. 99 n.2 [57]; *On Aphasia*, p. 56 n.1.

19. Freud, *Zur Auffassung der Aphasien*, p. 111 [68]; *On Aphasia*, p. 67.

20. Freud, *Zur Auffassung der Aphasien*, p. 99 [58]; *On Aphasia*, p. 56.

21. Freud, *Zur Auffassung der Aphasien*, p. 95 [54]; *On Aphasia*, p. 53.

22. *Ibid.*

23. Freud, *Zur Auffassung der Aphasien*, p. 95 [55]; *On Aphasia*, p. 53.

24. *Ibid.*

25. Freud, *Zur Auffassung der Aphasien*, pp. 95–96 [55]; *On Aphasia*, p. 53.

26. Freud, *Zur Auffassung der Aphasien*, pp. 131–32 [89]; *On Aphasia*, p. 87.

27. Freud, *Zur Auffassung der Aphasien*, p. 132 [89]; *On Aphasia*, p. 87.

28. Freud, *Zur Auffassung der Aphasien*, p. 83 [43]; *On Aphasia*, p. 42.

29. Freud, *Zur Auffassung der Aphasien*, p. 131 [89]; *On Aphasia*, p. 87.

30. *Ibid.*

31. Freud, *Zur Auffassung der Aphasien*, p. 133 [90]; *On Aphasia*, p. 88.

32. *Ibid.* As evidence, Freud cites an article by William Henry Broadbent, "A Case of Peculiar Affection of Speech, with Commentary."

33. Freud, *Zur Auffassung der Aphasien*, p. 133 [90]; *On Aphasia*, p. 88.

34. Freud, *Zur Auffassung der Aphasien*, pp. 104–106 [62–64]. Stengel translates Freud's *Sprachresten* as both "residues of speech" and "speech remnants," *On Aphasia*, pp. 60–62. Freud's running heads are unfortunately not visible in the text of the recent German reedition of *Zur Auffassung der Aphasien* from Fischer; as Valerie D. Greenberg has remarked and justly deplored, with respect

to the original the new edition differs considerably in typography, spelling, and paragraph structure. See *Freud and His Aphasia Book*, p. 10.

35. Freud, *Zur Auffassung der Aphasien*, p. 105 [63]; *On Aphasia*, p. 61. As the editors of the German edition note, Freud cites both the use of yes and no and the curse as examples of hysterical speech in his French essay "Quelques considérations pour une étude comparative des paralysies motrices organiques et hystériques," *Archives de neurologie* 26 (1893), p. 45.

36. Freud, *Zur Auffassung der Aphasien*, p. 105 [63]; *On Aphasia*, p. 61.

37. *Ibid.*

38. Freud, *Zur Auffassung der Aphasien*, pp. 105–106 [63]; *On Aphasia*, pp. 61–62.

39. Freud, *Zur Auffassung der Aphasien*, p. 106 [63–64]; *On Aphasia*, p. 62.

40. *Standard Edition of the Complete Psychological Works of Sigmund Freud*, vol. 6, *The Psychopathology of Everyday Life*, p. 261. "During the days when I was living alone in a foreign city—I was a young man at the time," Freud recounts, "I quite often heard my name suddenly called by an unmistakable and beloved voice." German in *Zur Psychopathologie des Alltagsleben*, p. 325.

41. Freud, *Briefe an Wilhelm Fliess*, letter 113, p. 218; *Complete Letters of Sigmund Freud to Wilhelm Fliess*, p. 208.

42. Freud, *Briefe an Wilhelm Fliess*, pp. 217–18; *Complete Letters of Sigmund Freud to Wilhelm Fliess*, pp. 207–208. Trans. modified.

43. Freud, *Briefe an Wilhelm Fliess*, pp. 218–19; *Complete Letters of Sigmund Freud to Wilhelm Fliess*, p. 208. Trans. modified.

44. Breuer and Freud, *Studien über Hysterie*, p. 5: "Der Hysterische leide[t] grössten theils an Reminiscenzen." English in *Standard Edition of the Complete Psychological Works of Sigmund Freud*, vol. 2, *Studies on Hysteria*, p. 7. Freud and Breuer place the sentence in italics.

45. Kafka, *Gesammelte Werke*, vol. 7, *Zur Frage der Gesetze und andere Schriften aus dem Nachlass*, p. 155: "Ich kann schwimmen wie die andern, nur habe ich ein besseres Gedächtnis als die andern, ich habe das einstige Nicht-schwimmen-können nicht vergessen. Da ich es aber nicht vergessen habe, hilft mir das Schwimmenkönnen nichts und ich kann doch nicht schwimmen."

Chapter Fifteen: Aglossostomography

1. Roland, *Aglossostomographie*, pp. 3–4.

2. *Ibid.*, pp. 33–34.

3. For a full account of the dangers of the partial loss of the tongue, see chapter 5, "Why Those Who Have Lost a Noteworthy Part of the Tip of the Tongue Do Not Speak Without Artifice."

4. De Jussieu, "Sur la manière dont une fille sans langue s'acquitte des fonctions qui dépendent de cet organe."

5. *Ibid.*, p. 10.

6. *Ibid.*, p. 7.

7. *Ibid.*, p. 7. De Jussieu notes, however, that when asked to name the letters of the alphabet, the girl did pronounce some better than others: the physician remarks that she was least impressive in her rendition of *c, f, g, l, n, r, s, t, x*, and *z*.

8. Jakobson, *Six Leçons sur le son et le sens*, lecture 1, in *Selected Writings*, vol. 8, *Major Works, 1976–1980*, p. 328. Cf. Jakobson's later comments on the same works in *The Sound Shape of Language*, which he co-authored with Linda R. Waugh, in *Selected Writings*, vol. 8, p. 99: "The study of speech sounds has often suffered from a kind of tongue-fetishism."

9. Jakobson, *Six Leçons sur le son et le sens*, p. 328.

10. *Ibid.*, pp. 328–29.

11. *Ibid.*, p. 329.

12. Poe, *Fall of the House of Usher and Other Writings*, p. 350.

13. *Ibid.*, p. 350.

14. *Ibid.*, p. 350.

15. *Ibid.*, p. 354.

16. *Ibid.*, p. 355.

17. *Ibid.*, p. 356.

18. *Ibid.*, pp. 356–57.

19. Barthes, "Analyse textuelle d'un conte d'Edgar Poe," p. 47.

20. *Ibid.*, pp. 47–49.

21. *Ibid.*, p. 49.

22. Svenbro, *Phrasikleia*, pp. 13–32; Pfohl, "Die ältesten Inschriften der Griechen"; Jeffery, *Local Scripts of Archaic Greece*; Guarducci, *Epigrafia greca*; Pfohl, *Greek Poems on Stones*, vol. 1, *Epitaphs*.

23. Maria Letizia Lazzarini, "Le formule delle dediche votive nella Grecia arcaia," in *Atti della Accademia nazionale dei Lincei, Memorie: Classe di scienze morali, storiche, e filogiche*, ser. 8, vol. 9 (1976), no. 795.

24. Pfohl, *Greek Poems on Stones*, nos. 158 and 15.

25. Svenbro, *Phrasikleia*, pp. 37–38.

26. *Ibid.*, p. 51; the work in question is Brugmann, *Die Demonstrativpronomina der Indogermanischen Sprachen*, p. 71.

27. Svenbro, *Phrasikleia*, p. 51.

28. *Ibid.*, p. 51.

CHAPTER SIXTEEN: *HUDBA*

1. The syntagma *materna lingua*, which one finds in a Middle Latin text dating from 1119, is the earliest known term for the "mother tongue"; but the vernacular Romance forms, such as the *parlar materno* of *Purgatorio* 26, follow soon thereafter. On the history of the expression "mother tongue," see Spitzer, "Muttersprache und Muttererziehung," in *Essays in Historical Semantics*, pp. 15–65.

2. See *De vulgari eloquentia* 1.1.2–3, pp. 28–33.

3. Elias Canetti, *Die gerettete Zunge*, p. 10; English translation in *The Tongue Set Free*, p. 4. In all following references, German page numbers precede those of the English translation.

4. *Ibid.*, p. 33; p. 23.

5. *Ibid.*, p. 34; p. 24.

6. *Ibid.*, p. 85; p. 66.

7. *Ibid.*, p. 86; p. 67.

8. *Ibid.*, p. 88; p. 69.

9. *Ibid.*, pp. 86–87; pp. 67–68.

10. *Ibid.*, p. 87; p. 68.

11. *Ibid.*

12. *Ibid.*

13. *Ibid.*, pp. 87–88; p. 68.

14. *Ibid.*, p. 88; p. 69.

15. *Ibid.*, p. 88; p. 69.

16. *Ibid.*, p. 89; p. 70.

17. *Ibid.*, p. 90; p. 70.

18. *Ibid.*

19. *Ibid.*, p. 94; p. 74.

20. *De vulgari eloquentia* 1.1.2.

21. Canetti, *Die gerettete Zunge*, p. 17; *The Tongue Set Free*, p. 10.

22. *Ibid.*, p. 17; p. 10.

23. *Ibid.*, pp. 17–18; p. 10.

24. Canetti, *Das Augenspiel*, p. 293.

25. *Ibid.*, p. 293.

26. *Ibid.*

27. *Ibid.*, p. 294.

28. *Ibid.*

29. *Das Augenspiel*, p. 284.

30. Asadowski, *Rilke und Russland*, p. 409.

CHAPTER SEVENTEEN: SCHIZOPHONETICS

1. Wolfson, *Le Schizo et les langues*.

2. *Ibid.*, p. 33.

3. *Ibid.*

4. Gilles Deleuze, "Schizologie," in *ibid.*, p. 6.

5. Wolfson, *Le Schizo et les langues*, p. 73.

6. *Ibid.*, p. 122.

7. *Ibid.*, p. 71.

8. *Ibid.*, pp. 71–72.

9. *Ibid.*, p. 118.

10. *Ibid.*

11. *Ibid.*, pp. 118–19.

12. *Ibid.*, p. 177.

13. *Ibid.*, p. 51. It is also important that, as one reads in a note placed before the inception of the text, the author originally wished to publish his book in a "reformed spelling," of which an extended example can be found in the appendix to *Le Schizo et les langues* (pp. 259–68).

14. *Ibid.*, p. 77.

15. Benjamin, "Karl Kraus," in *Gesammelte Schriften*, vol. 2, pt. 1, p. 344.

16. Kraus, *Schriften*, vol. 7, *Die Sprache*, p. 23.

17. At the end of his study of aphasia, Freud uses the odious expression in his discussion of the merits of Charcot's analysis of speech disorders. "Gewiss wäre es aber unrecht," he writes, "*an* die Idee Charcots ganz zu vergessen" (Freud, *Zur Auffassung der Aphasien*, p. 145 [p. 102 of the 1891 edition], my emphasis). Stengel translates, "It would certainly be wrong to dismiss Charcot's idea completely" (*On Aphasia*, p. 100), while a literal, albeit unidiomatic, translation would read, "It would certainly be wrong to forget on Charcot's idea completely."

18. Wolfson, *Le Schizo et les langues*, pp. 249, 233, 140.

19. *Ibid.*, p. 247.

Chapter Eighteen: A Tale of Abū Nuwās

1. Ibn Manẓūr, *Akhbār Abi Nuwās*, p. 55. On this passage, see Amjad Trabulsi, *La Critique poétique des Arabes*, pp. 114–15. The English translation cited here is largely that of Michael Cooperson, in Kilito, *The Author and His Doubles*, p. 14.

2. Kilito, *The Author and His Doubles*, p. 15.

Chapter Nineteen: "Persian"

1. Landolfi, *Dialogo dei massimi sistemi*, p. 73.

2. *Ibid.*, p. 74.

3. *Ibid.*, p. 75.

4. *Ibid.*, p. 76.

5. *Ibid.*

6. *Ibid.*, p. 77.

7. *Ibid.*

8. *Ibid.*, p. 78.

9. *Ibid.*, p. 79.

10. *Ibid.*, p. 78.

11. *Ibid.*, p. 80.

12. *Ibid.*

13. *Ibid.*, p. 82.

14. *Ibid.*, p. 83.

15. *Ibid.*, p. 79.

16. *Ibid.*, p. 92.

17. *Ibid.*, p. 79.

CHAPTER TWENTY: POETS IN PARADISE

1. On Ibn al-Qāriḥ's letter to al-Maʿarrī, see Blachère, "Ibn al-Qārih et la genèse de l'epître du pardon d'al-Maʿarrī." This passage is cited in Schoeler, *Paradies und Hölle*, p. 20.

2. Schoeler, *Paradies und Hölle*, p. 20.

3. The most complete edition is that of ʿĀisha ʿAbdarrahmān "bint al-Shāti": *Risālat al-ghufrān*. There have been several translations of the work into European languages, of which the most recent is that of Schoeler. Schoeler's careful German translation has been of help to me in my translations from the Arabic. In the citations that follow, the first page number is to the Arabic edition, the second to Schoeler's translation.

4. On possible Islamic sources for the *Commedia*, see the classic, if controversial, study by Miguel Asín Palacios, *La escatología musulmana en la "Divina Comedia,"* as well as Dieter Kremer's summary article, "Islamische Einflüsse auf Dantes 'Göttliche Komödie.'"

5. Al-Maʿarrī, *Risālat al-ghufrān*, p. 308; p. 171.

6. *Ibid.*, p. 308; pp. 171–72.

7. *Ibid.*, p. 309; p. 173. It is perhaps for this reason that Satan has so little patience for the poet's citations. As the wicked one explains to the protagonist of the work, what he wants from him is merely "information," and of a specific sort. "Wine," Satan observes to his human interlocutor, "is forbidden to you in this world, but it is permitted to you, by contrast, in the next. Do the inhabit-

ants of Paradise do the same thing with their immortal youths that Lot's compatriots did with theirs?"

8. The poem in question is the poet's *mu'allaqa* (a term that literally means "being hung"), which begins: "Stop, let us weep at the memory of a loved one and her dwelling at the place where the sands twist to an end between al-Dukhūl and Ḥawmal." For an edition, translation, and commentary of the poem, see Jones, *Early Arabic Poetry*, vol. 2, *Select Odes*, pp. 52–86, from whom I have borrowed this translation.

9. Al-Ma'arrī, *Risālat al-ghufrān*, p. 316; p. 177.

10. *Ibid.*, p. 290; p. 152.

11. *Ibid.*, p. 291; p. 153. The "fifteen meters" known to humankind are those defined in the classical Arabic system of versification traditionally attributed to al-Khalīl ibn Aḥmad. Depending on one's taxonomy, they can also be reckoned to be sixteen.

12. *Ibid.*, p. 292; p. 154.

13. *Ibid.*

14. *Ibid.*, pp. 292–93; p. 155.

15. *Ibid.*, p. 207; p. 79.

16. *Ibid.*, p. 209; pp. 80–81.

17. *Ibid.*, p. 238; p. 103.

18. *Ibid.*, p. 239; p. 104.

19. *Ibid.*, p. 246; p. 110.

20. *Ibid.*

21. *Ibid.*, p. 264; p. 130.

22. *Ibid.*, p. 279; p. 141.

23. *Ibid.*, pp. 279–80; pp. 141–42.

24. *Ibid.*

25. *Ibid.*, p. 360; p. 203.

26. *Ibid.*

27. *Ibid.*, p. 360; pp. 203–204.

28. Sura 20.115.

29. Al-Ma'arrī, *Risālat al-ghufrān*, p. 360; pp. 203–204. The etymology,

which seems to derive from a verse of Abū Tammām's, appears elsewhere in al-Maʿarrī, as ʿAbdelfattah Kilito has noted in *La Langue d'Adam*, p. 49. Amjad Trabulsi, ed., *Zajr al-nābiḥ "muqtatafāt*," pp. 100–101: "Do not forget your duties, for truly / You were called man [إنسان] because you are forgetful [نسي]."

30. Al-Maʿarrī, *Risālat al-ghufrān*, pp. 361–62; pp. 204–205.

31. *Ibid.*, p. 364; p. 206. As Kilito suggests, however, the debate might well go on forever. Even after the Adamic self-explanation, Ibn al-Qāriḥ is not satisfied. He argues that the verses could still have been written by Adam, albeit in Aramaic, and later translated into Arabic. The discussion ends only when Adam, willfully putting a stop to it, swears by God that no one of his age composed them. "When a prophet swears by God," Kilito comments sagely, "there is nothing more to add" (*La Langue d'Adam*, p. 50).

32. Kilito, *La Langue d'Adam*, p. 50. I have rendered Kilito's term "syriaque" as "Aramaic," since it refers to al-Maʿarrī's expression اللسان السريانية (p. 361), which I have consistently rendered into English as "Aramaic."

CHAPTER TWENTY-ONE: BABEL

1. Gen. 11.4.

2. Gen. 11.8.

3. Philo of Alexandria, *De confusione linguarum*, par. 187, p. 148.

4. *Ibid.*

5. On the history of representations of the Tower of Babel, see the monumental work of Arno Borst, *Der Turmbau von Babel*.

6. Dante, *De vulgari eloquentia*, 1.9.6. Cf. *Convivio* 2.4.14; *De Monarchia* 2.6.1; cf. also *Convivio* 9.10.8 and 23.5; *De Monarchia* 3.13. 6.

7. Dante, *De vulgari eloquentia*, 1.9.6–7, pp. 74–76; "Dicimus ergo quod nullus effectus superat suam causam, in quantum effectus est, quia nil potest efficere quod non est. Cum igitur omnis nostra loquela—preter illam homini primo concreatam a Deo—sit a nostro beneplacito reparata post confusionem illam que nil aliud fuit quam prioris oblivio, et homo sit instabilissimum atque variabilissimum animal, nec durabilis nec continua esse potest, sed sicut alia que

nostra sunt, puta mores et habitus, per locorum temporumque distantias variari oportet."

8. *Ibid.*, p. 75.

9. *Ibid.*, p. 76.

10. *Sanhedrin* 109a; English in Epstein, *Babylonian Talmud.*

11. *Ibid.*

12. *Ibid.*

13. *Ibid.*

14. *Ibid.*

15. *Ibid.*

16. Benjamin, *Gesammelte Schriften*, vol. 4, pt. 2, pp. 888–95.

17. Benjamin, *Gesammelte Schriften*, vol. 4, pt. 1, p. 10. As others have indicated, the classic English translation contains at this point an error whose gravity can hardly be overestimated: Harry Zohn omits the negative particle in Benjamin's sentence, transforming the statement into its contrary ("It should be pointed out that certain correlative concepts retain their meaning, and possibly their foremost significance, if they are [*sic*] referred exclusively to man" (*Illuminations*, ed. Hannah Arendt [New York: Harcourt, Brace and World, 1968], p. 70.)

18. Benjamin, *Gesammelte Schriften*, vol. 4, pt. 1, p. 10: "So dürfte von einem unvergesslichen Leben oder Augenblick gesprochen werden, auch wenn alle Menschen sie vergessen hätten. Wenn nähmlich deren Wesen es forderte, nicht vergessen zu werden, so würde jenes Prädikat nichts Falsches, sondern nur eine Forderung, der Menschen nicht entsprechen, und zugleich auch wohl den Verweis auf einen Bereich enthalten, in dem ihr entsprochen wäre: auf ein Gedenken Gottes. Entsprechend bliebe die Übersetzbarkeit sprachlicher Gebilde auch dann zu erwägen, wenn diese für die Menschen unübersetzbar wären."

19. Benjamin, *Gesammelte Schriften*, vol. 2, pt.1, pp. 239–40: "Vom Fürsten Myschkin darf man im Gegenteil sagen, dass seine Person hinter seinem Leben zurücktritt wie die Blume hinter ihrem Duft oder der Stern hinter seinem Flimmern. Das unsterbliche Leben ist unvergesslich, das ist das Zeichen, an dem wir es erkennen. Es ist das Leben, das ohne Denkmal und ohne Andenken,

ja vielleicht ohne Zeugnis unvergessen sein müsste. Es kann nicht vergessen werden. Dies Leben bleibt gleichsam ohne Gefäss und Form das Unvergäng-liche. Und 'unvergesslich' sagt seinem Sinn nach mehr als dass wir es nicht vergessen können; es deutet auf etwas im Wesen des Unvergesslichen selbst, wodurch es unvergesslich ist. Selbst die Erinnerungslosigkeit des Fürsten in seiner spätern Krankheit ist Symbol des Unvergesslichen seines Lebens; denn das liegt nur scheinbar im Abgrund seines Selbstgedenkens versunken aus dem es nicht mehr emporsteigt. Die andern besuchen ihn. Der kurze Schlussbericht des Romans stempelt alle Personen für immer mit diesem Leben, an dem sie teilhatten, sie wissen nicht wie."

Bibliography

Abrams, Daniel (ed.), *The Book Bahir: An Edition Based on the Earliest Manuscripts* (Los Angeles: Cherub Press, 1994).

Al-Jāḥiẓ, *Le Cadi et la mouche: Anthologie de Livre des Animaux*, ed. and trans. Lakhdar Souami (Paris: Sinbad, 1988).

Allen, W. Sidney, *Vox Graeca: A Guide to the Pronunciation of Classical Greek*, 3rd ed. (Cambridge, UK: Cambridge University Press, 1987).

———, *Vox Latina: A Guide to the Pronunciation of Classical Latin*, 2nd ed. (Cambridge, UK: Cambridge University Press, 1978).

Allony, Nehemia, *Torat ha-mishkalim* (Jerusalem: Hebrew University Press, 1951).

Andersen, Ole Stig, "The Burial of Ubykh," in *Abstracts for the Open Forum*, supplement to Nicholas Ostler (ed.), *Endangered Languages: What Role for the Specialist? Proceedings of the Second FEL Conference, University of Edinburgh, 25–27 September 1998* (Bath: Foundation for Endangered Languages, 1998).

Arendt, Hannah, *Essays in Understanding, 1930–1954*, ed. Jerome Kohn (New York: Harcourt Brace Jovanovich, 1994).

Asadowski, Konstantin (ed.), *Rilke und Russland: Briefe, Erinnerungen, Gedichte* (Berlin: Aufbau-Verlag, 1986; Frankfurt: Insel, 1986).

Ascoli, Graziadio, "Una lettera glottologica," *Rivista di filologia e d'istruzione classica* 10 (1882), pp. 1–71.

Asín Palacios, Miguel, *La escatología musulmana en la "Divina Comedia,"* 4th ed. (Madrid: Hiperión, 1984).

Aslanov, Cyril, *Le Provençal des juifs et l'hébreu en Provence: Le Dictionnaire* "Šaršot ha-Kesef" *de Joseph Caspi* (Paris: Peeters, 2001),

Augustine, *Confessions*, trans. R.S. Pine-Coffin (London: Penguin, 1961).

Baneth, David H. (ed.), *Kitāb al-radd wa'l-dalīl fī'l-dīn al-dhalīl (Al-Kitāb al-khazarī)* (Jerusalem: Magnes Press, 1977).

Barthes, Roland, "Analyse textuelle d'un conte d'Edgar Poe," in Claude Chabrol (ed.), *Sémiotique narrative et textuelle* (Paris: Larousse, 1973), pp. 29–54.

Barūn, Ibn, *Arabic Works on Hebrew Grammar and Lexicography*, ed. Pinchas Wechter (Philadelphia: Dropsie College for Hebrew and Cognate Learning, 1964).

Becker, Philipp August, *Die Heiligsprechung Karls des Grossen und die damit zusammenhängenden Fälschungen* (Leipzig: S. Hirzel, 1947).

Benavente Robles, Santiaga (ed.), *Tešubot de los discípulos de Menahem contra Dunaš ben Labrat: Edición del texto y traducción castellana*, rev. and completed by Angel Sáenz-Badillos (Granada: Universidad de Granada, 1986).

Bendavid, Aba, *Leshon miḳra u-leshon ḥakhamim*, 2 vols. (Tel Aviv: Devir, 1967–71).

Benfey, Theodor, *Vollständige Grammatik der Sanskritsprache* (Leipzig: n.p., 1852).

Benjamin, Walter, *Gesammelte Schriften*, 7 vols., ed. Hermann Schweppenhäuser and Rolf Tiedemann (Frankfurt: Suhrkamp, 1972–91).

Bergsträsser, Gotthelf, *Einführung in die semitischen Sprachen: Sprachproben und grammatische Skizzen* (Munich: Huebner, 1928).

Bishai, Wilson B., "Coptic Grammatical Influence on Egyptian Arabic," *Journal of the American Oriental Society* 82 (1962), pp. 285–89.

——, "Nature and Extent of Coptic Phonological Influence on Egyptian Arabic," *Journal of Semitic Studies* 6 (1961), pp. 175–81.

——, "Notes on the Coptic Substratum in Egyptian Arabic," *Journal of the American Oriental Society* 80 (1960), pp. 225–29.

Blachère, Régis, "Ibn al-Qārih et la genèse de l'epître du pardon d'al-Ma'arrī," in *Analecta* (Damascus: Institut Français de Damas, 1975), pp. 431–42.

Bolognesi, G., "Sul termine 'Indo-Germanisch,'" in P. Cipiriano, P. Di Giovine, and M. Mancini (eds.), *Miscellanea di studi linguistici in onore di Walter Belardi*, 2 vols. (Rome: Calamo, 1994), pp. 327–38.

Bopp, Franz, *Über das Conjugationssystem der Sanskritsprache in Vergleichung mit jenem der griechischen, lateinischen, persischen, und germanischen Sprachen*, ed. Karl Joseph Windischmann (Hildesheim: Olms, 1975).

Borst, Arno, *Der Turmbau von Babel: Geschichte der Meinungen über Ursprung und Vielfalt der Sprachen und Völker*, 7 vols. (Stuttgart: Anton Hiersemann, 1959).

Bovelles, Charles de, *Sur les langues vulgaires et la variété de la langue française: Liber de differentia vulgarium linguarum et Gallici sermonis varietate (1533)*, ed. Colette Dumont-Demaizière (Paris: Klincksieck, 1973).

Breuer, Josef, and Sigmund Freud, *Studien über Hysterie* (Leipzig: Franz Deuticke, 1893).

Broadbent, William Henry, "A Case of Peculiar Affection of Speech, with Commentary," *Brain* 1 (1878–79), pp. 484–503.

Broca, Paul, "Remarques sur le siege [*sic*] de la faculté du langage articulé suivies d'une observation d'aphémie (perte de la parole)," *Bulletins de la Société Anatomique de Paris, XXXVIe année* (1861), pp. 330–57.

Brodsky, Joseph, *On Grief and Reason: Essays* (New York: Farrar, Straus and Giroux, 1995).

Brugmann, Karl, *Die Demonstrativpronomina der Indogermanischen Sprachen* (Leipzig: Teubner, 1904).

Bühler, Georg, "Das gothische zd," *Zeitschrift für vergleichende Sprachforschung* 8 (1859), pp. 148–52.

Campanile, Enrico, "Le pecore dei neogrammatici e le pecore nostre," in A. Quattordio Moreschini (ed.), *Un periodo di storia linguistica, i neogrammatici: Atti del Convegno della società italiana di glottologia (1985)* (Pisa: Giardini, 1986), pp. 147–51.

——, (ed.), *Problemi di sostrato nelle lingue indoeuropee* (Pisa: Giardini, 1983).

Canetti, Elias, *Das Augenspiel: Lebensgeschichte, 1931–1937* (Munich: C. Hauser, 1985).

——, *Die gerettete Zunge: Geschichte einer Jugend* (Zurich: Erben, 1977; rpt., Frankfurt: Fischer, 1979).

——, *The Tongue Set Free*, trans. Joachim Neugroschel (London: Continuum, 1974).

Cannon, Garland, *The Life and Mind of Oriental Jones: Sir William Jones, the Father of Modern Linguistics* (New York: Cambridge University Press, 1990).

Catullus, Tibullus, Pervegilium Veneris, ed. and trans. F.W. Cornish, J.P. Postgate, J.W. Mackail, 2nd ed., rev. by G.P. Goold (Cambridge, MA: Harvard University Press, 1962).

Celan, Paul, *Der Meridian: Endfassung, Entwürfe, Materialen,* ed. Bernhard Böschenstein and Heino Schmull, with Michael Schwarzkopf and Christiane Wittkop (Frankfurt: Suhrkamp, 1999).

Cerquiglini, Bernard, *La Naissance du français* (Paris: Presses Universitaires de France, 1991).

Chomsky, Noam, *Aspects of the Theory of Syntax* (Cambridge, MA: MIT Press, 1965).

——, *Syntactic Structures* (The Hague: Mouton, 1957).

Chomsky, William (Zev), *Ha-lashon ha-ivrit be-darkhe hitpaṭḥutah* (Jerusalem: R. Mas, 1967).

Cohen, A., "Arabisms in Rabbinic Literature," *Jewish Quarterly Review* 3 (1912–13), pp. 221–333.

Cornulier, Benoît de, *Art poëtique: Notions et problèmes de métrique* (Lyons: Presses Universitaires de Lyon, 1995).

——, "Le Droit de l'*e* et la syllabilicité," *Cahiers de linguistique, d'orientalisme, et de slavistique* 5/6 (1975), *Hommage à Mounin*, pp. 101–17.

——, "Le Remplacement d'*e* muet par è et la morphologie des enclitiques," in Christian Rohrer (ed.), *Actes du Colloque franco-allemand de linguistique théorique* (Tübingen: Niemeyer, 1977), pp. 150–80.

Cowgill, Warren, "The Origins of the Insular Celtic Conjunct and Absolute Verbal Endings," in Helmut Rix (ed.), *Flexion und Wortbildung: Akten der V. Fachtagung der Indogermanischen Gesellschaft, Regensburg, 9.–14. September 1973* (Wiesbaden: L. Reichert, 1975), pp. 40–70.

Crystal, David, *Language Death* (Cambridge, UK: Cambridge University Press, 2000).

Curtius, Ernst Robert, *European Literature and the Latin Middle Ages*, trans. Willard Trask (Princeton, NJ: Princeton University Press, 1990).

Dante Alighieri, *De vulgari eloquentia*, in *Opere minori*, pt. 3, vol. 1, *De vulgari eloquentia, Monarchia*, ed. Pier Vincenzo Mengaldo and Bruno Nardi (Milan: Ricciardi, 1996).

Diem, Werner, "Studien zur Frage des Substrats im Arabischen," *Islam* 56 (1979), pp. 12–80.

Diez, Friedrich, *Etymologisches Wörterbuch der romanischen Sprachen*, 5th ed. (Bonn: A. Marcus, 1887).

Dorian, Nancy C., *Language Death: The Life Cycle of Scottish Gaelic* (Philadelphia: University of Pennsylvania Press, 1981).

———, "The Problem of the Semi-Speaker in Language Death," in Wolfgang U. Dressler and Ruth Wodak-Leodolter (eds.), *Language Death* (The Hague: Mouton, 1977), pp. 23–32.

Dressler, Wolfgang U., "Language Shift and Language Death—A Protean Challenge for the Linguist," *Folia Linguistica* 15, nos. 1–2 (1981), pp. 5–28.

Emerson, Ralph Waldo, *Selected Essays*, ed. Larzer Ziff (London: Penguin, 1982).

Eppenstein, Simon, *Ishak ibn Baroun et ses comparaisons de l'hébreu avec l'arabe* (Paris: A. Durlacher, 1901).

Epstein, Isidore, ed., *The Babylonian Talmud*, 7 pts. (London: Soncino, 1961).

Fauriel, Claude Charles, *Dante et les origines de la langue et de la littérature italiennes*, 2 vols. (Paris: A. Durand, 1854).

Fellmann, J., "A Sociolinguistic Perspective on the History of Hebrew," in Joshua A. Fishman (ed.), *Readings in the Sociology of Jewish Languages* (London: Brill, 1985), pp. 27–34.

Freud, Sigmund, *Briefe an Wilhelm Fliess, 1887–1904: Ungekürzte Ausgabe*, ed. Jeffrey Moussaieff Masson (Frankfurt: Fischer, 1986).

———, *The Complete Letters of Sigmund Freud to Wilhelm Fliess, 1887–1904*, trans. and ed. Jeffrey Moussaieff Masson (Cambridge, MA: Belknap Press of Harvard University Press, 1985).

———, *On Aphasia*, trans. E. Stengel (London: Imago, 1953).

———, *The Origins of Psychoanalysis: Letters, Drafts, and Notes to Wilhelm Fliess, 1887–1902*, ed. Marie Bonaparte, Anna Freud, and Ernst Kris (New York: Doubleday, 1957).

———, *The Standard Edition of the Complete Psychological Works of Sigmund Freud*,

24 vols., trans. James Strachey (London: Hogarth Press, 1957–1974).

———, *Zur Auffassung der Aphasien: Eine kritische Studie*, ed. Paul Vogel with Ingeborg Meyer-Palmedo, 2nd ed. (Frankfurt: Fischer, 2001).

———, *Zur Psychopathologie des Alltagsleben: Über Vergessen, Versprechen, Vergreifen, Aberglaube, und Irrtum* (Frankfurt: Fischer, 2000).

Gabba, Emilio, "Il latino come dialetto greco," in *Miscellanea di studi alessandrini in memoria di Augusto Rostagni* (Turin: Bottega d'Erasmo, 1965), pp. 188–94.

Gabelentz, Hans Conon von der, and Julius Loebe, *Glossarium der Gothischen Sprache* (Leipzig: F.A. Brockhaus, 1843).

Garbell, Irene, "Remarks on the Historical Phonology of an East Mediterranean Dialect," *Word* 14 (1958), pp. 303–37.

Gaus, Günter, *Zur Person: Porträts in Frage und Antwort* (Munich: Feder, 1964).

Gellius Aulus, *The Attic Nights*, trans. John C. Rolfe (Cambridge, MA: Harvard University Press, 1984).

Goidánich, Pier Gabriele, *L'origine e le forme della dittongazione romanza: La qualità d'accento in sillaba mediana nelle lingue indeuropee* (Tübingen: Niemeyer, 1907).

Gold, D.L., "A Sketch of the Linguistic Situation in Israel Today," *Language in Society* 18 (1989), pp. 361–88.

Greenberg, Valerie D., *Freud and His Aphasia Book* (Ithaca, NY: Cornell University Press, 1997).

Guarducci, Margherita, *Epigrafia greca*, 4 vols. (Rome: Istituto Poligrafico dello Stato, Libreria dello Stato, 1967–70).

Hamann, Johann Georg, *Sämtliche Werke*, 6 vols., ed. Josef Nadler (Wuppertal: R. Brockhaus; Tübingen: Antiquariat H.P. Willi, 1999).

Ḥarizi, Judah ben Shelomo al-, *Las asambleas de los sabios (Taḥkemoni)*, ed. and trans. Carlos del Valle Rodríguez (Murcia: Universidad de Murcia, 1988).

Heine, Heinrich, *Werke*, 4 vols. (Frankfurt: Insel, 1968).

Hirt, Herman Alfred, *Die Hauptprobleme der indogermanischen Sprachwissenschaft*, ed. Helmut Arntz (Halle: Niemeyer, 1939).

Holder, William, *The Elements of Speech* (1669, London: facsimile reprint, Scholar Press, 1967).

Householder, F. W., "On Arguments from Asterisks," *Foundations of Language* 10 (1973), pp. 365–75.

Isidore of Seville, *Etymologiae sive originum*, 2 vols., ed. W.M. Lindsay (Oxford: Clarendon Press, 1957).

Jacoby, Elfriede, *Zur Geschichte des Wandels von lat. ū zu y im Galloromanischen* (Berlin: Friedrich-Wilhelm-Universität, 1916).

Jāḥiẓ, Abī ʿUthmān ʿAmr ibn Baḥr al-, *Kitāb al-Ḥayawān*, 8 vols., ed. ʿAbd al-Salām Muhammad Hārūn (Cairo: Muṣṭafā al-Bābī al-Ḥalabī, 1938–45).

Jakobson, Roman, *Child Language, Aphasia, and Phonological Universals*, trans. Allan R. Keiler (The Hague: Mouton, 1968).

——, *Selected Writings*, 8 vols. (The Hague: Mouton, 1962–).

Jeffery, L.H., *The Local Scripts of Archaic Greece: A Study of the Origin of the Greek Alphabet and Its Development from the Eighth to the Fifth Centuries B.C.*, rev. with a supp. by A.W. Johnston (Oxford: Oxford University Press, 1990).

Jones, Alan, *Early Arabic Poetry*, 2 vols. (Reading, UK: Ithaca Press Reading for the Board of the Faculty of Oriental Studies, Oxford University, 1992–96).

Jones, Sir William, *The Collected Works of Sir William Jones*, 13 vols. (1803; rpt., New York: New York University Press, 1993).

Joüon, Paul, *A Grammar of Biblical Hebrew*, 2 vols., rev. and trans. T. Muraoka (Rome: Editrice Pontificio Istituto Biblico, 1991).

Jussieu, Antoine de, "Sur la manière dont une fille sans langue s'acquitte des fonctions qui dépendent de cet organe," *Mémoires de l'Académie Royale des Sciences*, Jan. 15, 1718, pp. 6–14.

Kafka, Franz, *Gesammelte Werke*, 12 vols., ed. Hans-Gerd Koch (Frankfurt: Fischer, 1994).

Kilito, Abdelfattah, *The Author and His Doubles: Essays on Classical Arabic Culture*, trans. Michael Cooperson with a foreword by Roger Allen (Syracuse, NY: Syracuse University Press, 2001).

——, *La Langue d'Adam et autres essais* (Casablanca: Toubkal, 1999).

Kincade, M. Dale, "The Decline of Native Languages in Canada," in R.H. Robins and E.M. Uhlenbeck (eds.), *Endangered Languages* (Oxford: Berg, 1991), pp. 157–76.

Klein, Hans Wilhelm, *Latein und Volgare in Italien: Ein Beitrag zur Geschichte der italienischen Nationalsprache* (Munich: Huebner, 1957).

Koerner, E.F.K., *Practicing Linguistic Historiography: Selected Essays* (Amsterdam: Benjamins, 1989).

——, "Zu Ursprung und Geschichte der Besternung in der historischen Sprachwissenschaft: Eine historiographische Notiz," *Zeitschrift für vergleichende Sprachforschung* 89 (1976), pp. 185–90.

Kokotsov, Pavel Konstantinovich, *K istorii srednevekovoi evreiskoi filologii i evreiskoi-arabskoi literaturi: Kniga sravneniya evreiskavo iazika s arabskim* (St. Petersburg, 1893).

Kontzi, Reinhold, ed., *Substrate und Superstrate in den romanischen Sprachen* (Darmstadt: Wissenschaftliche Buchgesellschaft, 1982).

Koschwitz, Eduard, *Überlieferung und Sprache der Chanson du Voyage de Charlemagne à Jérusalem et à Constantinople* (Heilbronn: Henninger, 1876).

Kraus, Karl, *Schriften*, 12 vols., ed. Christian Wagenknecht (Frankfurt: Suhrkamp, 1986–89).

Krauss, Michael, "The World's Languages in Crisis," *Language* 68 (1992), pp. 4–10.

Kremer, Dieter, "Islamische Einflüsse auf Dantes 'Göttliche Komödie,'" in Wolfhart Heinrichs (ed.), *Neues Handbuch der Literaturwissenschaft: Orientalisches Mittelalter* (Wiesbaden: AULA-Verlag, 1990), pp. 202–15.

Lambert, Pierre-Yves, *La Langue gauloise: Description linguistique, commentaire d'inscriptions choisies*, preface by Michel Lejeune (Paris: Errance, 1994).

Landolfi, Tommaso, *Dialogo dei massimi sistemi* (Milan: Adelphi, 1996).

Lazzarini, Maria Letizia, "Le formule delle dediche votive nella Grecia arcaica," in *Atti dell'Accademia nazionale dei Lincei, Memorie: Classe di scienze morali, storiche, e filologiche*, ser. 8, vol. 9 (1976), pp. 47–354.

Lehmann, W.P., and L. Zgusta, "Schleicher's Tale After a Century," in Béla Brogyányi (ed.), *Festschrift for Oswald Szemerényi on the Occasion of His 65th Birthday*, 2 vols. (Amsterdam: Benjamins, 1979).

Lepschy, Giulio (ed.), *History of Linguistics*, vol. 4, *Nineteenth-Century Linguistics*, by Anna Morpurgo Davies (London: Longman, 1994).

Leskien, August, and Otto A. Rottmann, *Handbuch der altbulgarischen (altkirchenslavischen) Sprache: Grammatik, Texte, Glossar*, 11th ed. (Heidelberg: C. Winter, 2002).

Maʿarrī, Abū al-ʿAlāʾ al-, *Risālat al-ghufrān*, ed. ʿĀsha ʿAbdarrahmān "bint al-Shāti" (Cairo: Dār al-Maʿārif, 1963).

——, *Zajr al-nābih "muqtatafāt,"* ed. Amjad Trabulsi (Damascus: al-Maṭbaʿa al-hāshimīyah, 1965).

Maimonides, *Le Guide des égarés: Traité de théologie et de philosophie*, 3 vols., ed. Salomon Munk (Paris: A. Franck, 1861).

Mallarmé, Stéphane, *Œuvres complètes*, ed. Henri Mondor and G. Jean-Aubry (Paris: Gallimard, 1945).

Mandelstam, Osip, *The Collected Critical Prose and Letters*, ed. Jane Gray Harris, trans. Jane Gray Harris and Constance Link (London: Collins Harvill, 1991).

Manẓūr, Ibn, *Akhbār Abi Nuwās* (Cairo: al-Itimad, 1924).

Meillet, Antoine, *Linguistique historique et linguistique générale* (Paris: Champion, 1965).

——, *La Méthode comparative en linguistique historique* (Paris: Champion, 1954).

Menéndez Pidal, Ramón, "Modo de obrar el substrato lingüístico," *Revista de filología española* 34 (1950), pp. 1–8.

Merlo, Clemente, "Lazio santia ed Etruria latina?" *Italia dialettale* 3 (1927), pp. 84–93.

——, "Il sostrato etnico e i dialetti italiani," *Revue de linguistique romane* 9 (1933), pp. 176–94.

Meyer, Leo, "Gothische doppelconsonanz," *Zeitschrift für vergleichende Sprachforschung* 4 (1855), pp. 401–13.

——, "Das Suffix *ka* im Gothischen," *Zeitschrift für vergleichende Sprachforschung* 6 (1857), pp. 1–10.

Meyer-Lübke, Wilhelm, *Einführung in das Studium der romanischen Sprachwissenschaft* (Heidelberg: C. Winter, 1901).

——, *Grammatik der romanischen Sprachen* (Leipzig: Fues, 1890).

——, "Zur u-y Frage," *Zeitschrift für französische Sprache und Literatur* 44 (1916), pp. 76–84.

Midrash Rabbah, 14 vols., trans. H. Freedman and Maurice Simon, with a fore-word by Isidore Epstein (London: Soncino, 1961).

Milner, Jean-Claude, *L'Amour de la langue* (Paris: Seuil, 1978).

——, *Introduction à une science du langage* (Paris: Seuil, 1989).

——, *Le Périple structural: Figures et paradigme* (Paris: Seuil, 2002).

Montaigne, Michel, *Essais*, ed. Pierre Villey (Paris: Presses Universitaires de France, 1978).

Nassir, A.A. al-, *Sibawayh the Phonologist: A Critical Study of the Phonetic and Pho-nological Theory of Sibawayh as Presented in His Treatise "Al-Kitab"* (London: Kegan Paul, 1993).

Nebrija, Antonio de, *Reglas de orthografía en la lengua castellana*, ed. Antonio Quilis (Bogotá: Publicaciones del Instituto Caro y Cuervo, 1977).

Nielsen, Niels Åge, "La Théorie des substrats et la linguistique structurale," *Acta linguistica* 7 (1952), pp. 1–7.

Olender, Maurice, *Les Langues du paradis: Aryens et sémites, un couple providentiel*, rev. ed., preface by Jean-Pierre Vernant (Paris: Seuil, 1989).

Opelt, Ilona, "La coscienza linguistica dei Romani," *Atene e Roma* 14 (1969), pp. 21–37.

Ouaknin, Marc-Alain, *Le Livre brûlé: Philosophie du Talmud* (Paris: Lieu Commun, 1993).

Ovid, *Metamorphoses: The Arthur Golding Translation of 1567*, ed. John Frederick Nims, with a new essay by Jonathan Bate (Philadelphia: Paul Dry Books, 2000).

Paris, Gaston, review of *Die aeltesten franzoesischen Mundarten: Eine sprachge-schichtliche Untersuchung*, by Gustav Lücking, *Romania* 7 (1878), pp. 111–40.

—— (ed.), *Vie de Saint Alexis* (Paris: Champion, 1872).

Petrus Helias, *Summa super Priscianum*, ed. Leo Reilly (Toronto: Pontifical Insti-tute of Mediaeval Studies, 1993).

Pfohl, Gerhard, "Die ältesten Inschriften der Griechen," *Quaderni urbinati di cultura classica* 7 (1969), pp. 7–25.

——, *Greek Poems on Stones*, vol. 1, *Epitaphs: From the Seventh to the Fifth Centu-ries B.C.* (Leiden: Brill, 1967).

Philipon, Edouard Paul Lucien, "L'U long latin dans le domaine rhodanien," *Romania* 40 (1911), pp. 1–16.

Philo of Alexandria, *De confusione linguarum*, ed. and trans. J.G. Kahn (Paris: Cerf, 1963).

Poe, Edgar Allan, *The Fall of the House of Usher and Other Writings*, ed. David Galloway (London: Penguin, 1986).

Pokorny, Julius, "Substrattheorie und Urheimat der Indogermanen," *Mitteilungen der Anthropologischen Gesellschaft in Wien* 66 (1936), pp. 69–91.

Proust, Marcel, *À la Recherche du temps perdu*, ed. Jean-Yves Tadié (Paris: Gallimard, 1999).

——, *Remembrance of Things Past*, trans. C.K. Scott Moncrieff and Terence Kilmartin (London: Penguin, 1981).

Pyles, Thomas, and John Algeo, *The Origins and Development of the English Language*, 4th ed. (New York: Harcourt Brace Jovanovich, 1993).

Richardson, Brian, ed., *Trattati sull'ortografia del volgare, 1524–1526* (Exeter, Devon: University of Exeter, 1984).

Riegel, Martin, Jean-Christophe Pellat, and René Rioul, *Grammaire méthodique du français* (Paris: Presses universitaires de France, 1994).

Roland, Jacques, *Aglossostomographie; ou, Description d'une bouche sans langue, laquelle parle et faict naturellement toutes les autres fonctions* (Saumur, 1630).

Sasse, Hans-Jürgen, "Theory of Language Death," in Matthias Brenzinger (ed.), *Language Death: Factual and Theoretical Explorations with Special Reference to East Africa* (Berlin: de Gruyter, 1992), pp. 7–30.

Schibsbye, Knud, *Origin and Development of the English Language*, vol. 1, *Phonology* (Copenhagen: Nordisk Sprogog Kulturforlag, 1972).

Schleicher, August, *Compendium der vergleichenden Grammatik der indogermanischen Sprachen: Kurzer Abriss einer Laut- und Formenlere der indogermanischen Ursprache, des Altindischen, Alteranischen, Altgriechischen, Altitalischen, Altkeltischen, Altslawischen, Litauischen, und Altdeutschen* (Weimar: Böhlau, 1861–62).

——, *A Compendium of the Comparative Grammar of the Indo-European, Sanskrit, Greek, and Latin Languages*, trans. from the 3rd ed. by Herbert Bendall (London: Trübner, 1874).

Schoeler, Gregor, *Paradies und Hölle: Die Jenseitsreise aus dem "Sendschreibung über die Vergebung"* (Munich: Beck, 2002).

Scholem, Gershom, *Judaica III* (Frankfurt: Suhrkamp, 1970).

———, *On the Kabbalah and Its Symbolism*, trans. Ralph Manheim (New York: Schocken Books, 1965).

Schuchardt, Hugo, review of *Irische Grammatik mit Lesebuch*, by Ernst Windisch, *Zeitschrift für romanische Philologie* 4, no. 1 (1880), pp. 124–55.

———, *Der Vokalismus des Vulgärlateins*, 3 vols. (Leipzig: Teubner, 1866–68).

Scragg, D.G., *A History of English Spelling* (Manchester: Manchester University Press, 1974).

Sībawayh, *Al-Kitāb*, 4 vols., ed. 'Abd al-Salām Muhammad Hārūn (Cairo: Al-Khānabī, 1966–75).

Silvestri, Domenico, *La teoria del sostrato: Metodo e miragi*, 3 vols. (Naples: Macchiaroli, 1977–82).

———, "La teoria del sostrato nel quadro delle ricerche di preistoria e protostoria linguistica indoeuropea," in Enrico Campanile (ed.), *Problemi di sostrato nelle lingue indoeuropee* (Pisa: Giardini, 1983), pp. 149–57.

Sirat, Colette, "Les Lettres hebraïques: Leur existence idéale et matérielle," in Alfred Ivry, Elliot Wolfson, and Allan Arkush (eds.), *Perspectives on Jewish Thought and Mysticism* (Amsterdam: Harwood Academic, 1998), pp. 237–56.

Smith, Sir Thomas, *Literary and Linguistic Works: Part III, Critical Edition of "De recta et emendata linguae Anglicae scriptione, dialogus"* ed. Bror Danielsson (Stockholm: Almquist and Wiksell International, 1963).

Sobhy, George, *Common Words in the Spoken Arabic of Egypt of Greek or Coptic Origin* (Cairo: Société d'Archéologie Copte, 1950).

Spinoza, Benedictus de, *Opera*, 4 vols., ed. Carl Gebhardt (Heidelberg: C. Winter, 1925).

Spitzer, Leo, *Essays in Historical Semantics*, preface by Pedro Salinas (New York: S.F. Vanni, 1948).

Svenbro, Jesper, *Phrasikleia: Anthropologie de la lecture en Grèce ancienne* (Paris: Découverte, 1988).

272

Szemerényi, Oswald J.L., *Introduction to Indo-European Linguistics*, 4th ed. (Oxford: Oxford University Press, 1990).

Tavoni, Mirko, "On the Renaissance Idea That Latin Derives from Greek," *Annuali della scuola normale di Pisa* 18 (1986), pp. 205–38.

Terracini, Benvenuto, "Come muore una lingua," in *Conflitti di lingue e di cultura* (Venice: Pozzi, 1957).

Tory, Geoffroy, *Champfleury; ou, Art et science de la vraie proportion des lettres* (facsimile reproduction of the 1529 ed., Paris: Bibliothèque de l'Image, 1998).

Trabulsi, Amjad, *La Critique poétique des Arabes jusqu'au Ve siècle de l'Hégire (XI. siècle de J.C.)* (Damascus: Institut Français d'Etudes Arabes à Damas, 1955).

Trissino, Giovan Giorgio, *Scritti linguistici*, ed. Alberto Castelvecchi (Rome: Salerno, 1986).

Trubetskoi, Nikolai Sergeevich, "Gedanken über das Indogermanenproblem," *Acta linguistica* (Copenhagen) 1 (1939), pp. 81–89.

——, *Grundzüge der Phonologie*, 3rd ed. (Göttingen: Vandenhoeck and Ruprecht, 1962).

——, *Principles of Phonology*, trans. Christiane A.M. Baltaxe (Berkeley: University of California Press, 1969).

——, *Studies in General Linguistics and Language Structure*, ed. and trans. Anatoly Liberman (Durham, NC: Duke University Press, 2001).

Valkhoff, Marius, *Latijn, Romaans, Roemeens* (Amersfoort: Valjhoff, 1932).

Valle Rodríguez, Carlos del, *La escuela hebrea de Córdoba: Los orígenes de la escuela filológica hebrea de Córdoba* (Madrid: Editora Nacional, 1981).

Victorinus, Marius, *Ars grammatica*, ed. Italo Mariotti (Florence: Le Monnier, 1967).

Vendryes, Joseph, "La Mort des langues," in *Conférences de l'Institut de Linguistique de l'Université de Paris* (1933), pp. 5–15.

Wallis, John, *Grammar of the English Language, with an Introductory Grammatico-Physical Treatise on Speech (or on the Formation of All Speech Sounds)*, ed. and trans. J.A. Kemp (London: Longman, 1982).

Weisgerber, Leo, *Die Sprache der Festlandkelten* (1931).

Wexler, Paul, *The Schizoid Nature of Modern Hebrew: A Slavic Language in Search of a Semitic Past* (Wiesbaden: Harrassowitz, 1990).

Windisch, Ernst, *Kurzgefasste Irische Grammatik mit Lesetücken* (Leipzig: Hirzel, 1879).

Wolfson, Louis, *Le Schizo et les langues; ou, La Phonétique chez le psychotique (Esquisses d'un étudiant de langues schizophrénique)*, preface by Gilles Deleuze (Paris: Gallimard, 1970).

Wurm, Stephen A., "Methods of Language Maintenance and Revival, with Selected Cases of Language Endangerment in the World," in Kazuto Matsumura (ed.), *Studies in Endangered Languages: Papers from the International Symposium on Endangered Languages, Tokyo*, November 18–20, 1995 (Tokyo: Hituzi Syobo, 1998), pp. 191–211.

Zafrani, Haïm, *Poésie juive en Occident musulman* (Paris: Geuthner, 1977).

The Zohar, 5 vols., trans. Harry Sperling and Maurice Simon (London: Soncino, 1984).

Index

De verborum significatione [On the
Meaning of Words] (Pompeius
Festus), 10.
De vulgari eloquentia (Dante), 18, 71,
163–64, 223–25.
Dialects, 61–62, 90.
Dialogo dei massimi sistemi [Dialogue
of the Greatest Systems] (Land-
olfi), 195–201.
Dialogo delle lingue [Dialogue of
Languages] (Speroni), 55.
Dictionaries, 105–106, 243 n.15.
*Dictionnaire étymologique de la
langue française* (Bloch-Wart-
burg), 105.
Diez, Friedrich, 79.
Diglossic half-language, 93.
Diphthongs, 186.
"Discourse on the Hindus" (Jones),
101.
Donatus, 53.
Dostoyevsky, Fyodor, 228–29.
Dubbî grammaticali, I [Grammatical
Doubts] (Trissino), 39.
Dunash ha-Levi ben Labrat, 47,
48.
Durard, Pierre, 149–51.
Dutch language, 184.

ECHOLALIA, 12, 190.
Ecology, 74.
Egypt, 90, 91–92, 203.
*Einführung in das Studium der
romanischen Sprachwissenschaft*
[Introduction to the Study of
Romance Linguistics] (Meyer-
Lübke), 83.
*Einführung in die semitischen
Sprachen* [Introduction to the
Semitic Languages] (Berg-
strässer), 94.

"Elegie auf den Tod eines Lautes"
[Elegy on the Death of a Sound]
(Kraus), 44.
Eliezer, Rabbi, 22.
Emerson, Ralph Waldo, 77.
Enantioseme, 158.
Endangered Languages Project, 58.
England, 39.
English language, 40–41, 99, 166,
172; Anglo-Saxon letters,
33–34; forgotten, as mother
tongue, 179–87, 190; Old
English, 80; phonology of,
16–17; Scandinavian elements
in, 79–80.
Enlightenment, 41.
Epistle of Forgiveness, The (al-Ma'arrī),
204–18.
Esenç, Tevfik, 61, 63, 64.
Essays (Montaigne), 73.
Ethics (Spinoza), 129.
Ethiopia, 90.
Etruscan language, 56, 80.
Etymologiae sive originum (Isidore of
Seville), 54.
*Etymologische Forschungen auf
dem Gebiete der indogermanischen
Sprachen* [Etymological
Researches in the Field of Indo-
European Languages] (Pott),
105.
Etymology, 104–106, 160, 184, 215,
217.
Europe, 104.
Eve (biblical), 154.
Evolution, Lamarckian doctrine of,
68.
Exclamations, 13–18.
Exegesis, 46.
Exile, language in, 45–51.

and, 189; language shift and, 91–
92; morphology and, 102; mother
tongue and, 164; of Hebrew, 94;
utterance in death and, 158.

Grammarians, 19, 20; Arab, 203,
205, 206, 212–13; English, 41;
European, 39, 40; Greek, 36, 53;
In ancient world, 89–90; Indo-
European linguistics and, 110;
Jewish, 48, 49, 50; language death
and, 62; medieval, 100–101;
Roman, 37.

Grammatik der romanischen Sprachen
[Grammar of the Romance Lan-
guages] (Meyer-Lübke), 84.

Graphemes, 33, 34, 39, 41, 124–25.

Grashey, Hubert E., 137.

Greece, ancient, 38–39, 159–60.

Greek language (ancient), 56, 89,
100, 221; first-person pronoun
in, 160; "Indo-Aryan" languages
and, 243 n.10; Indo-European
linguistics and, 101, 107, 110. *See
also* Letters, Greek.

Grimm, Jacob, 103, 105.

Grimm, Wilhelm, 105.

Gröber, Gustav, 82.

Grundriss der romanischen Philologie,
82.

Guide of the Perplexed, The (Maimonides), 23, 24.

Gutzmann, Hermann, 153.

Hārūn al-Rashīd, 187.

Hamann, Johann Georg, 42–44.

Hearing, sense of, 153.

Hebrew language, 19–25, 185, 221;
as "holy tongue," 54; in exile,
46–51; in modern Israel, 92–96;
lexical elements in Yiddish, 80;
medieval philology and, 100;

transition to Aramaic, 67; verbal
tense system in, 241 n.10. *See
also* Letters, Hebrew.

Heine, Heinrich, 35, 234 n.4.

Hell, poets in, 206–208, 209, 217.

Hellenistic period, 36, 53.

Hellwag, Christoph, 153.

Hercolano, L' (Varchi), 55–56.

Hermeneutics, 46.

al-Ḥarizi, 54.

Ḥumaid ibn Thaur, 212.

Hindus, 102–104.

Historians, 62, 70.

History, 77.

Hittite language, 243 n.12.

Holder, William, 41.

Homer, 33.

Horace, 54.

Householder, F. W., 116.

Hughlings Jackson, John, 134, 136,
138.

Humanists, Renaissance, 90.

Hysteria, 138.

Ibn Manẓūr, 191, 193.

Ibn al-Qāriḥ, 203–15, 217–18, 255
n.31.

Identity, national and racial ideologies, 85.

Idiot, The (Dostoyevsky), 228–30.

Idolatry, 226.

Imru' al-Qays, 207–208, 209.

Indo-European languages, 80–81,
85, 154, 243 nn.9–10; first-person pronoun in, 160–61; Israeli
Hebrew and, 94–96; recon-
structed forms of, 118; structuralism and, 113–14. *See also*
specific languages.

"In Memory of W. B. Yeats" (Auden),
126.

Sound shapes, 46.
Soviet Union, 34.
Spain, 39, 50, 80.
Spanish language; Argentinian, 99;
    Castilian, 16, 81; Grammarians
    of, 40; Latin phonetics and, 80.
    See also Ladino (Judeo–Spanish)
    language.
Speech; disorders of, 132–47; forget-
    ting and, 146–47; in absence of
    tongue, 149–53; limits of, 158;
    vocal apparatus for, 153–54. *See
    also* Language.
Speech remnants, 138–39, 140, 145.
Speroni, Sperone, 55, 56.
Spinoza, Baruch, 19, 20, 129.
Spirits, 36, 38, 39.
"starring" *(Besternung),* 108.
Strasbourg Oaths, 70, 74.
Stravinsky, Igor, 174.
Structuralism, 113–19, 185.
Studies on Hysteria (Freud and
    Breuer), 145.
Substrate theory, 78–79, 97.
"Suffix *Ka* im Gothischen, Das" [The
    Ka Suffix in Gothic] (Meyer),
    110–11.
Superstrates, 79.
"Sur la manière dont une fille sans
    langue s'acquitte des fonctions
    qui dépendent de cet organe"
    [On the Manner in Which a
    Girl Without a Tongue Acquits
    Herself of the Functions That
    Depend on this Organ] (Jussieu),
    151–53.
Svenbro, Jesper, 160, 161.
Swahili language, 183.
Synchronic studies, 115.
Syntactic Structures (Chomsky), 114,
    115, 116.

Syntax, 68, 118–19.
Syria, 90, 203, 214.
"Syriack" language, 45.
Szemerényi, Oswald, 109, 111.

TABLEAUX PARISIENS (Baudelaire),
    228.
Taḥkemoni (al-Ḥarizi), 54.
Taj, 46.
Tales of Abū Nuwās (Ibn Manẓūr),
    191–93.
Talmud, 46, 99, 226–27, 230.
Tamīm ibn Ubai, 212.
Targum, 46.
"Task of the Translator, The" (Benja-
    min), 228.
Taxonomies, 80.
Technology, 59–60.
Teeth, speech and, 153, 154.
Terracini, Benvenuto, 61–62, 63–64,
    67, 72.
Tha'alaba ibn 'Ukāma, 211.
Theology, 42, 153–54, 205, 226.
Time, language and, 71–72, 85–86,
    127, 205, 216, 218, 223.
Tocharian language, 243 n.10.
Tolomei, Claudio, 39.
Tongue: Absence of, 149–50; in Poe
    short story, 154–59, 161.
*Tongue Set Free, The [Die gerettete
    Zunge]* (Canetti), 165.
Tonic vowels, 69.
Torah, 20, 21, 22–23, 24, 226.
Tory, Geoffroy, 40, 124.
Transcription, 186.
Translation, 228.
Trissino, Giovan Giorgio, 39.
Trubetskoi, Nikolai Sergeevich,
    14–16, 17, 27, 113–14.
Tsvetaeva, Marina, 176–77.

Zone Books series design by Bruce Mau
Typesetting by Archetype
Image placement and production by Julie Fry
Printed and bound by Maple-Vail on Sebago acid-free paper